Politics of Innocence

D1612884

WITHDRAWN

STUDIES IN FORCED MIGRATION

General Editor: Roger Zetter, Refugee Studies Centre, University of Oxford

Politics of Innocence

HUTU IDENTITY, CONFLICT AND CAMP LIFE

Simon Turner

Berghahn Books
New York • Oxford

Published in 2010 by

Berghahn Books

www.berghahnbooks.com

©2010, 2012 Simon Turner
First paperback edition published in 2012

Library of Congress Cataloging-in-Publication Data
Turner, Simon, 1967-
  Politics of innocence : Hutu identity, conflict, and camp life / Simon Turner.
    p. cm. -- (Studies in forced migration ; v. 30)
  Includes bibliographical references and index.
  ISBN 978-1-84545-691-7 (hbk.) -- ISBN 978-0-85745-609-0 (pbk.)
  1. Hutu (African people)--Tanzania. 2. Refugees--Tanzania. 3. Humanitarian
assistance--Tanzania. I. Title.
  HV640.4.T34T87 2010
  305.896'39461--dc22
                    2010018503

British Library Cataloguing in Publication Data
A catalogue record for this book is available from the British Library

Printed in the United States on acid-free paper.

ISBN: 978-0-85745-609-0 (paperback)   ISBN: 978-0-85745-610-6 (ebook)

In memory of Ramadhan Abbas who opened many gates for me in the camp and whose political convictions cost him his life.

Contents

Acknowledgements

This book has been a long time in the making, and although it has at times been a lonely process, lots of people have been involved in one way or another. First, I am grateful to all the people in Lukole refugee camp who shared their thoughts with me, although I had little to offer in return. They would often ask me to 'tell the people in the big nations about our situation'. Although I could not promise them that the 'important people in the big nations' would listen to me, and I could not promise them that I would agree with their points of view, I hope with this book to shed some light on their lives, their hopes and their fears. I am especially grateful to Ramadhan Abbas, my assistant for more than a year, with whom a friendship grew. I am also grateful to the UNHCR and the Camp Commandant who let me come and go as I liked in the camp.

Although the thrust of this book is its fieldwork, it is first and foremost shaped by academia. Countless people have been involved in this long process: supervising, inspiring, commenting on chapters, reviewing the book, suggesting titles, or plainly giving moral support when things looked dark. Thomas Blom Hansen acted as a magic mirror; making my messy thoughts look impressively clear and clever. Steffen Jensen has been there 24/7 – ready to discuss anything from page layout to Zizek. Christian Lund, Jeremy Gould, Liisa Malkki, Peter Geschiere, René Lemarchand and Patricia Daley have all read the entire book at one stage or another and given valuable suggestions that I hope I have been able to incorporate into the final book. Others who have offered valuable critique on parts of the book include Finn Stepputat, Fiona Wilson, Giorgio Blundo, Pierre-Yves Le Meur and Marc-Antoine Perouse de Montclos. At Roskilde University my colleagues at the Institute for Development Studies gave me inspiration and moral support in the initial phases, while colleagues and friends at the Danish Institute for International Studies have helped me through the endless revisions towards the final product. Names that come to mind include Jesper Linell, Ane Toubro, Dietrich Jung, Thomas Brudholm, Nauja Kleist and Lars Buur. Finally, I was very fortunate to have my family with me while doing fieldwork, and our two years in Tanzania stand out as some of the best times we have had together.

1
The Troubled Nature of Innocence

On 21 October 1993, Burundi's first democratically elected Hutu president, along with other prominent politicians from the leading moderate 'Hutu' party, was abducted and later killed by Tutsi officers from the Burundian army. Within hours the news spread throughout the country, and rumours spread like wildfire about an imminent massacre of the Hutu by the Tutsi-dominated army. From hilltop to hilltop in this small, rural and densely populated country in the middle of Africa, it was rumoured that the army was planning a massacre like the one in 1972 where hundreds of thousands of Hutu were killed in Burundi's silent genocide. This time, however, they were determined not to be 'killed like animals,' and within hours Hutu villagers had put up road blocks all over the country, preventing the army from passing. They started hunting down and killing Tutsi by the thousands. An estimated 30,000 Tutsi were killed over the last days of October 1993, and a similar number of Hutu died when the army clamped down on them (Reyntjens 1995: 15). What followed was years of political instability, communal violence and civil war, causing hundreds of thousands to leave their homes and seek protection elsewhere – either inside Burundi or in neighbouring countries.

The cause of events is still unclear and depends on who recounts them. In a part of the world where secrecy and cover-ups are part of political culture, and where rumours and conspiracy theories therefore flourish, it is difficult to discern what actually took place in the days that followed the killing of the president. Whether the killing of the Tutsi was a carefully planned genocide or spontaneous outbursts of anger is heavily disputed, not only among scholars but also among those directly affected by them (Lemarchand 1996a), and establishing 'the truth' is a question for those involved of re-establishing some kind of moral order with victims and perpetrators. In this book I discuss some of these attempts to get to grips with what happened; namely, among Burundian Hutu who fled shortly after the violent events and settled in a big refugee camp just across the border in neighbouring Tanzania.

Once inside Lukole refugee camp, where I did ethnographic fieldwork in 1997/8, these people were no longer just Hutu or Burundians but labelled as 'refugees' with all the connotations that follow such a label. So when I explore their presentations of the events in Burundi, I am also exploring how this is linked to being a refugee under the benevolent, caring regime of humanitarian relief agencies. I am trying to understand how they come to terms with their violent past and how they relate this to their everyday experience of the exceptional space of the camp.

In the liminal space of the camp, refugees are considered by relief agencies and the general public as being outside the normal political life of citizen-subjects. The primary concern of the United Nations High Commissioner for Refugees (UNHCR) is to control and contain this population while at the same time keeping it alive and healthy, waiting for the day when the refugees may return to 'normality' and become proper citizens once again. However, in order to help refugees, one must assume that they need and want help; assume, in other words, that they are 'helpless'. One must also assume that they are the victims of circumstances, and to be the victim of circumstance – a central aspect in the UN declaration on refugees – means to be the victim of history and not the producer of history. Refugees are, in other words, assumed to be without political subjectivity. 'We are like babies in the arms of the UNHCR', as one refugee poetically phrased it to me. Furthermore, because the victims are helpless and without any agency, they are also by definition innocent: they are assumed to have had no part in what happened, and to have been made victims of history and of others' political agency. Humanitarianism revolves around the issue of helping 'bare humanity' – human beings who are victims of others and who are innocent per se. I will return to the conceptual issues that this rises, shortly.

However, the issue of innocence was less obvious in the case of the Hutu refugees. While they had obviously been the victims of massacres – possibly genocide – in 1972, their role in the violence of 1993 was more ambiguous. In 1972, Hutu had no idea what was coming to them. 'We were killed like animals', they would often say in the camp. They hardly had any common Hutu identity. They would often explain to me (as we will see in Chapter 7) that they were innocent before 1972, and also naive: 'We did not even know the difference between a Hutu and a Tutsi'. The watershed events of 1972 changed this, acting as a wake-up call and initiating political parties and Hutu ideologies. So when a similar event seemed to be on the horizon in 1993, Hutu had already lost their naivety and were not willing to become helpless victims once more. They finally lost their innocence when they decided to fight back and massacred Tutsi civilians in a pre-emptive strike.

With the International Criminal Tribunal on Rwanda (ICTR) establishing that the massacres in Rwanda – known as Burundi's 'false twin' – can indeed be classified as genocide, the image of Hutu refugees as pure victims has been further blurred. This had an effect on the huge camps hosting Rwandan refugees in Tanzania and, in particular, in Congo (DRC), when it gradually became clear that they not only sheltered the infamous Interehamwe and the former Forces Armées Rwandaises (Rwandan Armed Forces), but were also run by the same leaders that had orchestrated the genocide in Rwanda. This divided the humanitarian agencies with some, such as Médecins Sans Frontières (MSF), withdrawing from the camps, while others remained and turned a blind eye, insisting that one should not punish the innocent majority for the wrongdoings of a small minority. One might ask oneself how much this affected the image of Hutu refugees from Burundi as well. Not all the Hutu in Lukole refugee camp had taken part in ethnic violence; far from it. Most had fled general unrest or direct persecution and were genuinely in need of protection. But the issue of innocence had become blurred in the eyes of the international community. Issues of victimhood and innocence had become ambiguous in the eyes of the refugees themselves too, on the one hand claiming the victim position while one the other hand breaking this pattern and taking destiny into their own hands.

It is the objective of this book to explore how relief agencies and refugees alike reacted to this ambiguous position of innocence. On the one hand, UNHCR and other humanitarian agencies in the camp needed to produce the refugees in manageable categories in order to be able to help them. The refugees were 'framed' by the camp that set the limits as to how they could act, and they were framed by international relief agencies as innocent victims without a past and without political identities. This was something that the refugees had to deal with. On the other hand, this 'framing' never quite succeeded because refugees were not tabula rasa and they brought with them a past and a political history that was constantly reworked in the camp where new social and moral orders were being negotiated and fought out. This is where agency and creativity emerged. In understanding the everyday strategies and politics of the camp, it is in other words necessary to go beyond the confines of the camp and explore how refugees drew on master narratives of a broader geographical and historical origin.

Hutu refugees in Tanzania constantly reworked their bloody past in Burundi, just as they related to the ongoing conflict in their home country. This obviously created problems in relation to the attempts by the UNHCR to cast them as innocent victims without a past and without political subjectivities. However, their unclear role in the violent conflict also challenged their own narratives about being the victims of Tutsi evil. In this book we will explore how the UNHCR dealt with this ambiguity by splitting the camp population into victims and troublemakers and how the various political factions in the camp positioned themselves and each other variously in relation to innocence and responsibility. Finally, at the individual level, each refugee would cast their life story in relation to these master narratives, drawing ambiguously on the victim position as resource and constraint.

In her seminal work on among Burundian refugees in the 1980s, Liisa Malkki apparently goes beyond the confines of the camp both in time and space, as she explores the production of 'mythico-histories' (see esp. Malkki 1995a). She argues that refugees in camps created standardised versions of history in order to come to terms with their own violent pasts, casting themselves as the innocent victims of an evil Tutsi Other. These mythico-histories were intended, she argues, to restructure a world-view that had crumbled due to immense violence, flight and exile. The old world order no longer gave any meaning, so they were searching for a new one in exile. In Lukole, however, narratives of the past were not beautiful and dangerous mythico-histories – coherent narratives that were 'spontaneously and consistently' brought up in conversation. There seemed at first sight to be a more pragmatic, non-essentialist view of history in Lukole. I argue that this is because narratives in the camp did not merely emerge from the past that the refugees had experienced, or merely from the circumstances of life in exile (although this was certainly important). Whereas Malkki's focus is on the mythico-histories in themselves, I explore how they related to processes of social change in the camp, both in the sense of reflecting different social positions, and in terms of the ways in which such narratives were used in political struggles to gain hegemony in the camp. Furthermore, whereas mythico-histories seemed simply to 'emerge' in Malkki's account, I contend that they were closely linked to political ideologies. This obviously complicates matters for us, as political ideologies were not only formed by conditions in the camp but equally by the political field in Burundi and even global discourses on good governance, socialism, liberation, self determination, genocide and so on. It was such discourses that the narratives in Lukole had to draw on.

Available political ideologies provided the refugees with master narratives within which they could insert themselves and find temporary certainty. It appears that the difference in political dynamics between Mishamo, where Malkki did her fieldwork in the 1980s, and Lukole, where I did fieldwork more than a decade later, is due in part to shifts in the political field in Burundi and hence the position of the Hutu opposition.

As we shall see in Chapter 2, the postcolonial regime in Burundi was controlled by a small Tutsi military-technocratic elite that followed a strongly anticolonial, anti-feudal and modernist ideology and claimed, therefore, that ethnicity was a false invention by colonial powers in order to divide and rule an essentially united Burundian people. The mythico-histories that emerged among Hutu refugees in the camps in Tanzania in the 1970s and 1980s radically challenged this point of view and claimed that Hutu and Tutsi were essentially different races. This ethno-nationalist point of view became increasingly difficult to maintain in the 1990s, however, firstly because the regime in Burundi introduced democratic reforms while partially acknowledging the existence of ethnic groups in the country. In such a political field the ethnic card no longer had much value. Secondly, the position of the Hutu in international opinion had also changed since the 1980s. From being innocent victims of Tutsi persecution, the involvement of Hutu in killing thousands of Tutsi civilians in Burundi in 1993 and the genocide in Rwanda in 1994 had a crucial impact on the image of the Hutu, who were now all perceived as potential perpetrators of genocide. It was against such a powerful discourse that the refugees in Lukole tried to construct their narratives and thereby create a world-view that gave meaning and freed them from collective guilt. In other words, we must locate the construction of mythico-histories – or the lack of these – in a complex arena of social and political relations, some of which were generated within the camp – or by the camp – while others extended beyond the camp.

A striking feature in any refugee camp is the sense that its inhabitants have experienced a radical change in their lives, a 'catastrophic event' where physical surroundings, livelihood opportunities and modes of governing have all changed. One cannot help wondering how social relations and social imaginations must have changed as well. What is more, these changes have all occurred very abruptly, with the choice of packing a few possessions and leaving one's home often being taken within only days or even hours. Similarly obvious is the need among refugees to re-establish their lives after the catastrophic event that turned it upside down. When all that is known to them crumbles beneath them, when the myths and ideologies that they previously held in order to make sense of their world, are invalidated, new stories and new theories are needed to explain what happened to them and what is still happening around them. In other words, as a counterweight to the disruption and breakdown of known order, new orders are needed. This does not imply that what they 'put instead' is necessarily meaningful to others than themselves, or that it is consensual. It is contested, and is often about power struggles.

Such constructions of identity, such reconstructions of the past and attempts to fill the gap, do not happen merely on an individual level, devoid of power relations and other social constraints. As livelihood opportunities and modes of governing change, so do the social structures in the camp. People who used to wield considerable influence in Burundi may have had the ground ripped out from under them while others grabbed the opportunity of the liberating effects of the camp to secure themselves a powerful position. Some had privileged access to livelihoods such as trading with food rations, and some had privileged access to the UNHCR and other agencies, for instance through employment, while others were left to tend for themselves. These shifting relations of power in the camp were of paramount importance to the opportunities of the individual refugees and to the kind of identities they constructed. Not only did people in the camp make sense through narratives like Malkki's mythico-histories that have explicit moral lessons to tell; they also did so in more mundane, everyday, fleeting and unstructured ways, such as rumours and gossip. Finally, the ongoing power struggles over attempts to define hegemonic 'truths' about the conflict in Burundi in themselves structured the camp and hence gave it some kind of local meaning. The often violent struggles between political factions in the camp to define which version of Burundi's history was to dominate, divided the camp and its population into friends and enemies, safe zones and zones of insecurity, centre and periphery – all of which turned the camp into a meaningful place that could be interpreted locally through rumours and other stories. The way in which the struggles to define which version of the truth should prevail – whose story was to dominate – ordered the camp themselves. Power struggles between various factions created differentiated space in the formerly homogeneous, meaningless camp, and thus helped to make life more meaningful.

In sum, this book is about making sense of life under the benevolent regime of the UNHCR, and about being cast as innocent victims without political agency while simultaneously trying to get to grips with one's political and violent past in Burundi.

Refugees as Bare Life

Taking her cues from Mary Douglas and Victor Turner, Malkki argues that refugees are 'matter out of place', like initiands in rites of passage that need secluding in order not to pollute what she has so aptly termed 'the national order of things' (Malkki 1995b). By belonging neither here nor there, refugees become the residue that threatens to topple the established symbolic order, disturbing the Herderian 'garden of nations'. They expose, in other words, the constructedness of the relationship between people, place and identity. In the words of Giorgio Agamben, 'If the refugee represents such a disquieting element in the order of the nation-state, this is so primarily because, by breaking the identity between the human and the citizen and between nativity and nationality, it brings the originary fiction of sovereignty to crisis' (Agamben 2000: 21). Agamben argues that refugees are the symptom of the separation between birth and nation – between human being and citizen – and are therefore 'bare life' or *homo sacer* (life that can be killed but not sacrificed): 'only as such is it made into the object of aid and protection' (Agamben 1998: 133).

While such disenfranchised bare life is outside the *polis* – 'the city of men' – it is also an 'inclusive exclusion' and therefore productive. That is to say that any political community of citizens depends upon the exclusion of certain human beings that are reduced to bare life. As Nevzat Soguk (1999) convincingly argues, the refugee figure is constructed by nation-states as the 'necessary other' – a kind of Derridean supplement or constitutive outside. Not only do refugees lack a home, a nation and citizenship, they also lack 'proper agency, proper voice, proper face' (ibid.: 243). By producing the refugee as someone marginal and lacking, the normalcy of the 'citizen/nation/state constellation' is also produced, because citizens of nation-states get to have everything that the refugee lacks. So, as much as refugees disturb the nation, they also help define it by being what the national citizen is not.

It is important to stress that 'the refugee' is not only created through discourse – through naming – but also through state practices and, more importantly in this context, through the benevolent governing techniques of relief agencies. As Foucault would argue, the various difficulties and obstacles that refugees create need translating into a problem, to which the refugee agencies can then propose certain solutions.[1] 'It is in this field that the complex difficulties presented for the activities of statecraft by the movements and even the inertia of people are metamorphosed or reconceptualized as manageable problems within the logic of the sovereign state' (ibid.: 51). Whereas Soguk emphasises discourse, I will argue that it is the trivial daily practices of 'caring for' refugees that create the refugee as bare life – life that is outside the national order of things and hence life without political rights. It is through environmental awareness campaigns, women's empowerment programmes, food distribution, health clinics, elections for street leaders and so on that refugees are created.

Lukole refugee camp, shaped as it is by the relief agencies' top-tuned means of securing the lives of the refugees, easily lends itself to a Foucauldian understanding of biopower. Foucault (1978) describes a shift in modern society from a mode of governing based on sovereignty to a mode (or rather art) of governing based on biopower. Whereas sovereign power was deductive, based on the right of the king to take time, money, land and ultimately life, biopower is productive, its main objective being to maintain the well-being of the population as a whole. 'One might say that the ancient right to take life or let live was replaced by a power to foster life or disallow it to the point of death' (ibid.:138). Along with an increased focus on life and a shift away from deductive power to productive power, more and more mechanisms of control and regulation are shifted outside the sphere of the law with a 'growing importance assumed by the action of the norm' (ibid.:144). As Dean (1999) points out, the liberal art of government is a double movement of keeping the state lean and keen while expanding governmentality to other spheres: social services, schools, health care, psychiatry, NGOs and so on. Such 'natural processes' become loci of power relations as they are studied, measured, classified and regulated by specialists (doctors, psychiatrists, demographers, town planners). In the process, these specialists produce knowledge about – and hence create – criminals, delinquents, refugees, vulnerable groups and democratic citizens.

A forceful achievement of Foucault and 'the governmentality school'[2] has been to dissolve the opposition between government and freedom, enabling us to see how individuals in liberal democracies are governed by governing themselves in accordance with certain norms and values. I will propose that the attempts by the UNHCR and other humanitarian agencies to introduce refugee participation and community development in the camp can be perceived as a technique of government. Although the UNHCR is not a state, it can act like a modern liberal state in its everyday practices of governing the camp through norms as it attempts to foster life in the camp. Through participation and community development programmes it attempts to create self-governing citizen-subjects (Cruikshank 1999). However, despite the similarities, there are also aspects that are strongly at odds with what we normally understand by 'normal liberal democracy'. The fact that refugees are not allowed outside the camp, that they have no say in what to eat and how to build their huts (blindés), all makes the idea of creating self-governing citizen-subjects look rather absurd. It might seem more appropriate to compare the camp with colonial governmentality where colonial subjects were not perceived to be fit to enjoy the full rights of citizenship.[3] Their capacities to govern themselves could only be fostered through periods of compulsion and discipline (Hindess 2001).

Taking account of the exceptions – those spaces where biopower seems suspended – we may also see Lukole as an expression of Giorgio Agamben's camp as the hidden matrix and *nomos* of modern political space (Agamben 1998: 166; 2000: 37). Agamben offers a timely critique of and complement to Foucault's concept of biopolitics. Whereas Foucault operates with a temporal shift from sovereign power to biopower, Agamben argues – inspired by Carl Schmitt – that biopower is always underpinned by sovereign power. The camp for Agamben is related to the Schmittean state of exception (Schmitt 1985), created by a sovereign decision and related to the concept of a threat towards the stability of the political order (Agamben 1998: 168–71): 'the camp is the structure in which the state of exception is permanently realised' (Agamben 2000: 40). Here, the Tanzanian state decides that the refugees are a threat to the nation-state and puts them in this exceptional space, at once inside and outside the law, and the refugees are reduced to bare life, outside the *polis* of national citizens. The result is, as Nyers argues, that 'all notions of political agency are, in a word, emptied from refugee subjectivity' (Nyers 1998: 18). We must, however, not assume that the camp is the opposite of biopower. Agamben's main argument is that sovereign power and biopower are closely entwined. Biopower is about classifying and about turning 'people' into 'populations', 'transforming an essentially political body into an essentially biological body' (Agamben 2002: 84), and with each classification we get closer to 'biological life' or 'bare life'.[4] In this sense, the camp, which is the ultimate zone of sovereign power, is also the product of biopower.

I would argue that although the concepts of bare life and the camp are compelling, Burundian refugees in Lukole were not just any kind of bare life. For Agamben, the main point is that the camp is a space where normal law is suspended, suggesting that anything from Auschwitz to the *zones d'attente* in French international airports count as camps. Whether atrocities take place or not, does not depend on the law, he explains, but rather 'on the civility and ethical sense of the police that act temporarily as sovereign' (ibid.: 42). Although there undoubtedly are similarities between refugee camps, asylum centres, mining compounds, concentration camps and slave plantations,[5] I suggest that we must also explore the particularities that often emerge if we change our perspective a little and explore the camp from within.

In the case of Lukole, it is important to acknowledge that the camp was being subjected to a strongly moralising and ethical biopolitical project by humanitarian agencies. Whereas the Tanzanian camp commandant zealously controlled who entered and who left the camp, guarding the perimeters of this island in Tanzanian territory – an island that was outside Tanzanian law in order to secure Tanzanian law – it was international relief agencies, led by the UNHCR, that were in charge of the day-to-day 'care and maintenance' of the camp. They exerted a caring biopower, concerned with the life and health of the refugee population.

Furthermore, the refugees themselves sought to manoeuvre in this temporary space, thus creating pockets of sovereign power outside the reach of either the camp commandant's restrictions or the UNHCR's benevolent control. Although they were positioned as bare life by the Tanzanian state, they were not paralysed. And likewise, as much as the biopolitics of the UNHCR attempted to create moral apolitical beings, it never succeeded and history and politics would strike back. Due to the breakdown of class, gender and age hierarchies, the camp also became a liberating space for certain groups, an 'amoral' space of opportunities. While the refugees themselves also conceived of the camp as an exceptional space – a temporary suspension of moral order – they were constantly working on constructing their own political subjectivities. In other words, the camp was at once voided of politics by international agencies in their attempts to cast the refugees as pure victims, while it was also hyper-politicised in nature. As we shall see in later chapters, virtually all aspects of life were interpreted in terms of the oppositional political rivalry extant in the camp. This was due to the indeterminate nature of the camp, where nothing could be taken for granted any longer. The isolation of exile – the exceptional space of the camp, outside any normality

– perpetually suspended all regularities and institutions and created a space for politics, where politics is understood in the sense of attempting to create new hegemonies in a space where nothing is taken for granted.

The camp itself was a kind of 'excluded inside'. It was included because refugees constantly referred back to the political field of Burundi, inextricably linking the camp to the home country. And as much as Burundi influenced the lives and imaginations of Hutus in exile, the camp also became a part of Burundian reality. However, the camp was also excluded: although a part of the nation and its imaginations, it was also a parenthesis in time and place, a waiting room where refugees were meant to kill time before returning to 'normality.' By being outside the national order of things, the camp was an attempt at producing non-citizens, human beings without political subjectivities. This contradictory position of the camp as both inside Burundi and outside all nation-states, hence rendering the population both hyper-politicised and non-political, is the basic premise of this research, and in this book I attempt to explore this contradiction at several levels and from various angles. I explore how the camp and the refugees were produced by humanitarian agencies through everyday governmental techniques and how these agencies attempted to reconcile the contradictions of the camp – at once a non-place and seeped in history, at once victims and perpetrators, at once depoliticized and hyper-politicized. I explore how the refugees themselves related to their past and to the conflict in Burundi – where on the one hand, the past and the conflict had shaped the refugees and made them what they were, while on the other hand they were creating narratives about their past and about the nature of the conflict. I explore how the refugees reacted to being 'framed' – the attempts by the UNHCR to create them as helpless victims in need of empowerment. How did they interpret the camp? And how did they attempt to recapture it? In other words, the challenge is to grasp the dialectics of the camp as produced by and as the producer of history – and to remain open to its precarious, ambiguous position as neither here nor there.

Refugees in Tanzania

Being one of the most politically stable countries in the region, Tanzania has received large numbers of refugees and migrants over the years. During colonial times, Rwandans and Burundians would escape corvée labour in the Belgian protectorates and seek employment on the plantations in Tanzania (Daley 1993). Later, Rwandan Tutsi arrived in the Kagera region, following the 'social revolution' in Rwanda in 1959 and the violence that followed (Gasarasi 1990; Prunier 1995b). Many of these settled among Tanzanians in the border region while others were settled in specific 'villages' (Gasarasi 1984).

The first Hutu refugees arrived in Tanzania following the selective genocide in Burundi in 1972. Following a small rebellion in 1972 by a handful of Hutu in the south of the country, the Tutsi-dominated army launched a massive and repressive response, killing somewhere between 80,000 and 200,000 Hutu. They primarily targeted the 'Hutu elite', assuming that it was the elite who had planned the rebellion. In practice the army systematically tried to kill every Hutu with more than primary school education, leading René Lemarchand (1974) to call it 'selective genocide'. Hundreds of thousands of Hutu were forced to leave the country and settled primarily in Rwanda and Tanzania.

These refugees were resettled in settlements in scarcely populated areas far from the border where they were given large plots to farm and gradually became self-sufficient, even producing a surplus for the local market (Christensen 1985; Daley 1991; Malkki 1995a). In this way, the Tanzanian state perceived refugees within the general agro-developmentalist framework of Nyerere's *Ujamaa* (van Hoyweghen 2001; Chaulia 2003), and scholars and policy makers commended Tanzania for its hospitality towards refugees and its approach to refugee settlements in the 1970s and 1980s.[6]

In spite of the Tanzanian government's attempts at containing refugees in camps, substantial numbers of refugees have managed to live clandestinely in the border area (where they speak a language similar to the local population), in anonymity in Kigoma town (Malkki 1995a), or in Dar es Salaam, popularly known as 'Bongoland' – literally 'Brain-land' – because you have to be smart to survive there (Sommers 2001).

In the 1990s the country adopted a stricter attitude towards refugees, and the camps were oriented towards 'temporary care and maintenance' rather than self-sufficiency. Land was only made available for housing and not for agriculture, and the Tanzanian government and UNHCR encouraged repatriation rather than integration (Mendel 1997: 43).[7] This is often justified by the Tanzanian government – and taken as an explanation by the UNHCR – as a response to the vast number of refugees coming across the borders following ethnic violence in Burundi in late 1993 and, in particular, the 1994 genocide in Rwanda that brought 600,000 refugees to Tanzania within a very short time span.[8]

Saskia Van Hoyweghen finds the shift in Tanzania's refugee policies related to a shift in domestic politics away from *Ujamaa* and towards a liberal market economy. The result is that refugees have gone from being an economic resource to being a security issue (van Hoyweghen 2001: 3). Furthermore, as Chaulia (2003) argues, with the end of the cold war and apartheid, Tanzania no longer plays a role as a frontline state, supporting political refugees from South Africa, Zimbabwe and Namibia. Again, refugees lose their status as a resource – in this case in the political sphere. 'Freedom fighters' were never stripped of their national specificity or their political identities; they were part of an African national community. Present day refugees on the other hand are an irritation in the relationship with neighbouring states and seen as a threat to national security. The result of this shift is that refugee settlements are viewed as temporary solutions. They therefore typically have large populations of 100,000 to 150,000 people, and life is generally made hard for the refugees in order to prevent them from settling in too well. Hannah Arendt claims that our 'human condition' is premised on three kinds of human activities: as labouring beings, as political actors and as biological life forms (cited in Ong 2006: 22). With the fall of *Ujamaa*, refugees no longer play a role as labour and with the end of apartheid they no longer play a role as bearers of political rights. What is left, then, is biological life – and it is upon this kind of life that the UNHCR and international NGOs can act. Refugees are in other words stripped of any uncomfortable political subjectivity and treated as bare life.

Constructing Lukole

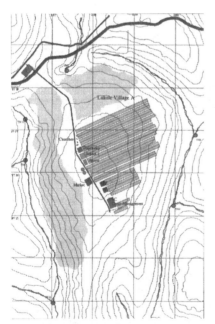 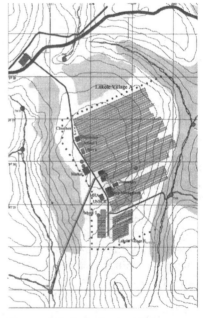

Figure 1.1: Lukole A, 1994 (Source: UNHCR).

Figure 1.2: Lukole A, 1995 (Source: UNHCR).

Figures 1.1 and 1.2 show how Lukole refugee camp[9] has developed. It was established in January 1994 as a response to the refugees that had fled Burundi after the assassination of President Ndadaye in October 1993. Originally, the 'caseload'[10] was 8,000 refugees. This number grew as a number of Burundian refugees who had lived in Rwanda also arrived in Tanzania in the aftermath of the 1994 Rwandan genocide. Some of these were put into Lukole (as can be seen from Figure 1.2), while others went to mixed Rwandan/Burundian camps in the district. During the following two years, the number of refugees fluctuated, but as the situation in Burundi worsened, the number grew steadily. In 1995, Palipehutu (Parti pour la Libération du Peuple Hutu) launched attacks in Muyinga province, starting a genuine guerrilla war just across the border from Ngara district. Tens of thousands of peasants from Muyinga fled to Tanzania in 1995 and 1996, and were mostly placed in Kitali Hills and Keza camps, some 70 kilometres away.

Whereas many of the first refugees to arrive in late 1993 and early 1994 had fled Burundi due to their political position and opinions, mainly as cadres in the moderate 'Hutu' party, Frodebu (Front pour la Démocratie au Burundi), the refugees who came across the border from Muyinga fled en masse from general insecurity. The latter were generally less politicised, less homogeneous in political outlook, and a significant number of them sympathised with Palipehutu. This resulted in intense political rivalry in the camps between Palipehutu and Frodebu, which escalated into violence around New Year 1996/7, leading to several deaths and people leaving the camp or being forced to move to other parts of the camp.

In December 1996 and January 1997, Rwandan refugees in Tanzania were forced to repatriate.[11] Following this, all the Burundian refugees who had been staying in camps with Rwandan refugees were gathered into one camp: Lukole. The majority of these came from the Kitali camp, and political differences between the refugees from Kitali and those from Lukole created problems that still haunted the camp while I was there, structuring the political and social fabric of the camp.

In spite of complaints from humanitarian agencies that the population density in the camp was already a health hazard, the Tanzanian authorities pushed ahead with plans to place close to 100,000[12] refugees in a camp that in late 1996 had held less than 20,000. Simultaneously, the Tanzanian authorities prohibited refugees from growing crops inside a 4 kilometre zone around the camp. Previously, they were able to supplement a meagre diet of maize, beans and cooking oil with crops that they were more accustomed to. From January 1997, they were only permitted to grow vegetables on their allotted plots inside the camp where they were also expected to build houses. These measures were intended to increase the 'push factor' in refugee repatriation efforts; in other words, the logic was that refugees might decide to remain if life in the camp became too comfortable. Thus, the camp turned from being a 'semi-permanent' refugee site in 1994 and 1995 to being a 'temporary' refugee site in 1997 (compare Figures 1.1 and 1.2 with 1.3).

Figure 1.3: Lukole A and B, 1997 (Source UNHCR)[13]

The refugees from Kitali were relocated to Lumasi, a camp right next to Lukole that had been vacated by Rwandans in December 1996. Some of these were moved a second time to plots in between the existing plots in Lukole. For every original street in Lukole, two new streets were established in between the old ones. However, due to pressure from the UNHCR, the remaining caseload was allowed to remain in Lumasi. However, in order to maintain the official policy of relocating all Burundians to Lukole, Lumasi was renamed Lukole B (UNHCR 1997: 1).[14] In March 1997 there were roughly 57,000 refugees in Lukole A and 42,000 refugees in Lukole B. During the second half of 1997, the Tanzanian authorities carried out a massive operation to 'flush out' illegal immigrants and refugees staying in villages in the border region of the country, who were given the choice to repatriate or go to the camp.[15] Those who went to the camp were allotted plots in separate villages in Lukole B, along with new arrivals from Burundi.

Planning the Camp

The maps of Lukole refugee camp, drawn by the UNHCR's site planner, give the impression of an extremely well organised space. The plots are of equal size and square in shape. They are arranged along good, broad feeder roads and are a far cry from the chaotic 'lived' space of squatter camps and *bidonvilles* in this part of the world. The uniformity of the dwellings (at least from a bird's eye perspective; the picture on the ground changes considerably) gives the impression that people have very little say in planning their space. It also gives the impression that efficiency and bureaucratic rationality are the driving forces behind planning.

However, if we take a closer look at the camp, we see certain inconsistencies in the spatial planning. Thus, space reflects social action but it also has a dynamic of its own that affects the social.[16] In this case, the spatial layout of the camp reflects previous planning practices and compromises between various social actors. Space represents a 'time lag' reflecting social actions of the past. In later chapters, we will also see how the refugees attempt to appropriate the 'space' of the camp and make it into their own 'place'. The cracks in the planner's order can be seen in the differences between Lukole A and Lukole B in terms of layout and plot size. If we are to understand this, we must look at the negotiations and compromises that have been made during the history of Lukole's construction.

The criteria for planning camps change according to the theories that the planners work by. At times they believe that it is important for the refugees to live in streets and at other times in 'villages'. In this manner, Lukole B was partitioned into villages while Lukole A was partitioned into streets and blocks because Lukole B was originally part of another camp – Lumasi – which was inhabited predominantly by Rwandan refugees prior to January 1997. The camps for Rwandans were organised according to village, *commune* and *prefecture* in Rwanda. As the leaders from Rwanda moved with their constituencies, they re-established themselves as leaders in the camps, making it convenient for the UNHCR to administrate. The UNHCR later abandoned this policy because of the ethical dilemma of supporting leaders who had helped plan the genocide and because these leaders' grip on the population was so strong that they could actively defy UNHCR activities. Lukole, on the other hand, was planned according to a logic of mixing refugees and allocating them plots according to time of arrival, regardless of their commune of origin. Thus, one can read the administrative past in the physical space of Lukole. Apart from contradictions within the UNHCR system that led to compromises between various experts, local political agendas also interfered with the bureaucratic dream, as did unexpected refugee movements in and out of Tanzania due to changing political situations in Burundi, Rwanda and Congo (DRC). While relief agencies were primarily concerned with the well-being of the refugees – reducing morbidity rates and so on – the Tanzanian government was worried about the destabilising effects of refugees as 'matter out of place' and tried to impede their movements; meanwhile, conflicts in Burundi, Rwanda and Congo (DRC) caused new 'waves' and 'influxes' in unpredictable ways. This led to a number of compromises, but as the maps reveal, planners attempted to keep the managerial dream alive. That is their only option, after all.

Entering Lukole Refugee Camp

Like most foreign visitors, researchers and relief workers, I first saw Lukole refugee camp from the air, coming in on a small UN plane from Mwanza, some 350 kilometres away. After leaving the sprawling lakeside town, we flew over villages of round huts connected by myriad small footpaths, and finally over what looked like uninhabited bush, before coming to the camp. First, the trees stopped and a web of paths emerged, dotted with people carrying firewood to the camp. Then, all of a sudden, the camp emerged, defying the surrounding countryside with its straight rows of blue and white huts, its equally straight roads, and its evenly distributed water stands. The neat grid was broken only by a few larger structures that turned out to be the food distribution centre, where the World Food Programme's (WFP) trucks were offloading hundreds of sacks of corn from ECHO (European Community Humanitarian aid Office) and USAID (The United States Agency for International Development) into huge storehouses, and, further along, square buildings surrounded by fences. These were hospitals and the offices of the UNHCR, NGOs and the camp commandant.

Roughly 100,000 Hutu refugees who had fled Burundi since 1993 lived on the 950 hectares that had been allotted them by the Tanzanian government. The UNHCR was in charge of keeping these people alive, and had created an efficient bureaucratic machine to deal with this challenging task. Every refugee was registered and given a ration card and a clearly demarcated plot with a street, block and plot number. Here, they could build a *blindé* (hut) as long as it lived up to certain regulations. They were told to dig a pit latrine of certain dimensions and at a certain distance from the *blindé*, and they were encouraged to keep their plot clean. They had to remain within a 4-kilometre zone, and at the time of my research they were forbidden to dig fields within this zone. On the cans of USAID oil they received it was clearly marked that the content was not to be sold or bartered. They received food rations, elementary household belongings – such as pots, jerrycans, blankets and plastic sheeting – and they were given free healthcare as well as free primary school teaching. In other words, they were kept alive and expected to do as little as possible.

When entering the camp by foot, however, the impression was quite different. Only from certain angles did I get a feeling of the grid that had been settled over these people. Although I could see the fences, the impression was much like that of any other Third World city. There was a hustle and a bustle of people walking, cycling, shouting, drinking, loading sacks of WFP corn onto pickups and bunches of green bananas off the pickups, while young men with shiny shoes and newly pressed trousers tiptoed round the puddles, trying to avoid the ever-present red mud, ostentatiously carrying a pen and a book in one hand, and a Rastafarian would be hanging out with his friend, the cigarette vendor, near the row of hairdresser shops.

The more time I spent walking around, the more varied the picture became. I discovered the areas of the camp that were quiet during the day, because all the able-bodied men and women were out collecting firewood or trying to earn a little extra by working for Tanzanians, the areas where the houses were mere shelters made of grass and the areas where most of the houses were mud brick and big enough to stand upright in. Some people stayed near their huts while others spent a lot of time around the market places. But even the market did not represent homogeneous space, because some people could afford to sit and drink Pepsi and bottled beer (usually smuggled in from Burundi) and eat brochettes in restaurants like La Vedette and One-One Love Bar, while others drank *gua gua* (banana beer) from glasses in the less prestigious bars, and most people made do with *mugorigori* (maize beer) from shared plastic cans in the open air or in improvised shelters of plastic sheeting. And when I took the time – a lot of time – to sit down in one of these bars and listen to the latest rumours and gossip, I realised that the camp was divided along other – less visible – lines as well. After months in the camp, people started telling me stories about the other political party, why so-and-so was killed, or how the Tutsi had infiltrated the Tanzanian police force and UNHCR. The political fault lines that structured life in the camp gradually emerged in contour, despite the efforts of the Tanzanian authorities and UNHCR to stamp out politics. However, even after a year in the camp, I never filled in all the gaps; there are aspects of camp life that remain unknown to me.

In order to grasp the complexities of this exceptional space, I have approached the camp from several angles and through diverse lenses. First, I approach the camp both as it is seen from the bird's-eye view of the relief agencies and the Tanzanian authorities and from the pedestrian view of the refugees who live there. This does not imply privileging one perspective over the other. The view from ground is no more authentic or real than the view from above; both are partial views. Seen from the angle of the ordinary refugee, the camp is an overwhelming place and the UNHCR is seen as an omnipotent and ever-present Big Brother, planning their lives in detail and concocting diabolic plans with the Tutsi and Western powers.[7] Seen through the eyes of an international relief worker, the camp is a mystery and can only be made comprehendible if translated into nutrition rates, mortality rates, degrees of vulnerability, water rations and security levels. Both views are limited and both views have the power to shape the camp and affect the other.

As a second distinction, I explore the camp both in terms of internal political dynamics, generated from shifts in social hierarchies within the camp and in terms of external dynamics, linking the camp with a broader political history of Burundi and the Great Lakes. The camp constitutes a space of suspension like the seclusion sites in rites of passage (Turner 1967). This permits old norms and hierarchies to dissolve and give way to a kind of amoral space where anything goes. However, not everything does go in the camp. Firstly, there are structures that the new authorities – the UNHCR and other NGOs – create, intentionally or not, within which the refugees must manoeuvre. Secondly, being a non-place (Augé 1995), a kind of waiting room suspended between the past of one's memories in Burundi – sweet as well as bitter – and one's dreams of a future Burundi, the camp is not totally delinked from the moral orders of Burundi. Indeed, Burundi saturates the camp.

These tensions – between the past, the present and the future; between the camp and Burundi; and between the camp from above and from below – have structured my approach to the camp and structure the remaining chapters of the book.

I did fieldwork in the camp for just over a year in 1997/8. I entered Lukole on my own, a piece of paper in my hand with the name of someone who might be interested in employment as an assistant. The advantages were clear: my car did not have the stickers of any agency on its sides,[18] and I was free to some degree to create my own position. There were, however, certain drawbacks to not having a clearly defined status in the camp: Since I could not be categorised as either aid worker, consultant or government representative, people in Lukole made their own theories about me. Some thought I might be a spy sent by the Tutsi who are smart enough to send a *muzungu* (white person) instead of a Tutsi (whom they would recognise at once). This kind of rumour was, of course, very disquieting for me as it seemed obvious that nobody would be interested in confiding in a Tutsi spy.

A more comfortable role ascribed to me by passers-by in the camp was that of a White Father. 'Komera Padre!' the children would shout, 'Hello Father!' Fortunately, my interpreter and guide was a great help in trying to explain my intentions in the camp, not only because he managed to translate and explain my purpose in a language that they could understand, but also because he could vouch for me. Being a respected person in the camp whose word carried a lot of weight, he vouched for my identity and initiated me into the camp.[19] As might be clear from the above, suspicion was a relatively big problem when doing fieldwork. With the Burundian government implicitly accusing refugees of being *génocidaires*, they obviously were not interested in recounting anything about their own involvement in any kind of violence in Burundi. Similarly, political parties and military training in the camp were sensitive issues, as all political activity in refugee camps was banned by the Tanzanian authorities.

The original suspicion towards me as a 'wild card' was gradually replaced by a certain amount of trust, thanks to my assistant. People began to find debating with me interesting and asked me to return. They saw my presence as a chance to gain access to the outside world, so that the 'big nations' might hear their side of the story. Generally, in Lukole there was an acute sense of being isolated and left to oblivion in the Tanzanian bush and a sense that the Tutsi were deceiving the international community; this fuelled a strong urge to get 'the truth' out to the 'big nations'. Sensitive issues – such as the nature of the conflict and its solutions, and political opposition –were often discussed after the formal interview. However, although my assistant gave me access to the camp, there are still areas on my map of Lukole that remain *terra incognita*, and I am convinced that it is my duty to leave some stones unturned.

Outline of the Book

I start my analysis outside the camp, exploring the repertoire of imaginaries of Burundi and its past that have been created over time, as it is this repertoire that actors in Lukole draw on in their struggle to create a moral order in the camp. Chapter 2 provides both an overview of the contested Burundian historiography and an attempt at placing these competing narratives in a historical and political context. While refugees produce histories in the camp – drawing on these metanarratives – they are also themselves the product of history. The second aim of this chapter is therefore to explore their historical production.

A central point of contention in these interpretations of the 'true nature of Burundi' is the question of whether Burundian society is fundamentally split between Hutu and Tutsi or whether this is simply a colonial legacy. I argue that in order to transgress the primordialist/instrumentalist dilemma that dominates analyses of ethnicity in Burundi, we must explore how these images of Burundi are bound up in larger narratives about progress, anticolonialism, tradition, inequality, and so forth. They are in constant flux and change radically at certain points in history. Thus the events of 1972 changed the image of Burundian Hutu, casting them as innocent victims of Tutsi evil, while the events of 1993 challenged their position as pure victims and called for new imaginings of Burundi.

In Chapter 3 the perspective changes to the present and to the bird's-eye view of the camp from above, as I seek to uncover the ways in which refugees are 'framed' by international humanitarian discourse and practice. I explore how the refugees are subjected to the governmental practices of international relief agencies, most notably the UNHCR. The grid of the camp is created by bureaucratic logics and specialist knowledge with the aim of creating the 'optimal solution' to the 'humanitarian crisis.' It is also the product, however, of ad hoc compromises between Tanzanian authorities and relief agencies. Furthermore, I try to grasp the apparent contradictions between regimes of bureaucratic control and a heavy emphasis on community development and refugee participation. Through a Foucauldian lens this can be seen as a benevolent mode of governing through creating self-governing citizens. I argue that the UNHCR in this way is able to objectify the refugees into two main groups in the camp – victims and troublemakers – the former being susceptible to community development while the latter undermine such projects. These categories are strongly gendered as women are assumed to embody 'the community' while men introduce trouble in the shape of politics. Finally, relief agencies attempt to sanitise the past and void the camp of politics by supporting various cultural activities in the camp.

In Chapter 4 we change perspective once more. This time we move from the bureaucratic view of the grid from above to the refugees' interpretations of their new surroundings and their new masters, as expressed in narratives of a loss of moral order. Although the UNHCR attempts, through sensitisation programmes and information campaigns, to produce certain subjectivities, these may not correspond with the ways in which refugees interpret their position in the camp. For instance, most refugees interpret the policy of promoting equality – especially between the sexes – as a threat, not only to the men and the elders but to the Burundian way of life as such, and hence to all segments of society. The symptoms of this decay are identified as a lack of respect for men, the elders and the 'big men' by women, the youth and 'small people'; the causes of this, meanwhile, are believed to be the UNHCR, the urban nature of the camp, and the experience of mixing with people of other cultures – Rwandans and Tanzanians in particular. In sum, the refugees interpret the exceptional space of the camp through tales of decay where the known moral order is perceived to be under pressure. In these tales gender, age, class and ethnicity are renegotiated in relation to the new surroundings, giving a sense of loss on the one hand and a sense of new opportunities on the other.

In Chapter 5 I move from the level of discourse to the level of social practices and from the aggregate level of the camp as a whole to issues of social differentiation within the camp population. Starting in three case histories of young men who hold key positions in the camp, I argue that three groups have taken advantage of the fact that the social order of Burundi can no longer be taken for granted; the street leaders, the NGO employees and the entrepreneurs. In all three groups, young men are strikingly present. They become 'liminal experts' who are able to play by the new rules and with the new rulers, outmanoeuvring the older generation. However, this process is not unidirectional or total. The camp does not mean that all former norms and habits cease to function. Most people juggle the diverse hierarchies of status markers from Burundi and from the camp, ambivalent as regards the Hutu virtues of 'the good old days' and the 'brave new NGO world' of the young liminal experts. And while these young men break down the old hierarchies of gerontocracy, they build up new ones in their struggle to rehabilitate the masculinity that they perceive to have lost to the UNHCR.

In spite of attempts by NGOs to void the camp of politics, two political parties dominate the camp to a degree that virtually all issues and conflicts are subsumed by this oppositional logic. In Chapter 6 I explore the political field in Lukole and show that political rivalry is intermeshed with personal networks about access to power and resources that come from the NGOs. But political rivalry is also a means for making sense out of a senseless place. Through political rivalry, rumours and violence, the homogeneous space of the camp is differentiated according to various meaningful hierarchies. Political struggle is about dominating the political field as well as defining and ordering this field, in this manner defining which principles of differentiation are to be dominant and meaningful. By following certain key events in the camp – as extended case studies – I demonstrate how politics, rumour and violence interact in attempts to hegemonise the camp and create ordered space.

Having set the stage by exploring Burundian historiography, available interpretations of the camp, and social and political differentiation within the camp, I return in Chapter 7 to the dispute with Malkki's research findings that was the original starting point of the book. Based on a number of detailed life histories of young men with different social and political backgrounds, I explore the construction of history in Lukole and the insertion of personal memories into broader narratives on Burundi's past and the nature of ethnic conflict. I argue that these memories relate to changes in the political field in Burundi and to the general narrative of the Hutu loss of innocence. The life history narratives reflect this dilemma as they all avoid explicit reference to violence and all emphasise a past of ethnic harmony. Related to the theme of losing innocence is a theme of 'opening one's eyes'. This is portrayed as an ambiguous and painful process, and draws out the same moral dilemmas that many of the narratives about the experience of camp life do. I argue that the political parties in the camp relate to these moral dilemmas in slightly different ways in their attempt to remain morally pure.

In the concluding chapter I attempt to pick up all the threads that have been laid out and look at the connections between the exceptional space of a camp where politics is discouraged and the past sanitised and the kind of political identities, histories and moral orders that appear.

Notes

1. In a similar manner, James Ferguson (1990) beautifully illustrates how development institutions construct 'development problems' to which they happen to have the solutions.
2. See Cruikshank (1999), Dean (1999), Foucault et al. (1991) and Rose (1999).
3. For a convincing study of colonial administration in Africa and the distinction between urban citizens and rural subjects, see Mamdani (1996).
4. Foucault argues that these classifications are based on race, the ultimate biological marker. For an insightful discussion of Foucault's understanding of race and an analysis of colonial biopower, see Stoler (1995).
5. See also Mbembe (2003) for a comparison with slave plantations.
6. See Gasarasi (1984: 49), Christensen (1985), Armstrong (1990: 204; 1991), and Anthony (1990).
7. For analyses of the shift in Tanzanian refugee policies, see van Hoyweghen (2001), Whitaker (2002a), Chaulia (2003) and Landan (2007).
8. Several studies show, however, that the 'impact' of refugees is not so negative as it is made out to be by Tanzanian authorities and NGOs, who are vying for donor funding to 'mitigate the negative impact' and 'rehabilitate' the environment, schools, infrastructure and medical facilities in 'refugee affected areas'. See Waters (1997), Whitaker (1999, 2002b) and Landau (2001, 2003).
9. Mostly, I call it a refugee camp rather than the official term, refugee site, as this was the term most commonly used by refugees and relief staff alike.
10. One of the bureaucratic terms used in UNHCR discourse. Others include 'relief operation, feeding figure and influx'. Bauman(1989) describes how the use of impersonal concepts makes it easier for the bureaucrats involved to make unpopular decisions. It is easier to cut down the food ration for a caseload than it is for women, men and children.
11. For discussions of this repatriation, see Whitaker (2002a).
12. In March 1997, the UNHCR carried out a registration of all refugees in Lukole (A and B). Here the total population was 98,371, as opposed to the planning figure of 107,985 before registration. The same report claims that the feeding figure as of 30 April 1997, was 101,957 (UNHCR 1997).
13. What is here labelled Village A and B in Lukole A, I elsewhere refer to as Lukole I and Lukole II in order not to confuse it with Lukole A and B.
14. In the following I will use the official terms Lukole A and B.
15. The accounts that these people told me of the ways in which the authorities had acted were horrific, and the operation has been strongly criticised by Human Rights Watch (1999).
16. For theoretical debates on the relation between society and space, see Pred (1986), Harvey (1990), Lefebvre (1991), Massey (1992) and Simonsen (1993).
17. For a discussion of conspiracy theories and ideas of 'big nations', see Turner (2002, 2004).

18. Johan Pottier (1996) discusses this issue. He claims, however, that 'no one wanders around freely' and that the only access is through the UNHCR or NGOs. I actually succeeded in transgressing these biases, perhaps because I took the time needed as opposed to consultants and other visitors.

19. My assistant was in no way an unbiased, neutral actor in the camp. However, since virtually everyone in the camp is forced to support one of the two political parties, it is doubtful whether I could have found an English-speaking person who was not involved, and I soon came to terms with this and learned to use it as a resource rather than a hindrance.

2
Histories of Conflict

In Lukole, the past was evoked in order to explain the violence that forced people to flee Burundi so as to establish clarification and cosmological order. The various ways of imagining Burundi that were reflected in these narratives do not tell us much about what 'really' happened in Burundi, and rather reflected present concerns in the camp. However, the narratives did not crystallise out of thin air but drew on a repertoire of discourses on the nature of Burundian society, constructed through historically located power struggles. It is the aim of this chapter to uncover the historical emergence of the repertoire of images and imaginations of Burundi's past. I argue that if we are to understand the changing discourses on ethnicity in Burundi, we need to place them in a broader context of political ideologies, including ideas about modernity, anticolonialism, tradition and development. We have to look at decolonisation and the one-party state's anticolonial paranoia. We have to look at the emergence of a politicised diaspora and its influence on the political field in Burundi. And we have to look at the influence of global discourses on democracy and good governance in determining the shifts in the position of ethnicity in Burundian politics.

Historiography in Burundi is incredibly powerful. As Lemarchand (1996a) points out, in Burundi there is the conflict, costing lives and causing others to leave their homes, and then there is the 'metaconflict', which is the conflict over what the conflict is actually about. Central to the metaconflict is the question of ethnic origins, which very crudely put is the question of whether ethnic groups and ethnic tensions are primordial, going back to the successive waves of immigration to the interlacustrine kingdoms of Central Africa; or whether they are newer constructs, the invention of colonial and neocolonial powers and the outcome of policies of divide and rule in Africa. This conflict is played out among political factions both in Burundi and in exile, and is also carried over into academia.[1] In fact, it is a debate that is difficult to avoid: if one chooses not to mention ethnicity, one is actually reproducing the policy of the Tutsi-dominated government that until the mid

1990s denied the existence of ethnic groups in Burundi. We must therefore tread with care when we engage with Burundi's history. History has gained a significant place in this metaconflict, where political entrepreneurs in Burundi and in particular in the diaspora are busy writing history books, pamphlets and homepages, trying to convince the world about 'the reality'– eager to 'put things right' and prove to the outside world that their version of history is the true one.[2] I explore how these political mythologies interact with scholarly discourse so that we may see how they influence popular beliefs in the camp. In other words, I attempt to write a historiography of Burundi and use my sources as artefacts, but I also attempt to place the production of such artefacts historically, hopefully striking a balance between source and artefact, history and historiography. One might say that I explore the historical production of politics in order to understand the political production of history.

Since independence, Burundi – like its 'false twin', Rwanda – has experienced large-scale violence in the name of ethnicity, and subsequently much of the literature on these two countries has sought to explain the violence by looking at history.[3] Genocidal violence has been explained as the result, among other things, of political manipulation of the peasant population by the elite (Chrétien 1996, 2003; Lemarchand 1996a), structural violence (Uvin 1998), colonial masculinity and militarism (Daley 2007), and the colonial production of citizens and subjects (Mamdani 2001). It is not my intention to critique these readings of history or to attempt to explain violence and conflict in Burundi through a new reading of history. Instead my starting point is postcolonial struggles over history and the ways in which history has been used in various political battles. In other words, I explore how conflict creates histories rather than explore how history creates conflict. Refugees in camps and elsewhere have been central both in the production of histories and in the struggle to define the true nature of the conflict. So although the refugees in Lukole are placed in an exceptional space – and expected to behave like non-political beings – they are central players in the political production of the past.

A New Beginning: Combating Colonialism and Tribalism

Although ethnicity was known and even manipulated[4] in precolonial Burundi, it remained rather ambiguous,[5] and despite the hardening of ethnic identities during colonization, the terms 'Hutu' and 'Tutsi' were not particularly politicized on the eve of independence in 1962. However, after some initial years of uncertainty and shifting power alliances, a new hegemonic order took shape in the late 1960s after Colonel Micombero came to power by coup d'état, and the ethnic conflict crystallised as the central antagonism in society. Although the new regime was dominated by Tutsi Hima,[6] from Bururi province in the south, Micombero's government was determined to conceal ethnicity, claiming that the terms Hutu and Tutsi were figments of the colonial imagination and that it was not in the interest of the nation to mention ethnicity. Anyone who mentioned the two groups was accused of destroying the natural unity of the Burundian people and helping neoimperialist powers weaken the country.[7] The government's 'White Paper on the Real Causes and Consequences of the Attempted Genocide against the Tutsi Ethny [sic] in Burundi' (Republic of Burundi 1972), written shortly after the massacres in 1972 as a defence of government policies, argues that ethnicity is an invention of colonialism and that any ethnic resurgence in the country must be attributed to neocolonial conspiracies.

> Do not forget that *genocide* is unknown to our history and culture, and even *the word is inexistant* [sic] *in our language.* How can it be differently? Tribalism was unknown before the arrival of whites. Before colonialisation [sic], our society had reached a degree of cohesion and *national unity that many European countries lacked.* If you have any doubts, question your ethnologists and historians. (ibid.: 10, original emphasis)

The White Paper claims that unity was the defining character of Burundi prior to colonisation, when tribe was an unknown concept to Burundians. As with many other political documents, this one refers to science (ethnologists and historians) for legitimacy and its claim to truth.

> If tribalism is to be mentioned think of the one *you dissipated into our society. You craftily took advantage of the naivety or the cupidity* [sic] *of certain of our citizens.* In a few years you *destroyed the secular product of our ancestors. You distinguished between the Burundese citizens libelling* [sic] *them as Hutu and Tutsi.* You did not stop there. *You convinced Hutu of the necessity of massacring Tutsi.* (ibid.: 11, original emphasis)

It is the colonialists that brought tribalism to Burundi and they did so by taking advantage of the naivety of the Burundian people. In short, they purposefully split a united people.

It is tempting to view the double-speak of the regime in instrumental terms, where a powerful group in society – in this case the Tutsi Hima from Bururi – consciously lies to the masses in order to stay in power. If, however, we are to comprehend the fact that a regime is explicitly antiethnic while at the same time obviously favouring one ethnic group over another in any other way than the famous ideological smokescreen, I propose that we need to explore other aspects of the dominant postcolonial ideology.

Apart from the ethnic dimension, Micombero's ideology was very modernist, developmentalist and anti-imperialist. Micombero was only twenty-six-years old when he seized power in 1966 and was by no means an exception,[8] representing a number of young bureaucrats and officers who were dissatisfied with the rule of the old elite and royal clans (Lemarchand 1970: 404–11; Chrétien 2003: 314–16). Lemarchand takes note of these new elites as they began to take shape in the mid 1960s:

> Their extreme youthfulness reinforced their sense of belonging to an 'out-group' while at the same time making them all the more vulnerable to the appeals of radicalism. And for some at least, these predispositions were further strengthened by their socially and politically marginal position in their own society. Their ideological leanings, in any event, differed sharply from those of the elder generations of traditional elites, animated as they were by a strong reformist zeal and a concern for secularism, social progress and technical innovation. (Lemarchand 1970: 404)

There was a certain sense that merit – especially Western education – should precede birthright and experience, in a sense giving Tutsi Hima from the south the opportunities that had been withheld from them by the Banyaruguru and the Ganwa[9] of the central region.

With its nationalist, anticolonial ideology, the government in Burundi under Micombero fed strongly on a Third World, Fanonist anticolonial discourse emphasising authentic African identity, national unity and a struggle against the colonial mentality of divide and rule. To become a member of the only legal political party, Uprona (Parti de l'Union et du Progrès National), one had to swear loyalty to the cause of national independence and opposition to divisive and bourgeois influences (Kay 1987: 7). In order for the nation to progress, it was not enough to become formally independent. One had to break with 'colonial mentality' which meant first and foremost breaking with the idea of ethnicity by reiterating that the Burundian people are united by definition. A document by the radical youth wing of Uprona, the Jeunesses Nationalistes Rwagasore (JNR),[10] states, in best Fanonist style, that 'we are witness to the decolonisation of an entire nation, and we want this decolonisation to penetrate the innermost recesses of our souls, not merely the surface' (quoted in Chrétien 2008: 33; see also Lemarchand 1970: 407). The revolution is depicted as an ongoing battle against neoimperialist powers that seek to divide and rule the country once again. If Africans continue fighting one another due to ethnic labels given them by Europeans, it is argued, they will remain underdeveloped. Hence, national unity was perceived as essential for 'progress' and 'development'.

The experience of the so-called Hutu revolution[11] in Rwanda in 1959, and the ensuing persecution of that country's Tutsi population, made the Tutsi elite in Burundi very vigilant about any ethnically based social movements. Consequently, it was feared that pluralism and liberal democracy would divide the Burundi population along ethnic lines and introduce majority rule, threatening the Tutsi's minority rights. Any critique of the government from the Hutu elite – whether ethnically motivated or not – would be interpreted in these terms. Threatened by what they perceived to be a Hutu peril, the country's leadership was in the grip of a kind of ethnic paranoia where only a close circle of trustworthy peers – mostly Tutsi Hima from Bururi[12] – were accepted into the higher echelons of the administration and military. While these young men in the bureaucracy and the army were – at least originally – up against the old high-caste Tutsi elite, they needed the Hutu peril in order to unite Tutsi and cover internal differences (Prunier 1995a: 2–3). In Jean-Pierre Chrétien's words, the Bururi group led a clan-based and regionalist 'politics of revenge' (Chrétien 2003: 315) against the historically privileged Tutsi from the central region which had been associated with the royal court. 'They also expressed the prejudices of an area where Hutu and Tutsi integration remained more limited than elsewhere' (ibid.: 33). With the anticolonial and anti-feudal discourse it was difficult for the old Banyaruguru and Ganwa elite to reassert its position without being categorised as feudal and neocolonial, and being accused of wanting to reintroduce Tutsi supremacy. The latter might seem bizarre considering the ethnic composition of the dominant group in the country. Nevertheless, together with the idea of the Hutu peril, the battle against reactionary groups succeeded in removing ethnicity from public discourse while keeping a small group of Tutsi in power and securing the backing of all Tutsi, irrespective of whether they were Hima or Banyaruguru.

This explains how an explicitly antiethnic ideology paradoxically supported a government in the hands of a small ethnic elite. The Hutu were constructed as inherently ethnic, always wanting to destroy national unity and introduce majority rule. However, this ethnicised Other was not ethnic by birth, according to government ideology. They had been made to believe that they were an ethnic group, first by colonialists (as the White Paper claims), and later by a Hutu elite that merely wanted to manipulate ethnicity for its own sake (often helped by foreign infiltrators).

The Commission Nationale Chargée d'Etudier la Question de l'Unité Nationale, appointed by the government to explore the ethnic problems in Burundi following the 1988 massacres in Ntega and Marangara, states: 'the vast majority of the population refused to take part in the massacres. A number of Hutu preferred to die rather than massacre their Tutsi brothers' (Republic of Burundi 1989: 18).[13] The Hutu masses were not interested in ethnicity unless incited by divisive and selfish leaders, the report claims, adding that it is the obligation of any progressive leadership to guide and educate the population and protect it from such divisive agitation. Hutu leaders and conservative Tutsi were, therefore, systematically kept out of office because the government perceived them as a threat to this modernising project.

According to the dominant discourse, the Uprona leadership knows the 'true nature of the Burundi nation' as it was before colonialism and as it will be in the future, and it is the burden of this enlightened leadership to spread this message and to make sure that it is not misunderstood. Obviously, in a situation where the masses have no idea what is best for themselves, liberal democracy is not advisable, according to Uprona. Uprona achieved these goals through an Eastern European-style one-party state in which youth, women and workers' organisations were organised under the party and played an important role in 'educating' the masses (Kay 1987: 7).

1972: A Violent Awakening

During the 1960s the Hima elite from the south continued its struggle to purge the country of monarchists and other counter-revolutionary forces. Intra-Tutsi competition resulted in the Hima from Bururi blaming the Banyaruguru from the north of creating an alliance with the Hutu in order to reinstall the monarchy. In this way, any 'softness' vis-à-vis the Hutu would be interpreted as counter-revolutionary and monarchist. On the other hand, it was obvious that the state was being increasingly built along newly forged patrimonial lines, supporting a small elite, and that it had great difficulties in delivering what it had promised in terms of development and progress. With a government that could not deliver on its promises and a fear of conspiracies among monarchists, Hutu and foreigners, the government became increasingly paranoid. One effect of this paranoia was to purge the administration, and in particular the army, of what were perceived as potential state enemies. Thus, the army was effectively cleansed of Hutu officers in 1969 while a group of Tutsi from the central region was convicted of treason and 'monarchism' in 1971 (Lemarchand and Martin 1974; Chrétien 2008: 33). The incessant provocation and harassment of Hutu by Tutsi officials created resentment among Hutu, and especially the Hutu elite, who found their avenues of upward mobility constantly thwarted, whether in the armed forces, in the civil administration or even in business. For instance, Hutu petty traders who were expanding their activities in the south were perceived as a threat by the region's Tutsi traders, and they in turn persuaded Tutsi officials to make life hard for them.

Between 7 and 8 o'clock in the evening of 29 April 1972, between 300 and 500 armed Hutu insurgents unleashed well-coordinated attacks on military posts and government installations in two southern provinces, Rumonge and Nyanza-Lac. Similar attacks were launched in Cankuzo and Bujumbura, although these were unsuccessful. After the attacks, the insurgents began killing Tutsi civilians indiscriminately in Rumonge and Nyanza-Lac. An estimated 2,000 to 3,000 people were killed, mostly Tutsi but also Hutu who refused to join the rebellion (Kay 1987: 5; Lemarchand 1996a).[14] There is no reliable data on the insurgency as the government obviously exaggerated the figures and the coordination of the attacks in order to legitimize the brutal clampdown by the army that followed. The careful timing of the events does, however, indicate that the insurgency was centrally coordinated. René Lemarchand argues that the insurgents consisted of a small group of dissatisfied students, schoolteachers and traders from the south as well as a handful of the Hutu elite in Bujumbura (Lemarchand 1996a: 93–94). That it only represented a small elite can be seen from the fact that hardly any Hutu joined or supported the insurgency. In fact there were many cases of Hutu and Tutsi combating the insurgency together. Jean-Pierre Chrétien supports this interpretation, although he emphasises the presumed influence of Mulelists from Zaire (Chrétien 2008). The repression of the insurgency took place immediately, developing from brutal counter-attacks by the army to systematic slaughter of all Hutu above a certain level of education. This genocidal violence was carried out by elements of the armed forces and by gangs of youth from the JRR (Jeunesse Révolutionnaire Rwagasore, formerly the JNR, Jeunesse Nationale Rwagasore), the youth wing of the governing Uprona party. The killings continued until August. Groups of soldiers and JRR youth would turn up in colleges and secondary schools either with lists of names of Hutu students or asking the students themselves to make such lists. The Hutu students would then be taken away on lorries never to be seen again. Tutsi who refused to collaborate were also executed.

As always in such cases, the death toll is difficult to know, with estimates varying between 80,000 and 200,000 deaths (Kay 1987: 5; Lemarchand 1989: 22; Chrétien 2003: 316; Daley 2007: 69). However, it was not just the scale of the killings that made them such an appalling event; it was also their intentionality. Lemarchand argues that 'far from representing the culmination of a long-standing, carefully elaborated master plan ... the systematic massacre of the Hutu elites came almost as an after-thought, long after "peace and order" had been reestablished in the south' (Lemarchand 1996a: 102). The fact that it might not have been a scripted master plan, does not mean, however, that it was not systematic and intentional and amounted to genocide. As in most cases of genocidal violence, the 1972 massacres were driven by a fear of being exterminated by the 'other', unless one acts promptly to stop them. Rumours and conspiracy theories about imminent attacks by European mercenaries, paid by the king, and fears of Hutu killings like the ones in Rwanda in 1959 and onwards, pushed Tutsi elements in the army and JRR to go for a 'final solution'.[15] Their fears of being exterminated by the Hutu did not lead Tutsi to want to kill all Hutu but to exterminate all potential Hutu leaders.[16]

At a concrete level, the result of the massacres was that the Hutu section of society was virtually decapitated of its elite, meaning that for years to come there were no qualified Hutu to enter the state administration and army. This was in line with the government perception that it was the intellectuals who had sowed the seed of ethnicity among the peasants, the latter perceived as being innocent due to their ignorance and naivety. In this manner it was also possible for the regime to maintain its non-ethnicist ideology, in spite of the genocide that it had carried out on a massive scale. It could maintain the perception that Hutu and Tutsi were essentially unified and that the violence was caused by outsiders and intellectuals.

It has been remarked how little the Hutu resistance was to the killings. Some collaborated with the army in rounding up fellow Hutu, and were afterwards told to dig their own graves. In the words of a teacher who was a student at the time, 'Everyone let themselves be led, like a sheep to the slaughterhouse' (Chrétien 2008: 50). This placidity strengthens the image of Hutu as hapless victims. As we shall see in later chapters, it also feeds into a larger Hutu narrative of being not only innocent victims but also of being 'blind' to what is actually going on around them. People told me again and again in the camp that Hutu had been 'blind to reality', while Tutsi had known all along. They also say that it was after 1972 that they 'opened their eyes' (see Chapter 7).

In the short term, the 1972 massacres seemed to have had very little effect on the political course of the government. With the loss of their elite, the rest of the Hutu population had been so terrorised by the violence that they posed no threat to the regime. The largest change was due to the approximately 150,000 Hutu who left the country and began organising politically, and, as we shall see in later sections, they were instrumental in the downfall of the 'Bururi clan' in the 1990s. Meanwhile, surprisingly little changed inside the country in the aftermath of the massacres. Micombero remained in power until 1976, when Jean-Baptiste Bagaza also a Hima from the same region as Micombero, seized power through a palace coup and declared the Second Republic. Micombero basically lost power due to maladministration and incompetence, and Bagaza craftily managed to lump together the First Republic and the colonial era 'as one long age of darkness' (Kay 1987: 9) and was able to maintain the notion that the 1972 massacres and all other misery in society was due to colonialism and neocolonialism.[17] Therefore, it was all the more important to be vigilant, he argued, institutionalising the revolutionary spirit and struggle against a reactionary bourgeoisie in the only legal party, Uprona. Ethnic terms were banned and various projects such as villagisation were instigated in order to promote national unity. Meanwhile, much effort was put into economic development as a way of overshadowing the Hutu–Tutsi conflict (Chrétien 2003: 316). In sum, Bagaza followed the same exclusionary ethnic politics as Micombero while moving away from politics and ethnicity.

Walking the Tightrope between Traditionalism and Developmentalism

The dominant ideology of the postcolonial government was marked by an ambivalent relation to precolonial institutions. On the one hand, it was explicitly anticolonial and by the same token evoked a picture of precolonial Burundi as the perfect, harmonious society that simply had been ruined by colonial rule. In this sense, ethnicity was assumed to have either not existed or to have been irrelevant prior to European occupation. This has been illustrated in the excerpts from the White Paper. On the other hand, the revolutionary rhetoric of the postcolonial ideology was obviously aimed at breaking with the power of the 'old guard', and youth, modernity and progress were to replace gerontocracy, tradition and stagnation in what Thomas Laely terms the new 'technocratico-pragmatic' development ideology (Laely 1992: 88).

This modernising, rationalistic ideology attempted to achieve the revolution by breaking with the 'feudal' and colonial past. However, being anticolonial, it also went against 'importing foreign solutions' to Africa (cf. Republic of Burundi 1989). Therefore, it sought solutions in an idealised precolonial past of national unity and equality. Africanisation policies were introduced, such as villagisation, the use of *bashingantahe* and the introduction of Kirundi as the only language of instruction in primary and secondary schools in the mid 1970s (Lemarchand 1996a: 108–9). This was done in the name of finding an authentic, African way to progress. African culture was supposed to produce unity and progress, and to secure the involvement of the community.

Using African indigenous institutions such as the *bashingantahe* would allegedly secure active popular support for the revolutionary state (Republic of Burundi 1989: 34). Among the institutions that the one-party state attempted to revitalise was the system of communal work (Guichaoua 1991). This drew on two historical references: the first was the Burundian 'custom' of helping one's neighbour in times of distress, while the second was the Belgian system of forced labour for communal works in the common interest of the community. This again drew on an image of peasants providing labour to the chiefs and the court. As with the policy of usurping the *bashingantahe*, it was a heavily centralised, top-down approach, controlled by Uprona. And as with the *bashingantahe*, the idea never really gained the full support of the population (ibid.)

So, although authentic African culture was allegedly grounded on solidarity and community spirit – with greed and divisiveness being foreign imports – the political system in Burundi became more hierarchical and centralised than ever. This was due to the patronising approach of the young Uprona leadership. It was also due to the institutional carry-over from

Belgian administration. And finally, it was due to the ways in which the rural population interpreted the new 'big men'. Here the fact that social status and political rank had become so intertwined with ethnicity (however much the government tried to deny it any discursive existence) had an impact on the way the leadership was interpreted by the peasants. These interpretations were due to the politicisation of the Hutu peasants after 1972 and, especially, from the late 1980s, when Palipehutu started campaigns inside the country.

Reimagining Burundi from Exile

As we have seen, 1972 was an eye-opener for many Hutu. However, it took some time for this traumatic event to translate into political ideology and a politicised ethnic identity. This process arguably took place in refugee camps in Rwanda and Tanzania, aided by a small diasporic elite in Europe. The mythico-histories that Liisa Malkki collected in Mishamo in the 1980s were examples of this politicised ethnic identity; they represented a search for explanations of the present in the past by a group of refugees whose life-worlds had been jolted by the massacres of 1972 and by their subsequent isolation in refugee settlements.

Apart from trying to establish ontological security for the refugees in the camp, these mythico-histories reimagined Burundi's past in radically new ways; they were, in Malkki's words, 'a subversive recasting and reinterpretation' (Malkki 1995a: 54) of the past. However, Burundi's past was not *terra incognita*; it had already been recast and reinterpreted several times by various powerful discourses – from the early European explorers' Hamitic thesis[18] to Uprona's anti-imperialist ideology. It is in relation to these discourses on the 'true' nature of Burundi's past that the mythico-histories tried to recast the past. The main point of contention between refugees in Mishamo and the dominant discourse in Burundi was that of ethnic groups and their origins. While the official discourse of Uprona was that ethnic groups were the invention of colonialists, the mythico-histories were intent on systematically 'proving' the age-old origins of Burundi's ethnic groups and their racial differences. Interestingly, the Hamitic thesis was brought back on stage in an attempt to prove not the Tutsi's inherent right to rule due to higher intelligence, but the Hutu's right to the Burundi nation due to autochthony. And whereas the post-independence government blamed the colonialists for destroying the national fabric, the mythico-histories of the Hutu refugees depicted the Belgians as protectors and moderators (ibid.: 74).

In Lukole, Palipehutu supporters who had lived in Mishamo told me that the founding father of the party, Rémy Gahutu, chose Mishamo as the place to start making the masses 'aware' because it was placed in virgin forest and people there were not distracted by other things. In Ulyankulu, another big refugee settlement located closer to the railway line that runs between Dar es Salaam and Kigoma, the refugees were far too busy doing business to care about their history.[19] The ideology of Gahutu and Palipehutu had to relate not only to the refugees' sense of despair in the camps, as Malkki argues, but also to the political field in Burundi. With the lack of other explanations in the camp, Palipehutu's reimagining of Burundi's past soon became hegemonic and the only authorised version in Mishamo.

After 'educating the people' in refugee camps in Tanzania and Rwanda, Palipehutu started running campaigns inside Burundi in the late 1980s, 'awakening' the peasants and making them 'aware' of their oppression.[20] In 1991, Palipehutu launched a series of armed attacks, including one on Bujumbura airport. Palipehutu was therefore instrumental in forming the political identity of the Hutu in Burundi and in pushing the government to take the issue of ethnicity seriously, eventually leading to democratic reforms in the early 1990s.

Rémy Gahutu's *Persecution of the Hutus of Burundi* (Gahutu n.d.)[21] gives an insight into Palipehutu ideology in the late 1980s. The book claims to provide a sober, scientific version of Burundian history as opposed to what the author sees as the biased propaganda that the regime has fed international opinion. He starts by outlining the country's three ethnic groups. Of the Twa, Gahutu states that: 'All historians agree that the Twa were the first inhabitants of Burundi. Of pygmy stock, the Twa had a rudimentary technology and did not use iron' (ibid.: 2). The Hutu, meanwhile, are said to have 'arrived in Burundi around 3000 BC. They presently make up 85% of the country's population, and are of Bantu stock ... They were a sedentary, peace-loving people and remain so today' (ibid.: 3–4). Gahutu goes on to add that 'Around 1500 AD, a third ethnic group gradually began to enter Burundi: the Tutsi. This group, of Nilotic stock, was originally one of the Hamitic peoples of North Africa and Somalia' (ibid.: 4). Clearly leaning on the Hamitic thesis of nineteenth and early-twentieth-century ethnographers, and referring to 'historians' and 'theories', Gahutu is challenging the government claim that ethnicity was invented by the colonialists. He claims that the Tutsi were peaceful at first and that they did not impinge on agricultural land because they were pastoralists. However, he rhetorically asks how it is that 14 per cent of the population was able to take power and rule over the majority of the country, and he wonders why the Tutsi learned the language and culture of the Hutu and not vice versa. He suggests that the Tutsi 'consciously learned the language and the customs of the Hutu in order to subjugate them more thoroughly' (ibid.: 5). Furthermore, the Tutsi subjugated the Hutu through the system of *ubugabire*, where they gave cattle to Hutu as gifts that effectively put the Hutu beneficiary into bondage.

In his analysis of the political parties around independence, Gahutu sees the apparent non-ethnic ideology of Uprona as Tutsi trickery, deceiving the naive Hutu electorate into believing that this was also a party for them. This theme, of the Tutsi having secret plans long before the Hutu are aware of them, is a persistent stereotype that also existed in Lukole.[22] This links to another theme that Gahutu refers to, namely that the Hutu 'bore no ill will toward the Tutsi' while the Tutsi did not hesitate to thwart the Hutu which has been the case from when the first Tutsi arrived and the Hutu welcomed them with open arms, he claims (ibid.: 45).

The main problem for the Hutu now, Gahutu claims, is that they are not united and that they are not all aware of their suffering. Another problem, he claims, stems from those Hutu who are tempted to become like the Tutsi. These 'turncoats' betray their true Hutu identity and hence not only the Hutu cause but also themselves. This 'blood and soil' ideology, of a true, authentic identity and a people that belongs to the soil due to their being the first to arrive, permeates his text: 'A close examination of the situation in Burundi show [*sic*] that the Hutu have lost a country which was rightfully theirs ... For a people to struggle, retake their country, and emerge victorious, their primary concern must be to strengthen their own identity' (ibid.: 49). Gahutu clearly sees the struggle as a nationalist one. The Hutu have a country which is rightfully theirs, only it has been stolen from them by someone else: the late comers and colonisers, the Tutsi.

Throughout his analysis of the postcolonial regimes, Gahutu focuses on the use of secrets and lies. These lies, covering up the Tutsi's 'customary cruelty' (ibid.: 46) and hiding the true intentions of the regime, have two audiences: the naive Hutu and the international community. In this way, the Tutsi government is able to deceive international public opinion into believing that it is the Hutu who are dangerous. Interestingly, in this connection he is very concerned with the ways in which President Bagaza attempts to deceive socialist countries like Tanzania. Among the seven lies that Gahutu identifies as being used by Bagaza to maintain power, two are about feigning socialism, one about organizing anti-democratic elections, and one about hypocritical solidarity with black South Africans. In other words, Gahutu is worried about the good image that Bagaza is trying to establish vis-à-vis certain international audiences. Although he disagrees fundamentally with the government on the question of ethnicity, Gahutu also adheres to a pan-African, socialist and Fanonist discourse. In this sense he speaks within the same hegemonic discourse, and it is therefore important for him to show that Bagaza is neither truly socialist, democratic nor pan-African.

In sum, Rémy Gahutu, founding father of the first substantial Hutu opposition party and the mythico-histories that circulated in the camps in Tanzania in the 1980s, fundamentally challenged the dominant discourse on ethnicity in Burundi. He did so by reversing the Hamitic thesis to prove the natural right of the Hutu to the Burundi nation. His language was ethno-nationalist, adhering to ideas of racial difference and believing in the close link between people and soil. It was also, however, a liberation ideology, fighting for the emancipation of a people perceived to have been oppressed, and in many ways resembled the anticolonial rhetoric of the regime in place. Gahutu and Palipehutu were instrumental in creating an awareness of an ethnic identity among the Hutu in Burundi, but soon they would be overtaken by political reality in the country.

Reopening the Field

In the 1980s, as the government began to lose legitimacy in growing sections of society, its exercise of control became ever harsher, with party cadres and the secret service infiltrating every part of society. This state of increased tension soon proved untenable. Old supporters began to lose sympathy for Bagaza's regime and allegations of mismanagement and corruption added to the problems of legitimacy (Lemarchand 1996a: 114–16). In 1987, Major Pierre Buyoya, also a Hima from Bururi, seized power in a bloodless coup, promising to normalise relations with the Church, clean out corruption and generally invigorate and rejuvenate the administration. He also signalled hope for democratic reforms and solving the 'ethnic problem.'

These gradual reforms led to the legalisation of political parties in 1992 and to multiparty elections for the National Assembly and presidency in 1993.[23] Palipehutu was never legalised and a number of its supporters chose to support Frodebu, a moderate, Hutu-dominated party. Frodebu won a landslide victory for the Assembly, as did its presidential candidate, Melchior Ndadaye.[24]

What were the consequences of these changes for the different ways of imagining Burundi? Basically, the government of Buyoya shifted from denying the existence of ethnicity to accepting the existence of ethnic groups to some degree. In the new Constitution of 1992, national unity is mentioned again and again. However, the Constitution also refers to ethnic groups by taking account of the 'diverse component parts of the Burundian population' (Reyntjens 1995: 9). As socialism and Fanonism were on the retreat in Africa in general, and as new demands for 'good governance' were emerging, the general rhetoric also shifted more in the direction of liberal democracy.

This shift in the country's dominant discourse also had consequences for the establishment of oppositional discourse. It was no longer enough to claim that ethnicity existed, as this was part of government discourse. Neither were references to socialism of much value any longer, in part because of changes in international opinion, in part because one could no longer accuse the government of only feigning socialism. The government was not even trying. The only way to establish a successful discourse of opposition was to play the same game. This game was made more difficult by the fact that, although ethnicity was now acknowledged, parties were not allowed to appeal to ethnic loyalties, as this would be inciting tribalism and thus go against the principles of 'good governance'. This is where Frodebu came into the picture. Frodebu managed a fine balance between being the party that appealed to the Hutu while not mentioning the liberation of the Hutu people or the Hutu nation.

Frodebu and its moderate leader, Melchior Ndadaye, won landslide victories at the elections for the National Assembly and the presidential elections in 1993. Ndadaye created a broad coalition government, including members of the defeated Uprona party. However, he only lasted three months in office before he was abducted and killed by Tutsi officers, throwing the country into a protracted constitutional crisis and waves of ethnic violence, followed by armed rebellions that have only recently come to an end.

At the time of my fieldwork in Lukole, Buyoya had again seized power in a coup d'état. Two rebel groups were fighting the Burundian army: Palipehutu-FNL (Front Nationale pour la Libération), a radical breakaway group of Palipehutu led by Cossan Kabura; and CNDD (Conseil Nationale pour la Défence de la Démocratie), created by Leonard Nyangoma and other Frodebu politicians who felt that the Frodebu leadership's attempts to solve problems politically were in vain. The majority of refugees in Lukole supported CNDD, and Nyangoma was something of a hero in the camp.

In Conclusion

No doubt the colonial administration was important in hardening an ethnic divide in Burundi. After independence, therefore, the postcolonial state radically reimagined Burundian history, blaming colonial indirect rule for introducing divisions into a united people. For the sake of re-establishing the 'original and natural unity' of all Burundians, it was seen as the duty of the revolutionary post-independence government to combat all 'colonial vestiges' and to eliminate 'colonial mentality'. According to the more vulgar discourse – such as that of the government's 1972 White Paper (Republic of Burundi 1972) – ethnicity had not existed prior to colonisation. The more refined version – as can be found in the work of Emile Mworoha (1987) and to a degree in the report by the Commission Nationale (Republic of Burundi 1989) – admits to the existence of ethnic groups but assumes that precolonial ethnic relations were unproblematic. Consequently, postcolonial regimes attempted to reconcile traditional Burundian institutions with a technocratic, modernist discourse, dismissing liberal democracy as a Eurocentric concept that would introduce divisions and hatred among Africans. Authentic

Burundian mobilisation of the masses was attempted through a mixture of socialist one-party sensitisation programmes and what were imagined to be democratic and just traditional institutions, such as communal work and the *bashingantahe* .

The government's doublespeak – denying the existence of ethnic groups while favouring a small Tutsi minority – resulted in very harsh punishment of anything that might resemble a Hutu uprising. This excessive use of force arguably made it difficult to maintain the idea that ethnicity did not matter in Burundi, and a growing Hutu ethnic self-awareness emerged, in particular in the refugee camps in Tanzania and Rwanda in the 1970s and 1980s. Hutu perceived themselves to have been oppressed and persecuted due to their ethnic origins and began to articulate an oppositional discourse – a new way of imagining Burundi – based on the idea of ethnic difference. The discourse of Hutu opposition – as exemplified in the writing of Rémy Gahutu and the mythico-histories circulating in Mishamo – ironically drew on the Hamitic thesis. But rather than legitimise Tutsi rule due to their alleged racial superiority, as the Hamitic thesis originally did when introduced by colonialists, it was now used to legitimise the Hutu's right to Burundian soil, portraying the Tutsi as invaders. Almost a century after the Hamitic thesis was thought up, it was not possible to claim rights or recognition on the basis of racial superiority, though one could claim the right to national territory and self-determination . By portraying the Tutsi as invaders, Palipehutu's struggle was portrayed as, essentially, a liberation struggle.

Finally, I have shown that the political field in Burundi moved once more in the early 1990s, in part due to the 'success' of Palipehutu, forcing the government to take account of ethnicity and share power with the Hutu. Again history took an ironic turn as the success of Palipehutu also became its downfall. With the democratic reforms, the ethno-nationalist discourse of Palipehutu lost ground to that of the more moderate Frodebu that envisaged a democratic, pluralistic (non-ethnic) Burundi. Palipehutu portrayed the Hutu as innocent victims of Tutsi conspiracies. However, the fact that they created this awareness among the Hutu population had the effect that when violence broke out again in 1993, they were ready to take the initiative, losing their innocence.

This repertoire of imaginings of Burundi was what the refugees in Lukole could draw on. The various stories could be appropriated, dismantled and reassembled in new ways, but they related to the political field in Burundi (and the region), and hence could not be used in any manner without consequences in Burundi. As we shall see in the following chapters, they slipped back and forth between the political field in Burundi and the region on the one hand, and local politics in the camp on the other.

Notes

1. See the dispute between Lemarchand (1989, 1990b) and Chrétien (1990a). See also Filip Reyntjens' critique of the 'École historique burundo-française', closely linked to Chrétien (Reyntjens 1990), and Chrétien's response (Chrétien 1990b); for further critique of this 'school', see Lemarchand (1990a).
2. For a discussion of the use of cyberspace in Burundi's metaconflict, see Kadende-Kaiser (2000) and Turner (2008). This conflict over history has also been acknowledged by the conflicting parties, who in the Arusha Peace Accords agreed 'to rewrite Burundi's history, so that all Burundians can interpret in the same way.' (quoted in Daley 2007: 42).
3. While the number of books and articles that try to explain the Rwandan genocide has reached astronomical levels, the amount of literature on Burundi's history remains modest to say the least.
4. See Adekanye (1996) and Laely (1997).
5. Among the modifying factors, one could mention the practice of *kwihuture*, where a wealthy and powerful Hutu becomes Tutsified, and the *bashingantahe* – advisors to the royal court and/or local village councillors – who would be Hutu and Tutsi (Laely 1992).
6. Generally the Tutsi are believed to comprise two sub-groups: the Banyaruguru (meaning those 'from above', though it is disputed whether this means from the hills or from higher status) and the Hima or Bahima. The latter were allegedly the lower-class Tutsi who had enjoyed only little influence prior to independence.
7. Reference to ethnic groups was officially banned during the Second Republic of Bagaza (1976–1987): see Kay (1987: 3).
8. The members of the National Revolutionary Council in 1967 had an average age of 27 years (Lemarchand 1996a). Typically, Lemarchand only takes note of their 'ethno-regional background' and not their age.
9. Princely lineages, also known as *baganwa* and *abaganwa*. Until the 1960s most political rivalry in Burundi had been between various Ganwa lineages. Lemarchand claims that the *ganwa* disappeared as an ethnic category and were assimilated into the Tutsi frame of reference by 1972 when Hutu–Tutsi antagonism dominated all other kinds (Lemarchand 1996b: 15).
10. Later renamed the Jeunesse Révolutionnaire Rwagasore. The JNR emerged after independence as a 'consistently radical, anti-Western and increasingly violence prone organization.' (Lemarchand 1996a: 62) consisting of a mixture of secondary and university students, school drop-outs and unemployed youth. What started as a loosely organised group of angry young men developed into 'a praetorian guard in the service of a Tutsi ethnocracy' (ibid).
11. I say 'so-called' because it is doubtful whether it can be called a revolution. For a discussion of this issue, see Prunier (1995b).
12. Both Burundi scholars and refugees in Lukole are not slow to remark that all three presidents from 1966 to 1993 (Micombero, Bagaza and Buyoya) were Tutsi Hima from the same commune in Bururi (Chrétien 2003: 412, n.69).
13. In 1988 ethnic violence broke out in two small communes in northern Burundi in which as many as 20,000 people were killed either by Hutu mobs or by the army in an operation aimed at 'restoring order' (Reyntjens 1993; cf.

Lemarchand 1996a; see also Chapter 7). The original French of the quoted passage reads: 'l'immense majorité de la population a refusé de prendre part aux massacres. Nombre de Bahutu ont préféré mourir plutôt que de massacrer leurs frères Batutsi'

14. For detailed witness accounts of the events, see Chrétien (2008).

15. The two countries would continue to mirror each other tragically in the future – inciting fears of worst-case scenarios both ways.

16. This has led Lemarchand and Martin to call it a 'selective genocide' (Lemarchand and Martin 1974).

17. For a fuller account of the differences between the First and Second Republics, see Kay (1987), Prunier (1995a) and Lemarchand (1996a).

18. Originally a theological term, claiming that Africans were descendants of Noah's son Ham, the Hamitic myth changed character during the Enlightenment from an idea of monogenesis to polygenesis. In the nineteenth century the Hamitic thesis was used to 'prove' that Egyptian civilisation was related to the Christian one, while the Bantu had completely different origins (see also Sanders 1969).

19. Interview: Jeremiah, 24 September 1997. All informant names have been changed to protect their identity.

20. Interview: Etienne Karatasi, chairman of Palipehutu, Denmark, July 1997. In a rather problematic publication, Alexandre Hatungimana similarly observes that the refugee camps in Tanzania are heavily politicised. However, he simply perceives this as a 'problem of propaganda' (Hatungimana 2008).

21. Gahutu's book is an unpublished document that has no date or place of publication. It is 55 pages long and claims to be translated from French by Hugh Hazelton and Peter Keating. Design and production: Productions Paperasse. I was given it Karatasi who had taken over as chairman of Palipehutu after Gahutu's death.

22. See Chapter 7; see also Turner (2005b).

23. Multipartyism, however, was only introduced at the higher levels of government. The new Constitution (1991) stipulated that local politics should be non-partisan and be given to the institution of the *bashingantahe*. According to the commission in charge of making a new democratic constitution, partisan politics constituted a threat against customary conviviality, everyday harmony and understanding, and even democratic values such as national unity and social peace (cited in Laely 1992: 76).

24. Filip Reyntjens has written extensively on this period; see Reyntjens (1993,1995, 1996).

25. Traditional council of elders and legal advisors to the court.

3
The Biopolitics of Innocence

Lukole was in many ways an exceptional space. Around 100,000 people with very different backgrounds had been crammed into this small area in the Tanzanian bush, where they were taken care of by high-profile international organisations and subjected to a number of extraordinary rules and regulations. They were not allowed to involve themselves in politics, leave the camp, or work or barter their food rations. They were given food and water and healthcare free of charge irrespective of whether they used to be a minister, a peasant or a street kid in Burundi. They were kept alive and healthy and were supposed to do as little as possible while they waited to return to 'normality'. The whole point with refugee camps is that they are temporary – exceptional spaces that act as a parenthesis in time and space, where refugees are kept on 'standby', neither in one nation nor the other, until a 'durable solution' can be found and they can be reintegrated into the national order of things. However, as opposed to the liminal space of ritual seclusion sites, there is no time limit on the limbo that refugees find themselves in and neither is there any guarantee that they will eventually be aggregated into society again. This exceptional space is thus full of paradoxes. On the one hand, Lukole was chaotic and unstructured while on the other hand it was extremely ordered and bureaucratised. Seen from the perspective of many refugees, there was a sense of social and moral breakdown and chaos. Seen from the outside, Lukole was far from chaotic. It represented ordered space, governed by quite specific rationalities and bureaucratic practices. It is this governing of Lukole and the kind of space and subjectivities that it produced to which we now turn.

We will start our entry into Lukole from above, from where we see the straight lines, the food distribution centres and the UN and NGO offices, and I will attempt to map this bureaucratic grid that one sees from a bird's-eye perspective, since it is this grid that the refugees must relate to and make sense of. In this manner, I introduce the camp and its construction by relief agencies and Tanzanian authorities. We will also explore the bureaucratic practices of the UNHCR and other agencies in their day to day 'care and maintenance' of the refugees and the consequences this had for the ways in which the refugees were 'framed'. At first glance, the control mechanisms and governing techniques of relief agencies and Tanzanian authorities appeared to limit the refugees' room for manoeuvre. However, governing need not only be restrictive or negative, as new categories and subjectivities are produced in the process. We must, in other words, be sensitive to the different ways in which order was created and refugees controlled by the Tanzanian authorities and the relief agencies respectively.

The Tanzanian authorities took a number of measures to contain these refugees. Once they have been secluded in the camp, they could not leave a zone of 4 km around the camp without special permission, and they were put under the authority of the camp commandant, the highest legal authority in the camp and the local representative of the Tanzania's Ministry of Home Affairs (MHA). The commandant did not answer to the district or regional commissioners, thus effectively placing the camp outside the normal jurisdiction of the Tanzanian state. The camp was at once in the grip of the state, trying to control and contain refugees through various harsh and restrictive measures, while simultaneously being placed outside the very same state as a kind of space of exception. Here, the words of the camp commandant were law. It is therefore tempting to see Lukole as an expression of Agamben's camp as the hidden matrix and *nomos* of modern political space (Agamben 2000: 37), a temporary, exceptional space, created by a sovereign decision (Agamben 1998: 168–71). Here, the Tanzanian state had decided that the refugees were a threat to the nation-state and had put them in this exceptional space, at once inside and outside the law, reducing the refugees to 'bare life', outside the *polis* of national citizens.

The main argument that I will advance in this chapter is that this is only part of the story. Although the concepts of bare life and the camp are compelling, Burundian refugees in Lukole were not just any kind of bare life. In the case of Lukole; it is important to acknowledge that the camp was subjected to a strongly moralising and ethical biopolitical project[1] by international relief agencies. Whereas the camp commandant zealously controlled who could enter and who could leave the camp, guarding the perimeters of this island in Tanzanian territory, it was international relief agencies, led by the UNHCR, that were in charge of the day to day 'care and maintenance' of the camp. They exerted a caring biopower, concerned with the life and health of the refugee population. In this manner, humanitarian relief agencies were attempting to create the 'refugee-as-victim', irrespective of the actual social and political background of individual refugees and their trajectory into the camp.

Counting, Controlling, Catering

The fact that the funds from international donors (upon whom Tanzania also greatly depends) for running the camp were channelled through the UNHCR and other relief agencies, indicates how important the UNHCR and other relief agencies were for the governance of the camp. In fact, the day-to-day business of living – organising registration, food distribution, health, education, building roads, and so on – was taken care of by relief agencies. And although the restrictions imposed on refugees by the MHA were very visible, the productive governing of the refugees by relief agencies had effects that were at least as strong.

The scale and efficiency of the relief 'operation' (a term used by international relief agencies, highlighting the technical, surgical approach to relief work) in Lukole was impressive. One cannot help but be impressed by the logistics of maintaining a constant 'pipeline' of food for such a big population along roads that in places are almost non-existent. In one of the remotest and poorest districts in Tanzania, the UNHCR managed to put an efficient system into place to distribute food, water, medicine, schooling and so forth fairly and evenly to 100,000 people. The Ngara 'operation' which at one point had involved more than half a million Rwandan and Burundian refugees, was generally commended for its efficiency by the thorough and pathbreaking Joint Evaluation of Emergency Assistance to Rwanda (Millwood 1996). The mere scale of refugee crises and the rapidity within which they develop, makes humanitarian relief operations some of the most elaborate and efficient bureaucracies of our age.

At the time of my fieldwork in 1997/8, the UNHCR was in charge of coordinating all relief activities in the camp, including refugee protection. In practice, responsibility for various 'services' in the camp was delegated to different 'implementing partners': national and international NGOs.[2]

Upon arrival in the camp, every refugee was registered by the UNHCR and each household was given a plot by the Tanzanian Red Cross Society (TRCS) upon which to build a *blindé* (hut). There were rules on where and how to build one's *blindé*. For example, people were not allowed to build fences around their plot – allegedly due to fire and health hazards. Similarly, for health reasons every household was obliged to build a pit latrine of a minimum depth and at a certain distance from their *blindé*. Each household was also given a food ration card, according to household size. Lost ration cards and changing ration cards due to births, deaths, divorces and so on caused a lot of problems for both refugees and UNHCR field staff. Of course, refugees would also try to cheat the system by having several ration cards or selling them when leaving the camp.

At one stage there was one large market in Lukole A and a further two smaller markets in Lukole B, but in early 1998 these were fused into one central market. The markets were regulated in several ways. Firstly, the UNHCR and TRCS decided where to place them. Secondly, each vendor had to pay a daily tax to the camp commandant. Finally, market committees were established among the traders. They would regulate the placing of various kinds of activities: bars in one section, maize dealers in another, butchers far away from the others for hygiene reasons and so on. They would also organise night guards and take care of hygiene. The shops and market stalls had to close by 6 P.M. and the bars by nine, according to MHA orders. Trading outside the designated markets was not permitted.

The World Food Programme (WFP) transported food – usually donated by aid USAID or ECHO – from Dar-es-Salaam by rail and then by truck to the rub-halls that CARE was in charge of. TRCS distributed the maize, beans, salt and oil in the two central food distribution centres once a fortnight. Instead of measuring out rations to each household, block leaders[3] would bring the ration cards of their constituency and then share it out afterwards.[4]

It was often in these situations that confrontations with Tanzanian staff occurred. At meetings refugees would complain that the Tanzanian distributors treated them with contempt and misused their power, often cheating the refugees of their fair share. This being one of the few direct points of contact between the governing institutions and the refugee population, it was here that their general sense of powerlessness surfaced. It was also typically the lower-level Tanzanian staff that was the object of their discontent, rarely the international staff. Tanzanians incarnated the constraints of the refugees in the camp in a very tangible manner, since it was they who handed out the insufficient and uniform food, although they had absolutely no say in the type or size of the rations. Similarly, it would be Tanzanians instructing the refugees to build latrines and not to cut down trees around the camp. The international staff would sit in offices in Ngara town and occasionally drive through the camp in four-wheel drive vehicles attending workshops and meetings. They did not do the 'dirty work' and hence retained a certain aura of the benevolent relief worker in the perceptions of the refugees.

This categorisation of relief staff by the refugees also related to other issues. There was a general feeling of being superior to the Tanzanian population as such. Seeing fellow Africans having so much influence on their lives, and earning so much more for the same work, made them resentful towards African relief workers.[5] It was therefore with great expectation that they welcomed the replacement of the African Education Foundation (AEF) by Norwegian People's Aid (NPA). While the former employed mostly East Africans, the latter employed a number of Europeans. Their expectations could also have been due to the fact that many of them knew NPA from experience in an earlier camp. However, NPA had operated at a time when funding was much more liberal because the Rwanda 'operation' still enjoyed a lot of publicity. AEF had been in charge while funding was slim and had therefore been equated with poor service delivery.

AEF ran a number of primary schools in the camp. In order to emphasise the temporary status of the camp, the Tanzanian authorities had not allowed the establishment of secondary schools. The primary schools followed a Burundian syllabus supplemented with English and Swahili. The teachers and head teachers were refugees. AEF was also in charge of health and ran three hospitals in the camp, staffed by expatriate (mainly Kenyan), Tanzanian and Burundian staff alike. Finally, 'community services' was run by AEF and played a central role in catering for the refugees. As we shall see shortly, central issues involving 'the community' were enacted by 'community services' that had previously been termed 'social services'. A large number of refugees were employed as 'community mobilisers' (previously 'social workers') with the task of mobilising the community to support 'vulnerable groups'.

In order better to govern the camp and deliver services, the camp population was divided into several sub-groups depending on their degree of 'vulnerability', in other words how needy they were evaluated to be. In a preliminary registration and demography report (UNHCR 1997) based on a registration exercise conducted between 28 February and 5 March 1997, two pages are devoted to 'vulnerability'. Here, twenty categories of vulnerability are identified, from relatively common groups such as 'EA – Elderly Adult', 'SP – Single Parent' and 'UAM – Unaccompanied Minor', to more complex categories such as 'SP/MD – Single Parent/Mentally Disabled' and 'FF/UAM – Foster Family/Unaccompanied Minor'. The latter categories are termed 'double vulnerables' in the report, and defined as 'individuals with more than one type of vulnerability' (ibid.: 9).[6] The UNHCR and implementing partners also operate with the term EVGs ('Extremely Vulnerable Groups') in their attempt to target those most in need of help.

Apart from achieving low mortality and morbidity rates, the effect of this was to categorise the population according to certain scientific criteria, effectively producing a population that could be subjected to governmental practices (Rajaram 2002). In other words, in order to cater for the camp population, the agencies in charge needed to count, categorise and control the refugees through various routine bureaucratic practices that had been developed to perfection (cf. Hyndman 2000). This bureaucratisation was a means of governing the camp, not through rules and restrictions – which was the main tool of the MHA – but through everyday practices of caring for the lives of the refugees.

It was my clear impression that most ground staff were generally committed to helping the refugees, but due to the bureaucratic imperative to count and control, a tug of war would often take place between relief staff and refugees. Relief staff would spend most of their time making rules and systems for ensuring that the refugees did not break them, while refugees would spend their time trying to bend the rules which they found unfair. This may seem paradoxical and it certainly frustrated many on both sides. However, in order to help the refugees in a way that made sense and ensured that everyone was treated as fairly as possible, bureaucratic machinery was unavoidable. Any refugee who disrupted the operation was perceived by NGO staff to be working against the good of all, and these systems were put in place for the benefit of the population as such. When a refugee cheated on food rations, they were taking food from other deserving refugees. When street leaders expressed a wish for blankets from the UNHCR in exchange for work, they were told that extra blankets were for elderly refugees who needed them more. In other words, the relief agencies had found a winning formula that would ensure the optimal result for the population as a whole, and they merely needed to convince the refugees of the sense in this. Behind these practices lay a will to help the victims of war and flight – and hence an assumption that it was the agencies that knew what is best for the refugees, who must be controlled for their own sake.

Combating Dependency

Despite the success of the 'relief operation' in terms of keeping the refugee population alive and healthy, humanitarian relief agencies were concerned that their generous handouts and impressive planning would produce passive clients who suffered from a 'dependency syndrome'. In private discussions, relief workers were troubled by the lack of initiative among the refugees and speculated how to make the refugees take more responsibility for their own lives. 'If you try to organise sports, the refugees will just ask for a new ball from the agency', an AEF youth coordinator said. This attitude annoyed the staff. Why were the refugees apparently not interested in helping themselves just a little? Why were they just waiting for handouts and not showing any initiative? Such frustration could result in stereotyping based on nationality. Thus, most expatriate staff held that the Rwandan refugees might be difficult, cunning and have criminal inclinations, but they certainly had more initiative than the Burundians. Also Zairean/Congolese refugees were known to have more initiative than Burundians. Burundians were generally known to be placid and lacking in initiative and drive. A report from Kitali Hills camp by Cathy Lennox-Cook (of GOAL, an Irish NGO) states that Burundians not only had a lower level of health and hygiene than the Rwandans in the camp, but they also lacked a 'community spirit' (Lennox-Cook 1996). Such stereotyping was not entirely racially based, however, and it was generally held that it was the kind of help given that produced dependency, and the differences between various nationalities were explained in social and historical terms. Thus, Rwandan Hutu allegedly had more pride and dignity than Hutu from Burundi because they were 'on top' in Rwanda before 1994. As we shall see in later chapters, similar stereotypes were held by the refugees themselves and had their roots in colonial classifications.

The dependency debate has a long tradition in refugee studies and elsewhere.[7] Much of the debate in refugee studies involves the idea that refugees are not inherently lazy but have been made so by the UNHCR's top-down approach and its failure to involve the refugee community in its decisions (see Harrell-Bond 1986; Kibreab 1993). The solution to this problem, they claim, is to introduce self-management, community development and participation. In the cases where the UNHCR has introduced such policies, critics accuse the organisation of having double standards and using participation as window dressing (see Hyndman 2000; Kaiser 2000). Thus, according to these critics, the solution to a dependency mentality lies in more and better participation and community involvement.[8]

The UNHCR and other refugee agencies have not been late to respond to this critique. The concern about apathy and the focus on 'participation' as the cure can be seen in virtually any policy paper of humanitarian relief agencies. In one cutting-edge document in humanitarian policy, it is stated that 'we shall attempt to build disaster response on local capacities', and that 'Ways shall be found to involve programme beneficiaries in the management of relief aid'.[9] Likewise, a UNHCR document proposes that the views of all sections of society, regardless of age or gender, should be included in planning (Anderson, Howarth and Overholt 1992), while in its mission statement, the UNHCR claims that: 'UNHCR is committed to the principle of participation by consulting refugees on decisions that affect their lives'.[10]

Obviously, there is a lot of distance between the policy papers produced at the head quarters in Geneva and the day-to-day practices of UNHCR and NGO staff in the camps. Whereas most international staff were genuinely committed to aiding victims of war, they often found themselves wound up in bureaucratic logics over which they had no control, and different NGOs reacted differently to this challenge. Often the better-funded European and North American NGOs, who could afford to train their staff in the latest approaches to relief work, were keener on community development than their underpaid Tanzanian and Kenyan counterparts. On the other hand, the local Tanzanian staff – whether employed by local or international agencies – appeared to have a more pragmatic and less naive approach to the refugees. Whereas international staff would often try to push their own agendas, impervious to the actual political manoeuvres taking place, because they assumed the 'refugee-as-victim' position, Tanzanian staff seemed more in touch with what was actually happening in the camp and would act from the position that refugees are (political) subjects with concrete histories rather than universal objects of humanitarianism.   The British NGO, Christian Outreach,[11] appeared to be very concerned with involving 'the community' in its activities. As their country director in Tanzania in 1996, Richard Reynolds, put it: '[T]he approach adopted by Christian Outreach incorporates the idea of development. A development philosophy, as opposed to *relief mentality*, can ensure that the *communities* within the camp population can *develop themselves and their capacities*' (Reynolds 1996: 14, emphasis added). We see here that participation and community development are a means to combat a relief mentality and regain a sense of dignity that, it is assumed by Reynolds, have been destroyed by relief and by the traumatic experience of flight. Rather than wanting to change power relations or devolve responsibility, involving the community is about mentalities – it is psychologised. Lack of involvement in decision-making decreases a sense of responsibility, which in turn causes lack of initiative in a vicious circle. Participation and community development are meant to break this circle and give refugees back a sense of dignity. In the words of the UNHCR, 'Refugee participation *helps build the values and sense of community* that contribute to reducing protection problems' (UNHCR 1991: 10, emphasis added). It is further argued in this document that traditional, pre-flight networks have broken down in refugee camps, and that alternative arrangements must therefore be provided. It is thus assumed that refugee societies have by definition experienced a disintegration of values and a loss of community, both of which they are assumed to have had prior to flight. In other words, participation is not merely perceived as a means of efficiently dealing with practical problems in the camp. It has the main aim of redressing the perceived social disintegration in refugee society, a means of installing 'values and a sense of community'. Participation is, therefore, meant to give the individual back their dignity and, more importantly, to re-establish refugee society as a community.

In her compelling study, Barbara Cruikshank explores this apparent contradiction between controlling and wanting to empower 'powerless' subjects in relation to modern, liberal government. She questions the underlying assumption that empowerment is a noble or radical political strategy and claims that the will to empower 'is neither clearly liberatory nor clearly repressive; rather, it is typical of the liberal arts of conduct' (Cruikshank 1999: 10).[12] Seen in this light, the idea of shifting power from the state to the population is in line with liberal governmentality, where rules from above are replaced by norms within the population (Foucault 1978: 144). State power is transferred to a population that in turn is being governmentalised. Self-help serves here as an example of how the individual citizen is instrumentally linked to 'society as a whole'. Moreover, it is a philanthropic technique that is exemplary of modern government; it is both voluntary and coercive (Cruikshank 1999: 48). The 'noble' cause of philanthropists is therefore to make powerful citizens out of powerless subjects. Liberal, democratic governance depends on citizens that are autonomous and self-governing, and this is what participatory schemes are about. Political apathy, not making use of democratic rights and voluntarily subjecting oneself to power thus become the worst enemies of biopolitics, and the ones that its proponents seek to eliminate through empowerment. Interestingly, in the view of participatory approaches, powerlessness is not perceived to be a structural problem in society. Rather, poor people's 'sense of powerlessness' or 'lack of self-esteem' is perceived as a personality problem, Cruikshank argues. Therefore, the main objective of participation programmes is to interest these people in their own empowerment, to alter their subjectivities. Instead of changing structures in society, the aim of participatory approaches is to make the participants 'feel' involved and to take responsibility. This certainly seems to be the case in a refugee camp where refugees have very little influence on the important decisions in their lives.

Ideally, being a democratic citizen, acting responsibly and governing oneself, leads to certain democratic, political rights and certain freedoms. But as both Hindess (2001) and Dean (1999) argue, not all populations in liberal government are seen fit for liberal freedom. Certain groups, such as welfare clients and colonial subjects, are perceived to lack the required capacities for autonomous conduct. These capacities, Hindess argues, can be developed either 'through compulsion, through the imposition of more or less extended periods of discipline [or] by establishing a benign and supportive social environment' (Hindess 2001: 101). Certainly, the kind of empowerment that was introduced in the camp was severely restricted and often took the shape of a 'spectacle' of democracy rather than genuine delegation of power. Being in the exceptional space of the refugee camp, normal political processes were suspended, and the refugees were simply being prepared for the day that they could become full citizens and members of the national order of things.

Relief agencies attempted to 'mobilise' the refugees in several ways. Educational programmes and information campaigns, including theatre troupes, sought to heighten their 'awareness' on technical issues such as environment, hygiene, sexually transmitted diseases and violence against women. It was not enough to tell the the refugees what they were and were not allowed to do; they also had to be convinced of the value of these rules and incorporate them in such a manner that boiling water and sweeping the *blindé* would seem natural to them, becoming a norm rather than a law. By learning to 'love the law' they would feel responsibility towards the rules of the camp, not only making camp management easier but also making the refugees more content. This was certainly the intention.

In Lukole, agencies had the answers ready when promoting refugee participation. The refugees needed educating in the art of self-management, but even then the possibility of making decisions of any significance to their lives in the camp was heavily circumscribed. They had no choice in what or how much to eat. They had no choice about not leaving the camp. They could not even choose to build their houses in clusters or circles if they so wished. Nevertheless, every block, street or village had a leader, elected by the refugees. These leaders attended fortnightly meetings with the UNHCR field officer or field assistant, an MHA representative, and representatives from relevant NGOs. Occasionally, the UNHCR's protection officer, security officer or another staff member with a special message for the refugee population would attend the meetings as well.

So what were the tasks of these leaders? Basically, they were meant to be intermediaries between the refugee population and the agencies in control. At a leaders meeting in Lukole B in June 1997, for example, they voiced refugees' complaints that they had lost their ration cards, that nurses treated them disrespectfully, and that Oxfam was pulling down their latrines. On the other hand, they were expected to disseminate information from the agencies to the population. This could be the security officer warning refugees to 'behave' or explaining to them why it is so important for Oxfam to make sure that they build mud-brick latrines ('It is for your own good').

I attended several of these meetings in order to get an impression of the ways in which the UNHCR dealt with the dilemma of wanting to empower refugees while wanting to do so in a certain way. The attitude of the international and Tanzanian staff at these meetings varied – from the arrogant, almost hostile, approach of some international staff to the equally patronising but more jovial note of some of the representatives of the Tanzanian authorities; from the friendly but ignorant attitude of European field officers to the equally friendly but more informed attitude of some Tanzanian field assistants. The following fieldnote extract illustrates the latter.

19 June 1997.
The UNHCR field assistant, a young Tanzanian woman, controls the meeting and sets the agenda. She speaks the local language, Kihangaza, which is similar to Kirundi and is friendly with the refugees – she jokes and listens. UNHCR has asked the refugees to establish committees in each village of the camp consisting of three men and three women. None of the leaders present have come up with a list of names for the committees. The UNHCR representative is angry with them – telling them off and telling them how important it is that they have these committees. The idea is that they should act as problem-solvers in relation to food distribution. Furthermore, they should disseminate information

from the agencies. Why this should be necessary when they already have village leaders is never made quite clear.

Although the young Tanzanian woman maintained the meeting in a friendly and relaxed tone, she had an agenda that the leaders must comply with. The UNHCR was not satisfied with the fact that 99 per cent of the leaders were men and was trying to establish a parallel system of committees. Although the leaders did not openly oppose the suggestion and appeared to play along with UNHCR rules, they purposely delayed the process. When the field assistant mentioned the committee lists, the leaders tried either to turn the conversation onto other issues or brought up a number of excuses.

In other cases, UNHCR staff members tried to get the refugee leaders to feel responsible towards UNHCR rules with a mixture of appeal and threats.

27 January 1998.
A key issue taken up by the UNHCR field officer is the problem with 'recyclers': people – in particular from villages B1 to B7 – would leave and go to Mbuba (a registration site for new arrivals from Burundi) in order to get new ration cards. Apparently, the refugee leaders have claimed that it only happens when people loose their ration cards and need a new one. UNHCR urges leaders to take people who have lost their cards to UNHCR – not to send them to Mbuba.

26 March 1998.
The protection officer from UNHCR is present and giving them a real talking to. There have been cases of members of one political party in the camp abducting and torturing members of the other party and alleged spies from Burundi. He is telling them that important people, leaders, 'some of you sitting here', are hosting Burundians from Burundi who are not officially registered in the camp. 'Please tell these people to go to Mbuba to be scanned and registered. We have certain sanctions. You could be relocated to Tanga, Tabora or southern Tanzania. Some of these people that you are hosting have been caught for making an illegal training facility, abduction and torture'.
Some of the leaders here bribed the local police to release these people. 'I hope you have enough money to bribe the field officer, to bribe me and to bribe the authorities in Dar es Salaam', he says, as the crowd remains awkwardly silent.

In these cases the relief agencies were appealing to the leaders to show a sense of responsibility towards the UNHCR's rules. They were called upon to turn their own people in if they broke the rules. This was done in part by trying to convince them that it was in their own best interests and in part by threatening them. Both the UNHCR and refugee leaders were feigning good intentions, while neither party actually trusted the other. When the UNHCR urged leaders to bring people to them when they had lost their ration cards rather than go to Mbuba, the UNHCR was playing along with the street leaders' game, although everyone present knew very well that the recyclers were using Mbuba as a strategy to get more than one ration card. However, the UNHCR was also threatening the leaders, implying that they could be held responsible for anything that their 'subjects' did. This was more obvious in the other case where the UNHCR appealed to the street leaders to turn in politicians hiding in the camp, and it was well aware that the majority of street leaders in that part of the camp supported the political party that was accused of abduction and torture.

The street leaders mainly just kept quiet in these cases. If they objected at all, they did not object to the fact that the UNHCR was forcing them to turn in their comrades, but to the fact that it was a difficult policy for them to implement and that the Tanzanian police were not helping them enough. In other words, they did not question the system as such; rather, they played along with it while dragging things out.

It is not my intention to criticise specific staff or the UNHCR as an organisation for having double standards with regard to participation. The field officers were driven by a will to empower. However, their paternalistic attitudes revealed a sense of knowing what was good for the refugees, of knowing that African refugees needed training, even disciplining, to become liberal citizens. Therefore attempts at 'involving the community', encouraging development rather than relief and promoting participation were about giving refugees a 'sense of community' and about combating 'lethargy', 'relief mentality' and 'feelings of lack of control over their own future'. In other words, the UNHCR and other agencies had succeeded in caring for the bodies of the refugees, and now they were intent on caring for their minds. The UNHCR assumed that war and flight had disrupted what was assumed to have been a harmonious society, and had made the refugees lose their cultural and social moorings. The liminal position that they had landed in, according to this logic, was dangerous because it made them 'vulnerable' to radical politics and violence. For this reason it was important for the UNHCR to instil some dignity in them while they were in the camp. The trick was to do this without introducing politics.

Good and Bad Participation: Community versus Politics

When they were set up, the Tanzanian government banned all political activity in the refugee camps.[13] Likewise, in spite of encouraging refugee participation, the UNHCR did its utmost to discourage political activity.

Peter Nyers argues that there is a binary opposition between humanitarianism and politics, 'the former element carrying positive connotations ("humanitarianism is compassionate, principled, impartial") while the latter is seen in negative terms ("politics is cynical, amoral, self-interested")' (Nyers 1998: 19). In other words, the various attempts to help refugees – based on a humanitarian ethos – are necessarily opposed to politics. For refugees to act as genuine victims, they are expected – in humanitarian discourse – to be helpless and passive. In other words, apathy has to be combatted, but not at any cost, since certain kinds of refugee activities and agency are perceived to be better than others.

Political activity was believed to disturb 'the community' and was equivalent to 'trouble'. However, as we will see in later chapters, the camp was rife with political activity, mostly concerning internal competition for access to power and resources between two political parties in the camp. It is to this trouble that we now turn in order to see how the UNHCR constructs categories that are believed to disturb the refugee community, in the process also constructing 'the community' as a category, and hence stabilising the image of the refugee-as-victim.

On 2 May 1997 a population meeting was called by the UNHCR with the participation of the camp commandant, UNHCR representatives, representatives from implementing partner NGOs and refugees in Lukole A. This particular meeting had been called due to deterioration in the security situation and to a petition submitted by the refugee street leaders, asking for the removal of the chief security guard for alleged misuse of authority.[14] This accusation was based on the fact that the chief security guard belonged to a different party from the majority of street leaders in Lukole A. This demonstrates that what the UNHCR perceived as a non-political, bureaucratic position was – correctly – perceived by the camp population as a position of power and hence worthy of political competition. Street leaders and security guards had access to resources and information and hence to power, which naturally lead to them being involved in the ongoing political power struggle between supporters of Palipehutu and CNDD in the camp.

It was decided by the UNHCR and MHA before the meeting that the security guards should be phased out and new ones recruited. Similarly, elections for new leaders would be held. It was the intention of the UNHCR to make sure these elections were 'free and fair'. These decisions were to be conveyed to the camp population at the meeting. What is interesting for our purposes is how the problem of political activity was construed in the discourse of the camp commandant and the UNHCR field officer. The camp commandant addressed the issue of criminal and political activity, as both were perceived to affect security in the camp. According to a UNHCR memorandum,[15] he warned that the time for 'taking action' on involvement in political activity was coming. UNHCR's field officer then relayed

UNHCR's concern about security issues. She took a softer approach, appealing to the refugees' own sense of responsibility rather than using the threat of force, encouraging them to restrain from politics – for their own sake. She advised the refugees to refrain from activities that disrupt security and endanger 'harmonious social life' among the 'great majority of the refugee community' who fled their country 'in search of peace and security'.

She also advised the refugees to assess the political involvement of candidates so as to avoid election of individuals who would like to use the forum for furthering their political interests 'at the expense of innocent people'. According to her discourse, politics is sordid, and political activity disrupts the harmonious community of the camp. Politicians are driven by selfish interests rather than the interests of the common good, and if they are given the chance a few such selfish individuals will destroy the life of the great majority of refugees who are 'innocent people'. She went on to give advice to the leader candidates. They should be ready to serve the people who entrust them with the responsibility of representing them on any forum. They should be ready to put aside their individual interests and provide service to the people they lead.

Refugee participation in leadership was supposed to be apolitical, with the leaders 'providing service to the people', complying with the common interests of the community as a whole rather than any particular interests of any specific group. Being void of politics, participation is also void of power relations and is merely a question of finding the optimal solution to the 'true interests' of the community.

The community was evoked as a counterweight to selfish political activity. To work for the community was to be self-sacrificing and disinterested, devoting oneself to the common good. It was assumed that empowering 'the community' would automatically serve the interests of the community as a whole. Such perceptions of the community imply almost sublime qualities, there is an almost organic texture to it, and any reference to the community is laden with positive connotations.[16] Finding a 'true community' is about finding a moral community where the individuals involved share common goals and interests.

The UNHCR had several practices through which it could nurture the community and formalise it into certain institutions.[17] One such institution was the street leaders, as we have seen. The problem with these street leaders – seen from the point of view of promoting community spirit – was that they tended to be too engaged in political competition. Furthermore, they were often young, able-bodied, semi-educated men,[18] and the UNHCR was worried that they would not promote the interests of the neediest refugees. Therefore, other means were used in order to try to reach the 'true community'. Among these were community mobilisers, the establishment of women's committees and community development projects.

What was once called 'social services' became known as 'community services'. It changed name in the early 1990s and was, in late 2000, in the process of becoming 'community development'. The idea was to enhance the self-help perspective. In the words of a community services officer: 'Our reason was that social services or social work was seen as more individual case management but community services was more what we were hoping to actually be doing i.e. involving the communities in whatever was needed including individual support'. For this officer, the community was linked closely to the idea of participation and empowerment, and was also meant to combat dependency and passiveness among refugees.

What must be seen as the most successful programme, from the perspective of promoting a sense of community and combating a relief mentality, was the use of foster families in the camps. When I was in Lukole there was no orphanage and the handful of street children that existed had been given *blindés* and put together in 'families'. All other unaccompanied minors had been placed in foster families. When hundreds of thousands of Rwandans arrived in the area within a short time in 1994, among whome there were thousands of children who had lost their parents, a policy of supporting foster families rather than orphanages was actively pursued. Community services staff among the UNHCR and implementing agencies at the time prided themselves on the good results they had achieved in this innovative approach. Orphanages were perceived to be alienating, destroying the social and moral fabric of children through the loss of their cultural moorings. It was therefore culturally sustainable to place children in foster families.

However, this system was not only perceived to ensure that the children had a culturally appropriate environment; it was also seen to benefit the community as such. It was assumed that by taking responsibility for the children, rather than leaving this to the NGOs, the refugees avoided the dependency syndrome, strengthening the social and moral fabric of the refugee community as a whole. The relief agencies' attitude to fostering is a good illustration of the prevailing sense that one has to sacrifice one's own interests for those of the community. The reward cannot be measured in individual wealth but rather in terms of dignity and community spirit. It must be noted that these families did not accept foster children of their own initiative, however, and that the practice was organised and systematised by the UNHCR and implementing partners. In other words, the community needed 'pushing' a little in order to get the policy off the ground.

However, this enforced solidarity is not merely a question of the refugees learning the art of governing – learning to become liberal citizens – as it is doubtful whether such unselfish acts of solidarity would be expected of citizens in other societies. Would British or French families be expected to sacrifice that much, except in times of war? It is as if, because the refugees were poor and had been through so much in terms of war and disruption, they could not afford to be demanding. In such situations of extreme human distress, one is expected, according to humanitarian discourse, to be able to sacrifice oneself for one's fellow suffering human beings. Refugees, incarnating 'bare humanity', are stripped of political subjectivity and hence expected not to be selfish (selfishness being linked to politics), but to rebuild their community for their own good and their own dignity. And if the refugees do not volunteer to do so of their own accord, they can be induced to volunteer (through campaigns and various kinds of material support for foster families) for the sake of community spirit.

Obviously, this sense of community was opposed to and posited as a cure against apathy and relief mentality. It was, ironically, also opposed to the kinds of behaviour in the camp that were farthest from being apathetic and passive. Political activity was one such type of behaviour that was perceived to subvert the community, another being cheating and misusing development projects. Both kinds of behaviour expressed refugees' agency, their taking the initiative, but they did so in the 'wrong way'.

Christian Outreach ran various community-based development projects where refugees could basically apply for funding for microprojects if they were based on community initiatives and if they were to the benefit of 'vulnerables'. This led to some practical problems, as refugees appeared to work out how to 'use' the system. Thus, Christian Outreach would receive applications for loans where the objectives of the project were formulated in a language that was strikingly similar to NGO language. Similarly, if Christian Outreach had decided that, say, 60 per cent of the profit should go to vulnerables, in order to ensure that the projects were actually benefiting 'the community' and not just some powerful individuals, they would be sure to receive a number of applications that proposed to give exactly 60 per cent of profits to vulnerables. Christian Outreach staff explained to me that they were frustrated by individuals misusing projects that were intended to be for the benefit of the community.[19] They perceived the 'problem' to lie with a few individuals that cheated and hence ruined everything for the majority of law-abiding and needy people. These individuals were the ones who fiddled the system of ration cards, sold blankets that were intended for vulnerables, and registered themselves twice or more (recyclers). A consequence of this dichotomisation between the community and a few bad individuals was that the NGOs were able to maintain a belief in the sublime qualities of 'the community' as an antidote to the dependency syndrome and ultimately a means of catering for the mental well-being of the camp population. By creating a category – the politicians and the misusers – that prevented the fulfilment of the community, relief staff could retain the illusion of the 'good' community. Simultaneously, by conferring the status of troublemaker on the first group, it was possible to maintain strongly controlled government 'from above' while also promoting participation. The underlying rationale here was that if the UNHCR did not control the process so tightly, troublemakers would misuse the system and promote self-interested politics to the detriment of the vast majority of 'innocent refugees'.

Gendering Refugees

Refugee women are commonly perceived by NGOs and the general public to make up the bulk of refugee populations.[20] Often lumped together with children in statistics, they are perceived as vulnerable victims in situations of conflict and war. The UNHCR, for example, states that: 'Among the people hit hardest by the violence and uncertainty of displacement are girls, elderly widows, single mothers – women. As a rule of thumb, some 75 per cent of these destitute displaced people are women and their dependent children'.[21] Collapsing women and children into one category reduces women to the level of infants. Women – like children – occupy the victim position and conjure up a sense of 'bare humanity'; they are to be felt sorry for and to be helped. Malkki points out that 'Perhaps it is that women and children embody a special kind of powerlessness; perhaps they do not tend to look as if they could be "dangerous aliens"; perhaps their images are more effective in fund-raising efforts than those of men' (Malkki 1995a: 11). She suggests that children – and by extension women – express better than adults 'bare humanity' with no specific culture or history, while adult men, on the other hand, represent the flipside of popular images of refugees: the 'dangerous alien' who brings dissident politics and foreign cultures with him. Thus, one might say that women epitomise the refugee figure as someone who lacks what national citizens have (culture, history, citizenship). In this manner, women are not only stripped of history and culture in humanitarian discourse; they are also stripped of any agency,[22] while men disturb the image of the refugee-as-victim.

In Lukole, the UNHCR had a number of programmes targeting various specific vulnerable groups, such as women, the elderly, children and youths. Adult men were not an issue in these benevolent programmes except when they caused trouble. They were summoned for meetings on camp security where they were warned not to take part in military training or political activity, and they were the objects of many reports, policies and strategies concerning domestic and sexual violence against women.[23] In all these cases, young men were defined as 'trouble'. By encouraging refugee women to be street leaders and security guards, the UNHCR was appealing to women as less troublesome and less politicised.

Such gendered stereotypes affected the governing of the camp and perceptions of politics, the community and dependency. While women were perceived to lack agency and epitomise the refugee-as-victim, they were also voided of sordid, self-interested politics. It was assumed by relief agencies that if women were empowered they would work for the good of the community as a whole, while men were assumed to misuse such power for their own political advantages. In this sense, we may say that men were believed to disturb the community and prevent it from developing into fullness, while women were believed to incarnate the community.[24] By placing 'trouble' and politics on men, the relief agencies were able to maintain the purity of the refugee-as-victim category. Furthermore, while the UNHCR and NGOs were attempting to introduce gender equality in the camp, they were also gendering the refugees in specific ways. This had often quite unintended consequences for both the ways in which refugees interpreted the camp and their strategies of regaining some kind of subjectivity.

Sanitizing the Past

Whenever there was a formal event in the camp, such as the election of a street leader, the celebration of African Refugee Day or the visit of the Tanzanian president, various dance troupes would entertain the camp with 'traditional' dancing and drumming. The best of these troupes were supported by various relief agencies which provided them with clothes and drums, encouraging the refugees to preserve their cultural heritage. Cultural heritage was also kept alive by supporting basket-weaving projects in which women made colourful traditional baskets and tablemats out of material from WFP food sacks. The objective was to support Burundian culture so that it was not forgotten in the camp and to prevent the refugees from becoming 'cultureless'.

The refugees, however, preferred listening to Bob Marley and Zairean pop than traditional drumming, and they never used the multicoloured baskets they were encouraged to make but preferred instead the more practical plastic containers made in China. By supporting dance troupes and basket weaving, the UNHCR was domesticating the past and exhibiting it in the form of cultural artefacts which represented an innocent Burundian culture devoid of any reference to politics or conflict. 'Why do you dance?' I asked one of the dancers from one of the most famous drumming and dancing groups, which practised almost every day of the week. 'In order to forget', was his answer. In other words, the past haunted the refugees as well as the agencies in charge of them. The camp was in principle an exceptional place, outside history. However, history did not just disappear, and it was therefore the task of the UNHCR to either void the camp of the past or to make sure that the past was depoliticised. In this sense, 'traditional

Burundian' customs and artefacts like the baskets and the dancing actually helped refugees forget their more painful past, as the dancer claimed. Rather than taking away their past, the refugees were given a sanitized, harmless past while they killed time in the limbo state of their present.

One form of cultural performance that was not supported by any agencies – or even known to them – was made by a 12-year-old boy who put on what my friends in the camp referred to as 'videos'. These 'videos' turned out to be performances using a shadow puppet theatre that the boy had made from a cardboard box, a piece of thin cloth, homemade oil lamps and puppets cut out of cardboard and stuck onto sticks. Those watching the performances were charged an entry fee of 20 shillings (about 3 U.S. cents). The show was performed after dark – when all the humanitarian agencies had left the camp – so that the oil lamps could have an effect, emphasising the covert nature of this cultural performance. The show was all about the Tutsi army fighting Nyangoma (the most famous rebel leader at the time), with people running away from helicopters and Bruce Lee and Rambo coming to the rescue. 'This boy is an extremist', my assistant said, momentarily uncomfortable with me being exposed to this kind of cultural expression. He soon forgot his political correctness, however, and we enjoyed the show. It was certainly a far cry from Oxfam's Sanitation Information Team, the educational theatre group teaching hygiene and decent behaviour, and it was quite different to the aestheticised performances of the 'traditional' drummers. This young boy was taking on the political past in a direct and uncensored fashion that was far more dangerous. He was questioning the refugees' neutrality and innocence, their status as victims, depicting a battle between good and evil where the goodies are not passive but fight the baddies, and where help does not come in the shape of food, shelter and community mobilisation but in the shape of heavily armed action heroes like Rambo and Bruce Lee.

In Conclusion

The camp made up a bureaucratic dream of efficiency and straight lines where the population was counted, measured, fed, nursed and generally kept in good health. The main aim of humanitarian intervention was to keep the population – the 'caseload' in humanitarian lingo – alive and well. However, it appears that the relief agencies were also keen on introducing 'participation' to the refugees. This may seem absurd in a refugee camp, where people's lives were heavily circumscribed by rules and regulations and their livelihoods strongly dependent on handouts. But empowering refugees was more directed towards the souls of the refugees than towards changing power relations in the camp, the idea being that the refugees should 'feel' empowered so as to avoid feeling apathetic. The question of empowerment was thus psychologised and pathologised and had little to do with societal power. It was therefore also void of politics.

In this way, participation was about strengthening the community rather than following self interests. It was assumed that 'real refugees' were victims who did not think of themselves first but sacrificed themselves for the community as a whole. Needless to say, this image is linked to the image of the female refugee. However, in the camp this ideal was constantly threatened by the refugees who did not act as real victims and who had their own agenda. They engaged in politics and used NGOs in order to reach their goals. This refugee was incarnated in the young man.

Seen from the humanitarian perspective, 'genuine' refugees are passive victims of violence that need helping and the role of humanitarian agencies is to provide such help in the best possible manner, providing food, protection, health and dignity. However, refugees do not always live up to the ideal of being hapless victims of war and persecution. Some left Burundi in order to seek employment or land, as was the case of those who migrated to Tanzanian villages near the border, only to be deported to the refugee camp in 1997/8, while others had been involved in fighting for the rebel forces, CNDD and Palipehutu, and could not be unequivocally conceived as passive victims of war.[25] In order not to appear to be providing bases for these rebels, as the Burundian government continually insinuated, it was necessary for the camp authorities and the relief agencies to drive out any political activity and make sure that the camp was only a place for genuine victims of war. Therefore it became of utmost importance to ban and combat any political activity in the camp. The UNHCR not only tried to rid the camp of politics through the 'negative' power of forbidding it but also tried to put something else in its stead, namely participation on the one hand and aestheticised cultural artefacts on the other.

By trying to create genuinely innocent victims without any past or culture, the humanitarian agencies were attempting to create *tabula rasa*, where politics was forgotten and the past was aestheticised into cultural performances. Such refugees were obviously easier to imagine repatriated and reconciled than the actual scheming, plotting politicised young men that we found in the camp.

Notes

1. This project is inspired by a Foucauldian approach to government. See Foucault (1978: 135–59), Dean (1999), Rose (1999) and Hindess (2001).
2. These were: CARE International, in charge of environmental programmes and logistics; the Tanzanian Red Cross Society (TRCS), in charge of camp

management and food distribution; and the African Education Foundation (AEF), in charge of community services, health and education in the camp. The latter were replaced by Norwegian People's Aid (NPA) shortly before I left in May 1998. In addition, Oxfam was responsible for water and sanitation, while other agencies that played minor roles included the United Nations Children's Fund (UNICEF), Ngara District Development Organisation (NDDO) and the Jesuit Refugee Service (JRS).

3. The camp was divided into 'streets' (in Lukole A) and 'villages' (in Lukole B), which were further divided into 'blocks'. Each block had an elected leader.

4. For a thought provoking analysis of the spatial reflections of the power relations involved in food distribution, 'head counts' and other managerial exercises in a refugee camp, see Hyndman (2000).

5. The local Tanzanian staff speaking Kihangaza – a language similar to Kirundi and Kinyarwanda – were the object of many rumours about them being Burundian spies. See also Turner (2002).

6. This report gives the following illustration to clarify. 'Example: "FF/SP, means foster family of single parent/ household head"' (UNHCR 1997: 9). I assume it helps to know the right 'dev-speak' to grasp this 'clarifying' example.

7. Barbara Cruikshank proposes that a fear of creating dependency dates back to philanthropic home visitors in Victorian times (Cruikshank 1999). Hall-Matthews, meanwhile, shows how the British colonial administration was worried about creating dependency through famine relief in India in the late nineteenth century (Hall-Matthews 1996).

8. For more critical analyses of new humanitarianism and the attempts to link relief and development, see Duffield (1996, 2001).

9. 'Code of Conduct for the International Red Cross and Red Crescent Movement and NGOs in Disaster Response Programmes'. Retrieved 1 October 2009 from: www.ifrc.org/publicat/conduct/code.asp.

10. UNHCR. 'Mission Statement'. Retrieved 1st October 2009 from: www.unhcr.org/pages/49ed8346.html

11. Christian Outreach was not actually working in Lukole when I did fieldwork in the camp. I did, however, talk to them and follow their work on several occasions: first, when they were in Ngara, prior to 1997; and second, in 1997, when they were in the Kigoma region.

12. By 'liberal arts of conduct' Cruikshank means the whole register of modes of governmentality that characterise modern liberal-democratic states. A forceful achievement of Foucault and 'the governmentality school' has been to dissolve the opposition between government and freedom, enabling us to see how individuals in liberal democracies are governed by governing themselves in accordance with certain norms and values. See also Foucault et al. (1991), Dean (1999) and Rose (1999).

13. This goes back to the late 1960s when the Organisation of African Unity (OAU) was determined to prevent refugees from using neighbouring countries as safe havens from where they could commit acts of subversion against their country of origin (Daley 2007: 169).

14. Security guards were employed by the UNHCR to assist the Tanzanian police in keeping law and order in the camp.

15. As these are internal 'Notes for the File', I cannot quote them directly.
16. As Elizabeth Frazer comments; 'community is not straightforwardly anchored in social relations ... communities 'rise above' or 'transcend' the muddle of relations' (Frazer 1999: 85).
17. Nikolas Rose points out that 'the community' is not merely something to be governed; it is also a means of government. Therefore, it needs to be 'celebrated, encouraged, nurtured, shaped and instrumentalised' (Rose 1996: 335). However, for community to become functional as a governmental practice, it needs technocratising. It is through these technical communities that the moral community can be encouraged and governmentalised.
18. Only one in a hundred of these leaders was female. See also Chapter 5 for a profile of the street and village leaders.
19. They did, however, privately acknowledge the irony that the individuals who are supposedly destroying the community are the ones who are showing initiative and taking things into their own hands.
20. This perception has been proved statistically wrong on several occasions. See, e.g., Daley (1991) and U.S. Committee for Refugees (2000).
21. UNHCR. March 1998. 'UNHCR Fundraising: The General Programmes – UNHCR's Core Activities'. Retrieved 18th October 2000 from: www.unhcr.ch/fdrs/gpapp.
22. Feminist scholars have tried to do away with this image by proving that refugee women show initiative and strength. See, e.g., Daley (1991) and Indra (1999).
23. Human Rights Watch has for instance published an elaborate report on sexual and domestic violence in the refugee camps in Tanzania (Human Rights Watch 2000).
24. Ironically, as will be seen in the following chapter, it was these young, politically active men – who constituted the vast majority of street/village leaders and the bulk of NGO employees – with whom the UNHCR and NGOs chiefly collaborated.
25. At the time of fieldwork, the armed wing of CNDD was known as the FDD (Forces pour la Défence de la Démocratie), while the armed wing of Palipehutu was the FNL (Forces Nationales de la Liberation). There was also a third rebel force in the country, Frolina. However, it was regionally based in the south and had no influence in Lukole.

4
Camp Life and Moral Decay

In this chapter, we shift from the aerial view of the planner and the bureaucrat to the pedestrian view of the refugee. We examine the ways in which the refugees interpreted being treated as an undifferentiated mass by the Tanzanian authorities and international relief agencies, how they interpreted their new environment and their new rulers, and how they contrasted this with life in Burundi. We explore their representations of the camp as a place of social and moral decay, and how they conjured up a picture of an idyllic harmonious past in Burundi. It is not a story about life in the camp in terms of everyday practices but rather an assemblage of the refugees' own stories – their reflections on life in the camp and their attempts to interpret and understand the camp. The UNHCR may have been trying to create refugees as innocent victims – introducing ideas of participation and gender equality – but how were these ideas received by those who inhabited the camp? How did they interpret the temporary, exceptional space of the camp and its modes of governmentality? In short, what does being in limbo look like from the inside?

In the camp I heard a number of tales about the social and moral decay that was allegedly taking place. Husbands and wives would fight and there were a great many divorces. Men took many wives in the camp and women became prostitutes. Young girls spoke too much and too loudly and they would wear short dresses and hang around at the market instead of working in the *blindé,* while men would spend all their time and money on beer and beat their wives for not showing enough respect. Young men would marry old women and old men would marry young women, and they would forget Burundian customs in the camp where nobody knew their neighbour and solidarity was lost. In the camp, so people claimed, the rich became poor and the poor became rich and the small people showed no respect for the 'big men' but treated them as equals. Because everyone received the same insufficient food rations from 'food distribution', the children no longer respected their teachers, the peasants treated the educated elite as equals and men could no longer provide for their wives who therefore would leave them. People assured me that this would never have happened in Burundi where everyone knew their place in society and behaved according to 'Burundian customs'. Through telling these tales – to me or to each other – they could put words to the experience of being put into a new environment and being subjected to new and foreign governing techniques.

The tales of decay were built up as a narrative of loss. Although some of the refugees had never lived in Burundi, and although gender, age and class relations were changing inside Burundi, Burundi was conjured up in the tales as the stable, harmonious opposite of the chaotic, immoral space of the camp. The loss that the refugees had experienced had very specific, historical roots, and yet the diversity of their Burundian past and their individual flight histories were suppressed, as the vague sense of loss was interpreted through these standard narratives. That said, however, the refugees also saw new opportunities arise in the immoral and liberating space of the camp. Burundian customs could be a straightjacket and they perceived the breakdown of these customs as an advantage for Hutu progress and liberation.

'UNHCR Is a Better Husband'

Lukole A II was established in 1994 for Burundians who fled after the genocide in Rwanda. For an outsider, this was a pleasant place to come to. The houses were all well established and made of mud and wattle or mud bricks, rather than the makeshift shelters that one could see elsewhere. Many people here had small businesses, making wooden bikes, collecting firewood for sale at the market to the elite refugees, or buying bananas from Tanzanians and selling them at the market. One young man, whom I got to know well, baked *mandazi* (doughnut-like bread rolls) that he sold to the restaurants. When I arrived somewhere like this in the camp, someone would give me a small wooden bench to sit on. A few of those living closest by would sit down with me and a crowd of curious neighbours gathered around. Some issues were discussed only with a few people while the others listened. People would come and go, as they heard the rumour that I was around or they got bored with the conversation. This particular day we were discussing changes in life after entering the camp, and a great many people were joining in the conversation. They seemed to agree that everything had changed for the worse, and when the subject turned to gender relations everyone joined in, men and women alike. Women, who usually see a virtue in being shy and reluctant to express themselves in public, joined in the debate and entered heated discussions with the men.

MAN: Yes, some women say that the UNHCR gives them food, so they do not respect the men. So there are many divorces.
OLD WOMAN: No. That's only the young women.
YOUNG WOMAN: That is not true.
MAN: Some women just wash themselves and put on nice clothes and go to the market, instead of working.
[*The women seem to protest.*]

In this conversation, from a visit to Lukole A II in August 1997, we see how women contested the man's statement about women losing respect due to the UNHCR. Furthermore, the older woman put the blame on the young women, provoking a young woman to disagree with the old woman. However, they all agreed that women ought to respect and obey their husbands. In other words, in spite of taking different positions vis-à-vis the narrative, they all related to it as a fact. Although tales such as this functioned as common narrative structures or interpretative schemes through which life in the camp was interpreted and pitched against an idyllic past in Burundi, they did not mean the same to everybody in Lukole. While both men and women must relate to tales of promiscuity, polygamy and prostitution, they did so differently, rejecting them, embracing them or contesting certain aspects of them.

I would hear the statement that the 'UNHCR [or the white man] is a better husband' again and again in the camp when men explained how women had stopped respecting their husbands because their husbands could no longer provide for them. In fact, sixty respondents in my survey of 464 randomly sampled adult refugees gave this exact response to the question 'Do you see any changes in the relations between men and women, after coming to the camp? (State which changes)'. Other responses with much the same effect would be: 'Men and women no longer respect each other' (93), 'disagreement' (85) and 'divorce' (55). In most interviews, a similar line of reasoning would emerge: In the camp, men do not provide their women with food and clothes. As it is the *muzungu* (white person) or the UN that provides, women no longer respect the men. They only respect the UN and *muzungu*.

In February 1998 I interviewed Pierre, a 24-year-old man who lived in village F2, known to be a rough part of the camp, allegedly dominated by uneducated young men who sympathised with Palipehutu and who had caused a lot of trouble in other camps. Pierre's parents fled to Rwanda in 1972 and he had only lived in Burundi for a few months in 1993. He had no schooling, was unmarried and had no occupation in the camp. This was my third conversational interview with him and we were discussing life in the camp. He described how humiliating it was to have to beg for food from the white man.

> We are begging from the *muzungu* to get something to eat ... It makes someone lose their pride. Because you are a man. And in Burundi customs, men don't go every time to beg for something.... Even in your country when there is somebody who is begging – for example disabled people who are begging for something in the markets – they are losing their pride. Refugees are compared with these people who are disabled in your country or somewhere else. Nobody respects him because every time he is forced to get food from the food distribution. Even these Tanzanians don't respect. We can't be respected because they know that we are fed by 'food distribution'.

'Food distribution' was where the TRCS distributed rations of oil, maize and beans that were the same for all refugees, irrespective of gender, age or social status. Being a refugee, in Pierre's view, was like being disabled, which was particularly humiliating for men who were meant to provide for their families. Being forced to beg meant that even Tanzanian men look down on him. As we shall see later, Tanzanians were usually looked upon with contempt by the Burundians, so not being respected by them was particularly humiliating.

Pierre went on to explain how this unfortunate situation caused problems between men and women.

> A few months ago some women got *kangas* [cloth] from *bazungu*,[1] from international ... from UNHCR. And when they went back to their *blindés* they were saying that now they get clothes from *bazungu* 'you are not our husbands because you don't give us clothes'. There are some women who say that 'we are fed by *bazungu*, and I will respect you when we will be back in our home country. Because in our home country you are going to give what you have to give me. But here you didn't'.

This quote illustrates the sense among men in the camp that the UNHCR was taking the role of the provider from them. In Lukole, the UNHCR would not only share rations out equally to all, they would also occasionally have 'special distributions' of specific 'non-food items' to 'vulnerable groups' such as women, the elderly or children. This resulted not so much in narratives of unfair treatment of men but rather in tales of having their masculinity taken from them because they could no longer act as superiors, distributing wealth to their inferiors. *Kangas* were given a lot of symbolic value in the camp. When asked about his business, a shopkeeper would often reply that he could now afford to buy some nice clothes for his wife. At parties and ceremonies in the camp, wealthy men would flaunt their wives' *Kangas*, and the audience knew exactly how much each item of clothing had cost. I recall being very astonished by the clapping and whistling that some couples received at such a party. Being an outsider, I could not see why some should attract so much more attention than others, until it was explained that people were applauding the expensive material in the wives' dresses. So when Pierre referred to *Kangas*, he was referring to quite an important symbol of social status. In short, when the UNHCR provided *Kangas* to the women they were taking respect from the men, as he said, but they were also homogenising men, as the difference between rich and poor was flattened.

Others echoed Pierre's concerns. Here a Twa[2] man bemoans life in the camp.

Life is much worse in the camp. We have no blankets or other materials. We have to beg. In Burundi we had *shambas* [fields]. We have no money to buy things for our wives. Our wives say: 'You are not feeding me. I'm fed by *wazungu* [whites]'.

For him the problem with women getting food from the UNHCR was that they no longer depended on their husbands, and that the men no longer had a role as breadwinners. When they lost respect, it was no longer the man who decided what was right and what was wrong in the family, and women did whatever they wanted. An older man who was a village leader with the nickname Savimbi, due to an impressive beard like UNITA leader Jonas Savimbi, explains:

SAVIMBI: In the Bible men and women are equal and also with UNHCR laws. But it is not good. A man has to give some orders in his house - and when a woman is equal to a man that means the woman also has to give orders in the house; some orders to the man. In Burundi it is forbidden women to give orders to men.
S.T.: Is that Burundi law of the government or..?
SAVIMBI: It's Burundi customs.

As we see from this quote, equality was not desirable. It was perceived not only to threaten male domination, as one might expect, but also Burundian customs. Once women started deciding things on their own, they may have been adhering to UNHCR law but they were undermining a far more fundamental law: the Burundian way of life. Savimbi was generally worried about the behaviour in the camp. People were drinking too much, he said, being a non-drinking Muslim himself.[3] He often had to stop fights between people in his village who had drunk too much. He also explained that the women wore short dresses. They never used to do that in Burundi, he explained, although he had only lived in Burundi for a few years since 1972.[4] Other examples of bad behaviour in the camp were young men who kept their hats on in front of elders. 'You wouldn't see that in Burundi', he explained.[5]

The image of a state of lawlessness or social and moral decay came through in the survey I conducted as well as in many of my interviews. In the survey, thirty-nine respondents mentioned polygamy as a problem. Other issues mentioned were wife-beating (10), prostitution (39),[6] and underage marriage and sex (27) – all in all, a picture of a society where social and moral norms were dissolving.[7] Sexual relations were at the forefront of people's concerns and appear to be important indicators of such decay. When the *mandazi*-baker, quoted earlier, mentioned that 'women put on nice clothes and go to the market', he was referring to the commonly held view that prostitution was rampant in the camp. He explained about the changes experienced with coming to the camp.

> Everything has changed. It is like a big city, like Dar[-es-Salaam] or Bujumbura. You can go to the market, meet a girl and chat with her. Then you can give her money and take her home.

Whether prostitution, polygamy, divorce and young marriage really had increased in the camp would be virtually impossible to estimate. The point here is the ways in which people perceived and explained change. Because sex – like race – is inscribed in the body, it is always given significance.[8] And in situations of change, as the refugee situation undeniably is, people use sex and sexual relations to 'monitor' the level of disarray. Change is interpreted through sex. Such tales of social and moral decay undoubtedly flourished in Burundi as well, just as they always have done around the world. In the camp, however, Burundi was conveniently remembered as static and harmonious and opposed to the camp.

Although women disputed the men's sweeping statements about lack of respect, they did not dispute the phenomenon but merely its prevalence. They contended that it was not all women that acted in this way, keeping their own path clean while not disputing the phenomenon as such. Secondly, they did not dispute the fact that women ought to respect their husbands, thus accepting the dominant gender ideology. In other words, men and women agreed that a Burundian (Hutu) woman should respect her husband, and they agreed – to varying degrees – that this ideal relationship was under threat in the camp. For instance, a group of women's representatives claimed that 'a man cannot give to his wife, and that is why she begins to behave badly'. Another group of women modified this opinion by saying that if a man does not buy clothes for his wife because he has no money, then she will be understanding and there will be no problem. In other words, if he genuinely cannot provide for her and is not drinking up the money, then she will show him respect.[9]

A special case was when women worked for one of the NGOs in the camp as a teacher, a medical assistant, a community worker or the like and the husband did not work. I discussed this in a group interview in Village E, Lukole B, where two young women working in Oxfam's Sanitation Information Team joined the conversation. A man explained how it could cause problems when a woman was employed by an NGO and the husband had no income.

> When she comes with her money, the wife becomes a husband. She has to decide everything. She has to buy clothes for her husband. That's why the wife will never respect the husband.

In other words, the breadwinner – in this case the wife – made the decisions. In response, the one who is being kept – in this case the husband – had to pay respect to the breadwinner. Note how buying clothes for the inferior part in the relationship was brought up as a symbol of this unequal relationship. One of the young women working for Oxfam replied that it need not be so in all cases, as it depends on the woman:

> Maybe that may happen. But it depends on the behaviour of the wife. The woman who does that, she is the one who doesn't know the power of the husband – who doesn't know how to treat a husband. The wife who knows how to treat her husband can take half of her money and give it to her husband.

In this way she agreed that it could cause problems. But if the woman was sensible – as not all women were, it appears – she would try not to antagonise him, and would give him half her wages. It was not an inevitable problem but a question of the individual woman's choices, according to this young woman.

From these accounts of women lacking respect in Lukole, as well as from other informal discussions in the camp, we can see that the ideal Burundian Hutu woman obeys and respects her husband. She is shy and quiet in public, and she works hard and dresses decently, whereas, I was told, women who are loud-mouthed are considered prostitutes and will find it difficult to get a husband.[10] The same seems to go for lazy and dressed-up young women. It is the father or the husband who should make the decisions and give orders in the home. It was these ideals that the refugees related to and it was in relation to them that they interpreted their surroundings and, in turn, acted upon these interpretations.

The constant sense that ideal gender roles were threatened in the camp lead individual refugees to act in certain ways, as when women shared half of their wages with their husbands, or men spent their first earnings on buying *kangas* for their wives. Similarly, ideal gender relations were created and recreated as ideals by the constant fear that they were being undermined by life in the camp and by the UNHCR's policy of equality. Every time someone complained about polygamy, divorce, young people marrying or lack of respect, they were reproducing the supposed opposite: an ideal without divorces, prostitution, disrespect and so on. This ideal was produced in the camp and reflected the feelings of anxiety and uncertainty that were produced in and by the camp. The vague feeling that things were no longer as they used to be was translated into tales of immoral sexual relations and women's bad behaviour in the camp, while the picture of ideal gender relations 'back home' was simultaneously constructed in exile.

This social and moral decay was like a disease that had hit a healthy society, and women's 'misbehaving' became a central symptom, hence the preoccupation with women's behaviour, female sexuality and the female body in the accounts. Does this, then, render the male body irrelevant? I would argue not. In fact, masculinity was exactly what was at stake in the camp, being threatened by equal food rations, women's committees, clothes distribution to vulnerable groups, and so forth. The phrase 'UNHCR is a better husband' illustrates very aptly this feeling that masculinity was being taken from the male refugees and appropriated by the UNHCR. So although women were often to blame – or at least seen as a symptom – of the problem, it was male pride that was at stake. Pierre explained how men were not given respect – not only by women but also by Tanzanians – and it was this respect and recognition from other men that was important.[11] Later, we shall see how these men attempted to rehabilitate their masculinity through various internal power struggles to gain control over the camp and make it a liveable space. In this struggle to 'perform' one's masculinity, women were mere auxiliaries. It was perceived as a fight between men, and recognition was sought from other men.

What is interesting about this tale of social and moral decay in gender relations is that it not only alluded to disintegration and centrifugal forces but also to a single causal factor, an agent that caused all this misery; namely, the UNHCR or the *muzungu*. The everyday governmental practices of the UNHCR, such as the distribution of food and clothes, were seen as a direct threat to social and moral order, as men became like women and women like men. So when the men fought back, they were not just fighting micro-powers and bureaucratic practices of biopolitical ordering, they were fighting what they perceived to be an agent: the UNHCR.

'The Children Teach Themselves Many Games'

David was twenty-six-years old and belonged to the young elite in the camp, employed by an NGO in 'community services'. He almost finished secondary school in Burundi before being forced to flee and he spoke very good English. He married a woman in the camp and had a child. I was interviewing him about his life, about the conflict in Burundi and about the changes that he experienced in the camp compared to Burundi. After rather hesitant and inconsistent responses to questions on leadership in the camp as opposed to in Burundi, he was not in doubt when asked directly what had changed in people's behaviour.

> Some things have changed because ... when Burundese refugees ... came to Tanzania they mixed with Rwandese people. Then they had some changes in their culture. And also the children – the very young children – their respect to their parents, it has decreased. Because here we live as a town, but in Burundi it was in village. And now here the children are together. They are together in the night, during the day, and they are teaching themselves many kinds of games.

In his mind, the urban nature of the camp caused children to run wild and lose respect for their parents. However, when asked whether the 'games' that they made up were bad, David replied that they could be bad or good. Such ambivalence in relation to the camp and the new behaviour that had emerged there, was pervasive. Mixing with other cultures was also identified by David as a cause for children's changed behaviour. I will return to the issue of mixing shortly, as it has broader implications for understandings of Hutu identity and the ambiguous effects on that identity of being exposed to Tanzanian and Rwandan culture in the camp.

Often these tales would relate to the perception of Lukole as a town or city. Some friends of mine in the camp explained that children in the villages in Burundi would never run up to a European and beg. They may want to practise their French or English, that is all. Only in the capital city Bujumbura, Rama and Ndege said, would you find children begging as they did here in Lukole. So what were the problems of a city? Later in the interview, David explained how adults used to keep an eye on each other's children in villages. In the camp this did not happen because you did not know your neighbour. Like the city, the camp represented to David an alienating, anonymous space where individuals did not feel any obligations or responsibility towards each other.

The urban nature of the camp was often epitomised in the market. The market was where the action was and was often contrasted with the *blindés*. When asked how they spent their time, many refugees would answer that they 'stay in the *blindés*', a euphemism for doing nothing and that one was not involved in 'business', scout's clubs, employment or dance troupes. The elite in the camp would always talk about people 'in the *blindés*' or 'in the streets' as mere uneducated peasants as opposed to important people or 'big men'. The market, on the other hand, contained all the attractions and temptations of a city. Here, one could get drunk and forget one's troubles. For 100 shillings[12] one could go to the video hall and watch a Vietnam film with Chuck Norris, an action-packed Bruce Lee film or Bob Marley music videos. In the better bars there were tiny rooms that could be rented by the hour. One could be more or less anonymous, free of all the bonds and norms that constrained people in the villages. In the marketplace you could try your fortune. If you could not start your own business, you could try to find some casual work offloading pickup trucks or you could resort to petty theft.

This was where children went to think up 'new games'. In tales of prostitution and promiscuity, the market and the urban nature of the camp also played a central role. And as we shall see in the discussion of class relations, the market constituted a place where new fortunes could be made: it was dangerous, threatening morality and Burundian customs, but it was also tempting. In short, the market represented the virtues and vices of the city and of modernity. These perceptions of the market (as the epitome of the urban, modern, alienating nature of the camp as such) varied according to social position. Thus, the elite perceived the market area as the most dynamic space, providing economic opportunities, leisure opportunities and contact with international agencies. For the poorer refugees, however, the market was more ambiguous. Some poor young men explained to me that they enjoyed being near the market but mostly chose to stay away as the temptations were too many and they were afraid that they would end up as thieves. The ambiguous nature of the marketplace was also reflected in the individual's perception. The *mandazi*-baker explained that it was fine to go to listen to music at the market, but women should not go there. On the other hand, he liked going to chat up a young lady there himself. The temptations of the market were, in other words, perceived to be more harmful to some groups than others. Women who went to the market to enjoy themselves were considered prostitutes while it was not a problem for men to go there to listen to music or drink beer. Similarly, the temptations were perceived to be too strong for children. Women, the poor and children were subjected groups that needed controlling as they were too weak to handle the freedom and temptations of the marketplace. Curiously, the market could also be a threat to the elite. The *mandazi*-baker said in relation to social decay that one could see someone with a university degree hanging around the market listening to music or visiting people. In other words, this was okay to do if you were an ordinary person but if you were a 'big man' with a degree, you should not be wasting your time like that.

Children's disrespect was seen as a symptom of something gone wrong in Burundian culture, and quasi-urban conditions were perceived to be the cause of these symptoms. When discussing women's behaviour, this also came through as a cause, although the cause that was put forward more often was the UNHCR and food distribution. In relation to children's behaviour, the UNHCR and equal rations was also mentioned. A group of young men involved in petty trading at the market, explained.

> They think that everyone is equal to another, they don't respect. The non-respect is caused by bad life. It may happen that you meet a child saying that everybody is equal in the camp because they are getting food from the same area.

Getting food from food distribution, the children allegedly saw themselves as equals with adults. Equality was not desirable in this aspect of life either, according to the tales of decay, as Burundian customs prescribe that society is hierarchical, not only between men and women but between old and young.

In spite of the tales of children's disrespect of adults, it was my clear impression that the youth's lack of respect for elders was far less of an issue. In the questionnaire that I used for my survey, I asked: Are there any other changes[13] in the way people behave after coming to the camp? Among the answers, only twenty-three out of 464 respondents mentioned that the youth no longer show respect. I had expected this kind of response to be more prominent, and my surprise led me to inquire into the issue.

David was one of the people with whom I discussed the issue of age and respect. We were discussing leadership in Burundi and the camp when I brought up the issue of elders. He claimed that it was mostly the old people in the villages who made the decisions and from whom people sought advice. They were more respected than the others, he said. He got confused when I asked about leaders in Lukole. Yes, they were young, he said, because they could speak English and Swahili and had been to school.[14] But if there was a problem between neighbours, they would go to the old men to have it solved.

The village leader in B3, himself a thirty-year-old, explained how elders were respected but could not be elected, due to lack of speed and adaptability. Others claimed that there were fewer old people in the camp than in Burundi because they either died in the camp or preferred to remain in Burundi. Yet none of them complained about lack of respect. Either they claimed that nothing had changed or that the youth had become the leaders – but this was said as a matter of fact. Even in interviews with old men, the issue was surprisingly absent. Savimbi, a man in his forties or fifties, complained that the youth no longer took their hats off in the presence of elders. But apart from that, he did not comment on the crumbling power base of the elders.

When interpreting women's and children's behaviour, the refugees tended to see it in the light of a notion of hierarchy, any change being a threat to the status quo. However, when interpreting the crumbling power base of the elders, the blessings of a hierarchical social order were somehow absent. Such changes were merely acknowledged and even explained but rarely bemoaned, perhaps due to the fact that the young men actually were running the camp and setting the agenda, perhaps because these relations were changing in Burundi as well.

What was lost in the camp was the self-evident legitimacy of patriarchy. It was no longer obvious that age or sex defined your place in society, as age and gender came within the field of opinion and discourse.[15] Which opinion prevailed depended on power relations between various groups in the camp. It appears that gender ideals were strongly defended in the tales of decay, while tales of lost respect for elders were virtually absent. In other words, the respect for elders had been strongly challenged while gender ideals had been defended. Tales of decay do not tell the truth about social relations in the camp, but they show how taken-for-granted social orders were questioned and needed defending. Once again, we see that objective changes in social structures in the camp did not determine the tales of decay and loss. Despite there being little evidence to show that women were becoming more powerful in the camp, tales still flourished there about women becoming equal with men and not showing them respect. And conversely it appears – as will be argued in Chapter 5 – that young men had gained powerful positions in the camp without this resulting in a proliferation of tales about the youth no longer respecting the elders. The symptoms that were found in the tales of decay are not to be confused with real effects in the social structure, just like the 'causes' of social and moral decay that the refugees pinpointed (the UNHCR, thee urban nature of camp, cultural mixing) are not to be confused with the 'real' causes of their feelings of loss. If anything, there is an inverse relationship. That is to say that women's behaviour was identified as a symptom due to their inferior position, while the elders' marginalisation – either in the camp or before –meant that tales of lack of respect for elders were muted.

'The Children Can See That I Eat the Same Food As They Do'

The final symptom of social malfunction in the tales of decay concerned crumbling class relations in the camp. The young men in the market that we saw above explained how class differences were flattened and respect for 'big men' was lacking:

> When a man who in Burundi was respected – such as an educated one or a trader or someone who had a great job in Burundi in the government – when he meets with others, they suppose that they are equal. They have the same level because they are all in the camp.

In this tale it is assumed that there used to be respect for the people who were more than mere peasants in Burundi while here in the camp it was impossible to maintain that respect because they were all equal. This homogenising also made one anonymous: those who were 'somebody' in Burundi were just 'anybody' now. Curiously, some of these young men were doing relatively well in the camp, occupying social positions that they would not have held in Burundi. One had a bicycle that he used for transporting people and goods to and from the junction at the main road, where refugees traded with Tanzanians. Another sold oil from rations illegally, always fearing the authorities. In other words, they were not the kind of respected men in Burundi that they refer to in the quote, but were instead among those who had gained from the breakdown of social hierarchies in the camp.

The *mandazi*-baker, also a self-made man with moderate success, touched on the same issue: 'Those who had things in Burundi may lose them, while those who had nothing may become rich in the camp'. In his view, the camp turns social distinctions upside down, as the rich have become poor and the poor have become rich. As with the other tales, the main theme is lack of respect for those who ought to be respected due to their naturally superior position in society. Equality in the camp – the fact that they all receive the same food rations, whether they once were peasants or ministers – breaks down respect for 'big men'. The main cause of this, according to the tales of decay, was obviously located in the food rations. But proximity of neighbours – the urban layout of the camp – was also partly to blame, as this young schoolteacher testified:

> In Burundi teachers lived in their home and children came little to visit that area. Here we live together and maybe children are my neighbours. And then they don't respect me well. I can give an example: when we go to get food, I go there and I meet my pupils and they say, 'This is my teacher'.

The schoolteacher – a man who was educated and ought to be respected as a 'big man' – was forced to live close to his pupils. In this manner, they could see that he was also forced to eat maize and soybeans.[16] The young traders explained 'someone has passed all day without eating and just his neighbours noticed that'. To be a 'big man' it was important to be able to give the impression that one was qualitatively better than others. If the teacher lived apart from the others in the village with a big fence around his compound,[17] he could maintain the illusion that he was different and better, and the school children need never know that he ate the same food as they. To be powerful and important is to have something that others do not have access to – to have a secret.

This links up to the widely held belief in the camp that the Tutsi had a secret that they zealously guarded. It is the secret to governing Burundi and remaining in power and the reason why they tried by all means to prevent Hutu from getting an education. If only Hutu got the right education (in economics, law, political science or the like) they would soon reveal the secret and Tutsi power would fall.[18] For this reason, Hutu were only allowed education in technical fields such as agriculture and engineering, according to people in Lukole. This concept of secrecy and having access to certain kinds of knowledge that others did not have seemed to be applicable to inter-Hutu relations as well. Living so close in the camp, these 'big men' risked revealing that they were just the same as everybody else. The teacher's problem was, in other words, not only that he was equal to his pupils, but also that they knew this.[19]

When lamenting that there was no respect for big men, the refugees referred to the presumed hierarchical order of Burundi being threatened by the centrifugal forces of the refugee camp. But don't we also sense ambivalence in these tales? Is there not an element of optimism in them as well? When they say that the rich become poor, they immediately add that the poor become rich. One of the characteristics of being 'betwixt and between' is that, along with the negative effects of old social structures being suspended, there are certain positive opportunities for new social forms to appear (Turner 1967: 99). So, people in Lukole may have regretted that the old world no longer stood, that the rich and powerful no longer enjoyed the same respect as they used to. But they – or some of them at least – also saw the liberating effects and possibilities of the camp. Young men from peasant families, like the young traders above, could try their luck in the camp where they had all to gain and nothing to lose – and sometimes they were successful. The camp, like the juggernaut of modernity (Giddens 1991) was at once a horrifying and a liberating experience.

Mixing as Loss and as Resource

In the tales of decay, mixing often emerged as a cause of decay. David claimed that problems with children's behaviour had been caused by mixing with other cultures. There was also an implicit notion of cultural pollution in anxiety about women's behaviour. In the survey I conducted, respondents would simply state 'mixing', 'mixing with other cultures' or 'loss of own values' as a problem in the camp. This cultural mixing was perceived as a result of contact with Tanzanians but was also explicitly linked to mixing with Rwandan Hutu in the camps. This mixing was not, however, seen as entirely negative and was interpreted in the light of Hutu–Tutsi stereotypes.

There was a large presence of Rwandan refugees in camps close to Lukole until December 1996, and large numbers of Lukole's present inhabitants had lived in camps with mixed Burundian and Rwandan populations. Furthermore, a number of Burundians in Lukole had lived in Rwanda for some period of time.[20] This meant that they had been very exposed to Rwandans and that a number of stories about them circulated in Lukole. The Hutu refugees in Lukole had a rather ambivalent attitude towards Rwandan Hutu, who were generally believed to be more industrious and assertive than their Burundian counterparts. On the one hand, they despised their brutal character and their rude behavior: as one person put it, 'Burundese and Rwandese were different in customs because Rwandese, if they don't have permission, they do what they want. But Burundese can't do so'. The Rwandans would not be afraid to break the law, while the Burundians prided themselves on being good law-abiding citizens. This image of the Burundians as following the law of the UNHCR and Tanzanian authorities would be evoked time and again. Burundian Hutu were also shyer than Rwandans, according to these narratives, and Rwandan Hutu were like Burundian Tutsi in their behaviour.

However, the Burundian refugees could also see the advantages of such behaviour and would envy and admire the Rwandans their strength and courage. After spending some time with Rwandans in the camps or as refugees in Rwanda, they claimed that they were learning to be assertive like the Rwandans: 'Because Burundese used to live with Rwandese some have adopted their behaviour. Because Rwandese are not shy. So some Burundese now are digging outside the camp. They began to act as Rwandese'. By 'digging outside the camp' this person was referring to refugees farming outside the camp, in spite of a ban by the Tanzanian authorities. The naive Burundian would follow the law and starve in the camp, while the Rwandan and the new kind of Burundian would ignore the rules and have plenty of food. Businessmen in particular would be glad to say that they had learned from the Rwandans. Cultural mixing with them certainly had its benefits in terms of business opportunities. The question is whether it had its price in terms of the moral degradation of Burundian culture. This dilemma reflects their ambivalent relationship to their own 'Hutu-ness'.

Hutu were generally perceived in the camp to be shy, polite and honest as opposed to the lazy, cunning and scheming Tutsi. These are widely held beliefs in Burundian society that have their roots in colonial labelling.[21] Most refugees in Lukole would claim that there are no somatic differences between Hutu and Tutsi[22] but that you can tell the difference in their behaviour. The main difference, they would assure me, is that a Hutu will show their feelings straight away. They will get angry and then they will forget and forgive. Tutsi, on he other hand, 'hide' their emotions, and they can carry a grudge for a long time. As much as they were proud of their Hutu virtues, people in the camp also sensed that these virtues had become a vice in their relations with the Tutsi. For as well as being honest and open, the Hutu were also slightly naive, and would believe anything that the more intelligent – and less honest – Tutsi told them. According to their own understanding, they had been the victims of Tutsi trickery and deceit for centuries and would often mention the need to be smarter themselves in the future. In other words, they needed to shed aspects of their Hutu-ness and become more assertive and cunning if they were to manage the harsh realities in a camp or in a future Burundi. As the refugees saw it, this assertiveness could come from the Rwandan Hutu, who had been 'on top' from 1959 to 1994.[23] The Rwandan Hutu were constructed as 'the modern man' who - free of bonds and obligations – could pursue their own fortune and happiness as they liked. On the other hand, they lacked the comfort of customs, family bonds and mutual obligations, and they were morally corrupted (as can be seen from their rude behaviour and lack of respect for the law).

Tanzanians were usually looked down upon in Lukole. They were perceived to be poor, dirty, uneducated and badly dressed – in short, uncivilised peasants. This negative view of Tanzanians usually surfaced in complaints about Tanzanian staff members, whom the refugees found it hard to accept as superiors, as the above quote from Pierre illustrates. Not being respected by Tanzanians was terribly humiliating for him. On the other hand, when discussing some Burundian refugees who had been living in Tanzanian villages for years and had just arrived in the camp, my Burundian assistant explained that they behaved like Tanzanians. When I asked him to elaborate, he said that they wore dirty clothes and their children were polite.[24] In his narrative, Tanzanians represented the opposite of Rwandans by being 'more Hutu than the Hutu'. They were supposedly more ignorant and rurally backward than even the Burundian Hutu, as illustrated in the comment about dirty clothes. At the same time, they incarnated the positive aspects of Hutu-ness by being more peaceful and polite, indicating that they held a sense of community even stronger than the Burundian Hutu.

Following the logic of Mary Douglas (1966), one could claim that mixing with either Rwandans or Tanzanians caused impurity and hence danger. However, what is interesting about these ethnic stereotypes is: firstly, the refugees' ambivalent relations towards them; and secondly, they both – in opposing ways – were constructed as representing aspects of Hutu identity – they represented the ambiguous identity of the Burundian refugees in Lukole. In other words, Rwandan Hutu represented what the refugees might end up like if they did not take care to protect their customs and values, while the Tanzanians showed to them how they would end up if they continued to live a rural, uneducated life, turning their backs on 'progress' and (political) power. So, 'mixing' was not just perceived as impurity and danger. Mixing – taking the best from both worlds – could be seen as a source of strength, a strategy to learn the ways of the world and manoeuvre in this new setting where you would not get very far with old and stagnant values and customs.

Finally, mixing could be done with people from other parts of Burundi. This, however, could lead to bad behaviour, some claimed, though they also said that this kind of mixing, living close to people that you did not know before, could also be positive. As one village leader put it:

> Everything has changed. For example, in Burundi there were many difficulties between neighbours. But here, if you consider in the camp, it is few – few people who make troubles with others. If here people don't have something to eat, he can go to ask his neighbour for maize grain, and he just gets it. But in Burundi, if you went to ask for that, it was ridiculous – it was not good.

In other words, being forced together was not perceived only to have negative consequences. And the camp was not pitched unequivocally as a site of decay against a harmonious Burundian past. The refugees were in an ambiguous position, between a loss of the *Gemeinschaft* of the 'good old days' and being given the opportunity in the camp to open their eyes, learn new tricks and develop new relations. This relates to a general Hutu narrative about the loss of innocence. As we shall see in Chapter 7, the issue of Hutu naivety as both a virtue and a vice, and the necessity of 'opening one's eyes' and becoming more aware and assertive, is central to narratives about the conflict in Burundi, and feeds into the perception of abandoning the position as the innocent victim.

On Understanding Tales of Decay

This chapter has attempted to explore the ways in which the experience of being cast as 'bare life' was interpreted, and especially represented, by the refugees. In spite of the heterogeneous composition of the refugee population, the bureaucratic space of the camp was homogeneous and homogenising, and the governing techniques of the relief agencies tended to 'flatten' the population. Tales of decay were articulated reactions to these homogenising and flattening effects of camp life, conjuring up an opposing picture of Burundi as hierarchical but harmonious and praising the alleged social differentiation of Burundian society.

When refugees complained about increased prostitution, lack of respect and forgotten customs, they were putting into discourse certain concrete historical experiences that had had more or less traumatising effects on them. These experiences had forced people in Lukole to try to reinterpret their surroundings but their experiences were not identical, as every refugee had followed his or her own trajectory before ending up in Lukole. Hence the need for narratives or 'tales' that retrospectively 'fix' the loss, define what was lost and define what went wrong. Perhaps the changes that they claimed to have taken place in exile were already taking place in Burundi. Perhaps relations between men and women and between the youths and elders had been challenged in Burundi over the years. However, the camp brought them to the surface and made them visible. Furthermore, the fact of living in the camp allowed the refugees to interpret these changes as results of the camp. In this way the changes were seen as the result of flight and exile and the ideal picture of Burundi was drawn as the opposite of the camp; as solid and static.

The refugees identified three causes of social and moral decay in their tales of decay: equal rations from the UNHCR, the alienating urban nature of the camp, and cultural contamination by Tanzanians and Rwandans. These causes had certain symptoms: the collapse in gender relations; to a lesser degree, eroded generational relations; and, sometimes, the loss of class hierarchies. Although gender relations had not necessarily changed dramatically, and although women had not become equal with men, gender appeared to be the dominant interpretative scheme through which the refugees were able to express their feeling of loss. What the refugees found the most threatening about the camp was the fact that life no longer was in their own hands and that they were at the mercy of powerful external forces in the shape of relief agencies, local Tanzanians and Rwandan refugees. They sensed that their previous knowledge was no longer of much use for navigating everyday life in the camp. Ironically, the relief agencies' attempts to empower the refugees and help them out of this sense of powerlessness were most often interpreted as having quite different effects to those intended. Therefore, instead of equal food rations setting men and women free to govern themselves on an equal setting, the rations were perceived in terms of hierarchy and rank. Not only did they threaten patriarchy, as one might have predicted, they were also perceived to be the expression of a new patriarchy where men were reduced to the level of women and children, while the UNHCR took their rightful place as household head.

This is epitomized in the phrase 'UNHCR is a better husband'. While empowerment and community development programmes were interpreted as alienating, they also provided new opportunities for those refugees who were able to make use of them – although for other purposes than those intended by the relief agencies. In the following chapters we will see how certain groups of young men in the camp manoeuvred and made the best of the opportunities created by the camp – in a sense subverting attempts to create helpless victims.

The camp represented a space that was at once threatening and liberating, opening up new avenues whereby individuals could shape themselves in new ways. The immoral space of the market place and the immoral behaviour of the Rwandan Hutu fascinated at least as much as they appalled. Cultural mixing with Rwandans, for instance, was perceived not only as a loss of purity but also as an asset in the camp. These negotiations of moral spaces in the camp were intertwined with larger debates about what it meant to be a good Hutu and a general reworking of ethnic stereotypes in the region. Along with a yearning to uphold Hutu moral virtues was a wish to cast off the stigma of the naive Hutu and assert one's rights – although this entailed loosing one's innocence. The tales of social and moral decay brought into play questions of moral being in a place that was essentially immoral. In spite of the moral, altruistic intentions of the humanitarian regime, this regime created – or attempted to create – an exceptional space where human beings had no history or any political subjectivity, reducing them to bare life, ironically void of morality. The tales of decay were therefore attempts to re-establish a moral space by counterposing the present in the camp with the past in Burundi, enabling refugees to judge what was right and what was wrong and distinguish who was good from who was bad.

Notes

1. *Bazungu* is the Kirundi plural of *muzungu*. In the following quotes both the Kirundi plural prefix *ba-* and the Swahili *wa-* are used. People would also use the Anglicised plural: *muzungus*.
2. The third ethnic group in Burundi, comprising roughly 1 per cent of the population and usually treated as outcasts by Hutu and Tutsi alike. In the camp, they still made pots as they had traditionally done in Burundi.
3. This attitude was relatively rare in the camp. In fact, I was surprised to notice how rarely drinking was mentioned as a sign of social and moral decay.
4. Like so many other refugees in Lukole, his flight trajectory is rather complex. He fled to Rwanda following the massacres in 1972, and after a few years went to

Tanzania. When the Hutu Melchior Ndadaye was elected president in 1993, he returned to Burundi. He fled again to Tanzania in 1995 when fighting between Palipehutu and government soldiers broke out in his commune, Giteranyi.

5. I return to the issue of generations below.

6. Interestingly, it appears that women's extramarital affairs are dubbed 'prostitution' while men's are called 'polygamy'.

7. In broader terms people also mentioned dishonesty (36), theft (40), selfishness (45), drinking (25) and laziness (25) as problems.

8. See also Robert Connell's discussion of 'body-reflexive practices', where he argues that bodies matter as both objects and agents of practice (Connell 1995: 60).

9. Spending money on beer was one of the most common accusations against men, not so much because beer drinking was perceived as immoral but because it was seen as a waste of the household's money.

10. As in many cultures, older women appeared to be more or less exempted from these norms.

11. Gilmore argues along similar lines that masculinity is fragile and a man always has to prove himself to other men for recognition (Gilmore 1990). Following Connell's concept of hegemonic masculinities (Connell 1995), Michael Kimmel argues that men can never live up to this hegemonic ideal. This gives urge to constant fears of not being a real man (Kimmel 1997).

12. 1 U.S. dollar = c.600 shillings.

13. This question followed another on changes in gender relations.

14. In later chapters I will explore how a group of young, semi-educated men have emerged as the official and unofficial leaders in the camp.

15. This point is inspired by Bourdieu (1977: 159–71).

16. Curiously, the wealthy Tutsi in Burundi used not to eat in public, giving the impression that they did not eat solid food at all but lived exclusively off milk and beer (Albert 1963: 186). Several middle-aged Tutsi have since explained to me that they never saw their father eat while they were children.

17. People do not actually live in villages in Burundi but in hamlets spread out on the hilltops.

18. See also Chapter Seven, and Turner (2005b).

19. As with Tutsi secrets to governing, the power lies in the act of concealment, for the secret is that there is no secret. See Turner (2005b).

20. According to my survey, 27 per cent had lived in Rwanda at some point in time.

21. Liisa Malkki makes some brilliant observations on Hutu and Tutsi stereotypes in a refugee camp in the 1980s (Malkki 1995a). Other descriptions that tend to see them as true ethnic characteristics rather than as stereotyped constructions include Maquet (1961), Trouwborst (1962) and Albert (1963).

22. This proposition is different to the one put forward by the refugees that Malkki (1995a) talked to in the 1980s, who clearly charted body maps of ethnic difference.

23. This period runs from the Hutu 'social revolution' to the genocide, and covers the time when the Rwandan state was dominated by a Hutu elite.

24. This was in fact the first time a child in Lukole had greeted me with shikamoo – a *Swahili* greeting that expresses respect for seniors.

5
'Big Men' and 'Liminal Experts'

Let us briefly recall the image of Lukole seen from the air in a UNHCR six-seater aeroplane, revealing the humanitarian bureaucrat's dream of red macadam roads making a neat grid, straight lines of blue and white *blindés*, and the fenced compounds of the humanitarian agencies. We saw how the camp made up not only a tightly organised but also a tightly confined space. However, even from the air one could spot the cracks in the bureaucrat's dream. Footpaths, made by the movement of thousands of pairs of usually bare feet, wound their way through the camp, breaking the strict geometry of UN roads and creating lived space. And it was not only within the camp that rules were defied. The footpaths also sprouted into the bush in all directions, marking in space the fact that refugees did not remain in the seclusion zone, waiting to be fed and waiting for the day they could eventually return home. They fetched firewood, running the risk of being caught by CARE's environment guards or, worse still, by local *sungu sungu*, Tanzanian vigilante groups. They went to dig fields that they had rented from Tanzanians or they sold their labour to Tanzanian farmers. As these paths faded out and became invisible to the spectator in the plane, we could no longer follow the routes of the refugees who had decided to live in Tanzanian villages, or of those who crossed the Ruvubu River into Burundi to visit relatives, to check the security situation, to smuggle coffee or to join the rebels. Neither could we see when they boarded minibuses, pretending to be Tanzanians and putting on their best Swahili, and went to Mwanza to buy goods to resell in the camp or to Ngara post office where they would phone party headquarters in Nairobi or Brussels.

In order to see this, one must move beyond the bird's-eye perspective of the UNHCR and beyond the nostalgic perspective of the tales of decay, because Lukole was neither merely the tightly organised space of the bureaucrat nor the fragmented space of the tales of decay. The space was recaptured – or at least its inhabitants tried to recapture it – and transformed into lived space. Strategies of recapturing Lukole could be directed against the centrifugal forces of the camp, towards gaining cultural coherence and reconstituting Burundian customs as they ideally used to be. But then again, a great many refugees had no interest in reverting to a glorious past which was based on patriarchy and gerontocracy. In this chapter we follow three young men who in various ways had managed to make use of the liminality of the camp and carve out a space for themselves and become 'big men'. I explore 'how they combined different registers of power (economic, "traditional" and "modern" political) in order to achieve "bigness"' (Lentz 1998: 48). They recaptured the camp by making use of the liberating forces of liminality and became what I term 'liminal experts'.

Since the 1990s a number of studies have explored the emergence of informal economies (Roitman 2005), twilight institutions (Lund 2007) and criminal networks inside and outside the state in Africa (Bayart, Ellis and Hibou 1999; MacGaffey et al. 2000), emphasizing the twilight zones between formal and informal, public and private, state and non-state, legal and illegal. With the collapse of the developmental state and people's faith in modernity (Ferguson 1999), the *fonctionnaire* is no longer a role model for young Africans. Instead, they seek adventure in the illicit economy where the role model is the trickster, the *bricoleur*, the *feyman* (Ndjio 2008). Common to these studies is the idea that it is the shape of late capitalism and globalization – 'millenial capitalism' in the words of the Comaroffs (Comaroff and Comaroff 2000) – that has created this new entrepreneurial class that operates in this twilight zone between the licit and the illicit, the visible and the invisible. In today's Africa it is necessary to operate within multiple moral economies or systems of norms, and therefore the brokers and middlemen who know how to straddle several of these and to translate between them become central figures (Olivier de Sardan 1999).

In the case of Lukole, brokers and middlemen were obviously also central figures – whether in the semi-legal economy of bartering food rations, as NGO employees, mediating between NGOs and the population, or as formal leaders who also had an invisible and heavily politicised side to them. However, whereas the position of the *bricoleur* is central in present day Africa due to neoliberalism and a breakdown in faith in the developmentalist state, their central role in the camp was slightly different. They recaptured the camp through their ability to operate in the liminal space between the UNHCR's advanced social engineering and the tales of moral decay; they became liminal experts. When I say 'recapturing' Lukole, I do not imply some heroic figure fighting against the constraints of 'power' but rather I see the liminal expert as strategic. The fact that the taken-for-granted social order had been seriously questioned in the camp, opened up new modes of interpretation, widening the terrain of indeterminacy and hence of situations where the answer was not given beforehand. Strategising emerges in this indeterminacy, in the 'gap' in the system, which leaves room for decision-making.[1]   However, the terrain is never completely unstructured and undecided, as people bring with them experiences, memories and habits that structure their strategies. Following Van Velsen (1967) and Mitchell (1983), we may claim that individuals have to operate within conflicting and competing societal rules and norms, leaving room for manoeuvre and strategic choice in each specific context (cf. Bourdieu 1977). It was on this terrain that the 'liminal experts' – those who in the camp were simply referred to as 'big men' – operated.

In the following I introduce three young men who in different ways had managed to carve out spaces for themselves, each of them making the best of their liminal situation, although in quite different ways. The three young men exemplify a phenomenon that I was struck by in the camp, namely a number of very young men who held extremely influential positions as street leaders, NGO employees or entrepreneurs. Apart from the formal street and village leaders who enjoyed a great deal of respect and were important people in the camp, I got the impression that there were other categories of 'big men' who were to be found in other places that allowed them to position themselves strategically, either as entrepreneurs or through employment with an NGO. They may have even combined a job with an NGO with a small business on the side. These three kinds of 'big men' had different roles and were different in social composition, although they also often overlapped and cooperated.

Steven: Being Where the Action Is

Steven was a polite, soft spoken young man, choosing his words carefully and doing his best to answer all my questions as best he could. He was twenty-five-years old and unmarried. He did not want to marry in exile, as he said the responsibility of a family would hinder the possibility of continuing his studies. He dreamed of studying economics. A great many young men with hopes of continuing the studies that they were forced to discontinue in Burundi shared his hopes for further education. And a great many also chose to be single for this same reason. Steven's father and brother lived in the camp but he usually stayed with a friend close to the market and the NGO offices – as opposed to 'down the hill' where his father's plot was.

Steven was a few months short of finishing secondary school when President Ndadaye was assassinated, at which point Steven fled to Tanzania. Steven's background was atypical in the sense that his father migrated to Tanzania long before Steven was born and Steven's mother was Tanzanian. This probably explains why his English and Swahili were so good. He moved to Burundi with his father at the age of nine, and all his schooling took place there. However, he was typical of a number of other young men born in Burundi, who spoke these languages and held good positions in the camp, working for humanitarian agencies.

When I first met him, he was working as a primary-school teacher and had done so since arriving in the camp in 1994. We met him in the previous chapter, complaining about the school children's lack of respect. A few months later, he became chief security guard for Lukole A. The security guards were employed by the UNHCR and were responsible for security in the camp in collaboration with the Tanzanian police, who established a 24-hour police post in the camp in 1997. The security guards protected public places like the food distribution centre, the market and the graveyards, and they patrolled the rest of the camp night and day. They were unarmed and were allowed to arrest people for petty offences and keep them locked up for up to three days. More serious crimes were transferred to the Tanzanian police. In Lukole A, with a population of roughly 70,000, there were about sixty security guards. In other words, Steven had been given a large responsibility for someone his age.

He was given the position after the UNHCR had sacked all the previous guards and 'screened' all new and old applicants to clean out the political activists among them. As may be recalled from Chapter 3, this was due to a conflict between the camp chairman and the previous chief security guard, who, according to one version of the story told to me by Steven, had accused the chairman of being active in CNDD and had managed to have him imprisoned for a few days. On the other hand, the camp chairman had complained that the security guards were Palipehutu supporters and that their arrests were biased. These accusations and counter-accusations led the UNHCR to try to depoliticise the security guards. This was when Steven was employed.

Ironically, Steven was deeply involved in politics – only he was pro-CNDD rather than Palipehutu and hence more in line with the camp chairman. Due to the strict ban on political activity in the camp it was not easy to determine who belonged to which party and what the parties were actually doing in the camp. However, after being in the camp for some months and learning not to ask too directly or push the issue too hard, I gained the confidence of quite a few refugees and learned something, if not all, about their political sympathies and activities. This had a certain snowball effect, since those who had confidence in me would vouch for me. There is no doubt that Steven was a CNDD supporter and, judging from the network of 'big men' in the camp that he knew, he was an influential member.

I was fortunate to be able to follow Steven for a while in the camp and have since corresponded sporadically with him by e-mail. Apart from his job as chief security guard, he began teaching French to UNHCR staff in Ngara town. He later went to Nairobi to try to study. He failed to find any sponsorship for his studies, but managed to learn some basic computer skills before returning to Lukole where he applied for resettlement in Canada. For some reason, he failed to turn up for the interview and moved to a camp in Kigoma region, where he married 'after a long despair of soon regaining school,' as he said in a letter in March 2001. As of September 2005, he had two children and both he and his wife worked for international NGOs. He still hopes to go to the West and continue his studies.[2]

Steven belonged to a large group of young men (and some women) which had managed to find employment with NGOs and which made up a substantial and influential elite brokering between the camp population and the powerful relief agencies. But who were the NGO employees? And how did they differ from the camp population as a whole in terms of social composition? Humanitarian agencies employed refugees in a number of positions. The UNHCR employed security guards. AEF employed more than 200 primary school teachers, around 100 community mobilisers and a handful of supervisors and coordinators, as well as more than 200 refugees in its clinics (medical assistants, nurses, laboratory technicians, guards, cooks, and so on). Oxfam, in charge of water and sanitation in the camp, employed close to 200 refugees, mostly as guards to watch the boreholes and water tanks. They also employed large Sanitation Information Teams (roughly 75 refugees) to spread information on how to boil water, wash hands and build latrines the right way. Finally, TRCS, in charge of camp management, had almost 200 refugees employed as food distribution workers, guards, plotters and construction workers. NGO employees did not receive wages but so-called 'incentives', as they were in theory already fed by WFP. A schoolteacher would receive 14,000 shillings (about U.S.$20) a month while the maximum monthly incentive allowed – for a supervisor or a doctor, for instance – was 22,000 shillings.[3]

It is the people employed as community mobilisers, teachers, medical assistants and in the Sanitation Information Teams that are of particular interest here, as they made up the educated elite in the camp. The refugees employed by NGOs generally had a higher level of education than the average population.[4] Whereas 17 per cent of the population above the age of sixteen had more than primary school education, at least 85 per cent of the NGO employees in my survey had more than primary school education. Furthermore, 31 per cent of the population in general claimed to have no formal schooling, while this was not the case for any of the NGO employees.

The NGO employees were also generally better trained in European languages than the average population, with 86 per cent claiming to speak French against 27 per cent of the population in general, and the number of English-speaking NGO employees being roughly four times the number of English-speakers to be found in the general population. However, NGO workers did not speak significantly more Swahili than other refugees. While

French was a language that was linked to formal schooling in Burundi, and Swahili was learned in the public space of the camp, English was a mixture of the two, since the better educated had in theory been taught English in secondary school but it was only in the camp that they actually learned to speak it. I knew people who had learned English while working for NGOs like NPA and GOAL, while others had actually taken lessons from the few refugees who spoke the language reasonably well. Some would follow literacy classes with the American and Irish Catholic priests in the camp. English is the language of the future, people would say, referring to the perception that French is losing its hold in central Africa.

Both English and Swahili were seen to be the best languages to know in the camp as they allow you to 'express yourself' to the NGOs, UNHCR and Tanzanian authorities. In terms of status, English was considered more prestigious than Swahili, just as European or North American agencies and staff were considered more prestigious and more honest than their Tanzanian or Kenyan counterparts. Being able to approach the *wazungu* or the Tanzanians was clearly seen as an asset, and people who mastered these skills were often used as brokers by their friends, relatives and neighbours. Language skills also allowed for upward mobility, as the ability to speak English could give one access to a job as a coordinator or supervisor with an NGO. Here, French was not of much use and was seen as something of a social marker left over from Burundi. It was prestigious in the sense that it marked a certain level of education and social position, but it was perceived to be rather anachronistic and of little use for social mobility in the present or future.

Finally, the surveys I conducted indicate that NGO employees were very young, with an average age of twenty-nine years. In other words, through the jobs created by NGOs, a group of young, semi-educated, mainly male refugees was created and given a pivotal position in the camp as intermediaries between the refugees and the agencies. In this sense they resembled the leaders. But whereas the leaders were the official representatives and intermediaries in charge of governing the refugees, the NGO employees carried out the everyday practices of governing. They informed about hygiene, they helped the 'vulnerables', they taught the children, they mobilised the youth and they took care of security. This is where biopower was exercised. But they were not merely the instruments of biopolitics, and they manoeuvred strategically according to very different agendas to the NGOs.

The employees made use of their strategic positions as intermediaries between donor funds and beneficiaries. The camp population's access to essential resources – such as medical help, education and security against theft and robbery – went through these intermediaries. Therefore, it became important to be on good terms with an NGO employee who could ask favours in return, thus creating the basis for patron–client relationships. Jobs with NGOs were so attractive that people would pay to be allowed to work for an NGO. If you as an employee got someone a job, you could ask for half of their wages. When asking people in Lukole B – the poorer part of the camp where new arrivals were housed – if they had any employment, they would reply, 'No we haven't got enough money'. This really surprised me – assuming that the objective of employment was to earn money and not vice versa – until they explained about the bribes involved.[5]

> VILLAGE LEADER: These people who came recently don't know where to find the job. They don't know the mechanisms of the camp. These people who have already got jobs here in Lukole, charge them some taxes in order to get a job. And these people are very poor. They don't have shillings to pay. That's why they don't have jobs.
> S.T.: You should complain to Tanzanian staff that the Burundians tax them shillings.
> VILLAGE LEADER: Where can we go to complain? And those Tanzanians, sometimes they tax us shillings. [*He laughs.*]

This exchange illustrates the attractiveness of being employed by an NGO. It also reveals a perception that NGO employees made up a close-knit and impenetrable network.

Steven fits the profile of an NGO employee that attained a pivotal role in the camp. From being a secondary school student in Burundi, he became chief security guard, responsible for keeping a check on crime in a camp with a population the size of a fair-sized town and with a murder rate somewhat higher. According to their own explanations, the reasons why he and a number of other young men gained such prominent positions was in part due to their formal education and in part due to a number of personal abilities: to cope in the camp and become a 'big man' one had to be open, not afraid to approach a *muzungu* and have a certain nerve to assert oneself, they claimed.

These personal abilities were metonymically linked to the vague idea of being 'shy' or not, an issue that was often brought up in discussions in the camp. Not being shy epitomised the meaning of education, language and mobility in the refugees' understanding of the changes that they felt were taking place in Lukole. Those who mastered these abilities and who adapted to the changes were at the forefront of recapturing Lukole. To not be shy meant to dare to voice one's opinion in public in front of a number of foreign and 'superior' people. It meant knowing the new rules of the refugee game and knowing how to bend them to one's advantage, rather than being taken advantage of by the new rulers.

As mentioned in earlier chapters, 'shyness' was seen as a Hutu virtue. To be shy was to show good manners. An inferior was meant to be shy towards a superior, whether that was in terms of age, gender, class or ethnicity. However, as has also been mentioned, the refugees expressed an ambiguous relation to shyness. As much as it was still praised as a virtue, it was also considered a vice. This was most clearly expressed in relation to Rwandan Hutu refugees who allegedly were not shy. In Lukole, people would take pride in having learned 'tricks' from the Rwandans such as cheating the UNHCR. When discussing the UNHCR's coming verification exercise with a group of refugees in October 1997,[6] they expected very high figures. I argued that the figure had decreased by 25 per cent in the Kigoma camps after a similar verification a few months earlier because it had allowed the UNHCR to weed out all the refugees with more than one ration card. 'But people here are cleverer', they said. 'We also cheat the verification. We have defeated UNHCR'. They explained that it was because Burundians in Lukole had lived with Rwandans, as opposed to the Burundians in Kigoma who were quite green in the refugee game. 'The Rwandans were very clever. They knew what medicine to use to remove ink'.[7] In this sense, it is 'clever' to cheat UNHCR. The longer you had lived in the camp and the more you had learned to shed your shyness, the better you would cope, they believed.

NGO employees like Steven took advantage of the fact that the old hierarchies of Burundi were no longer valid, and carved out a place for themselves by shedding their Hutu naivety and their position as inferiors. Through linking up with the international agencies in the camp, they made themselves indispensable as brokers. They were adept at the language of humanitarian workers, not only literally through their command of Swahili and English but also in terms of knowing about food rations, community development projects, hygiene sensitisation programmes and all the other codes that needed deciphering in order to handle and please the international NGOs. For Steven the exceptional space of the camp was liberating – freeing him from tradition and history. However, the liberating dehistoricised space did not make him a pure victim or reduce him to bare life. On the contrary, it created him as a strategic, political being.

James: Between Mobility and Sedentary Knowledge

James was the village leader of B2 in Lukole B. It was a village of people who had lived in Tanzanian villages for years and who were rounded up by the Tanzanian authorities in late 1997. He had fled Burundi in 1993, and was among the first to arrive in Lukole when it was established in 1994. However, in 1996 he decided to try to earn some money and left the camp to work for a rich refugee smuggling coffee out of Burundi.[8] After a while, he moved to a Tanzanian village and worked as a builder until he was rounded up and put into Lukole B. Perhaps his longer experience of camp life made him a natural leader in a part of the camp where most of the inhabitants had only just arrived and still did not know what they term 'the mechanisms of the camp'; that is, how to make food rations last for two weeks or what a 'community mobiliser' or a 'vulnerable' is.

James was twenty-five-years old, although he looked so young that during his election which I attended in January 1998, the UNHCR field officer thought he was too young to vote. He was unmarried because he feared being forcefully repatriated, and having a family would be too much of a responsibility in such a situation, he said.

During the election, he kept rather quiet. However, he beat the previous incumbent, who was also young but better educated. Apparently, people were fed up with him because he drank too much and was too loud mouthed. James converted to the Seventh Day Adventist Church after a close shave with death while visiting Burundi in 1995, so he did not drink at all. He also beat the jolly old man who made people laugh when he presented himself for elections, and who had worked for UNICEF years before. At the elections, James seemed to have a group of young lads hanging around him most of the time. When he won, everybody rejoiced and the crowd carried him over their heads.

I interviewed him later on his own in AEF's offices, where he did not seem too comfortable. He had no job and no business in the camp. He had almost finished primary school but was interrupted during his studies, in part by 'the troubles' in 1991[9] and in part because his father had left for Uganda and James had to help his mother in the fields. He went back to school in 1993, hoping to continue on to secondary school and get a job in the administration or the army, but he had had to flee shortly after.

James reckoned that he was elected for his personality. In the intimacy of camp life, it only takes a few days to learn about somebody's personality. He explained that it is important for a leader to be humble and kind.

> There were leaders who were respected such as these ones who gave good advice or who had tried to solve problems in a good way. But these people who were not shy – or more proud – because these people who were more proud, these people were not respected.

Although shyness could be a hindrance in the camp, it still was perceived by some to be a virtue, while being too 'proud' was associated with Tutsi arrogance.

James voted for Frodebu in 1993 but he assured me that he was not interested in politics. 'Politics is dealt with by these people who have been in school – who are educated.' This was a very common response in the camp.

James represents quite a different 'type' than Steven. He was not as educated, he was not so keen on politics, and he did not appear to be in the limelight of international organisations. There were, however, some similarities in terms of age and in terms of the role that he played as an intermediary between the population and the international agencies and Tanzanian authorities. Generally, James was in a more ambiguous position in terms of recapturing the camp. He was not exclusively an expression of the new forces of liminality, nor of the attempts to bring back the old days to limit the disruptive effects of liminality.

The leaders made up a more complex group than the NGO workers in terms of age and class. Instead of James I could equally have chosen Savimbi, the uneducated forty- to fifty-year-old who first fled Burundi in 1972 and had been a farmer in Tanzanian villages; or the 30-year-old leader of B3 who, in spite of having only seven years' schooling, constantly walked around with a pen and pad and kept his clothes clean as if to mark his rank; or the 22-year-old from Lukole A who also worked as a social worker for the AEF and spoke fluent English. It was, however, the youthfulness of the street leaders that surprised me when first coming to Lukole. I had expected to see only men in their forties or older at the leaders' meetings, but 29 per cent were in their twenties, 47 per cent were in their thirties, and only 24 per cent were forty or above.[10]

Why were there so many young street and village leaders in the camp? To answer this we can look at some of the explanations that the leaders themselves gave as to why people in the camp would choose someone with so little experience. They mentioned similar virtues to those for NGOs; namely, mobility, language and education. This is summarised in the more abstract 'not being shy'. The village leader of B3, mentioned above, explained:

> VILLAGE LEADER: Yesterday we got information that today we will have a meeting with the representative of [the] *wilaya* [Tanzanian town council]. Today at four o'clock. And because I am quite young, I took a megaphone and went around villages – all villages, thirteen villages – and told them that you will have a representative of [the] commune who will come here to hold [a] meeting....
> S.T.: So yesterday you were told by whom?
> VILLAGE LEADER: [The] camp manager.
> S.T.: So you were very quick. Immediately you took a megaphone and went....
> VILLAGE LEADER: Yeah, yeah. And because I am quite young I have to deal with many activities in a short time. But if it is an old one, he can't. That's why they have to elect someone who is very quick: someone who is very quick and who is intelligent.

Here, liaising with camp authorities and those who were in charge of resources in the camp was seen as an important role of the leader, who had to be able to react fast to any new situation. Furthermore, as one leader explained, leaders had to be able to 'explain the problem fluently'.

> According to Burundi customs, we usually respect elders. But if there is a problem, he is not fast – to go to explain the problem. It may happen that when they are going to food distribution, it may happen that some people don't have food. And the leader has to go to explain the problem – and he has to explain fluently the problem. Because when he doesn't explain the problem fluently, the people who miss the food, they don't have. They don't have it.

Although expressing oneself fluently was not necessarily exclusively an ability of the youth, it was linked in his discourse. It went with the idea of not being shy and being able to express oneself openly that I found with the NGO employees. It also linked with being able to speak foreign languages, especially Swahili and English. In principle, the meetings between leaders, the relief agencies and Tanzanian authorities took place in Kirundi with an interpreter. However, Tanzanians would often speak Swahili and it would often go untranslated. Also, in more informal situations, like the one the leader mentioned above where he was called to help at food distribution, Swahili and English would be an asset. Knowledge of languages was pointed out by the refugees themselves as an important asset for leaders – especially the young, extrovert ones.

> When they are going to deal with problems with Tanzanians they have to speak Swahili. When you don't know to speak Swahili you can't express yourself. Because most of those workers – those people who are working with NGOs, different NGOs – are Tanzanians. And Tanzanians don't know how to speak French. They know how to speak Swahili and English. It is good to know Swahili language.

In spite of the ideal leader speaking Swahili (and perhaps English) the fact is that only about half of them did.[11] This affirms our picture of the leaders as a mixed group. But it also shows that people played on a register of elements when defining an ideal leader in the camp. In trying to come to terms with being positioned as helpless victims in the exceptional space of the camp, they did not only worry about the crumbling positions of 'big men' but they tried to find new ways to evaluate a 'big man'. In the camp, people reckoned, mobility and language must be virtues that were useful, in order to communicate with the all-powerful UNHCR. But they also evaluated the concrete leader according to other criteria, ones that drew on the ideal leader in Burundi and helped preserve some kind of continuity. So when electing a leader for their particular street or village, people measured the candidate partly according to how good at communicating with NGOs they were, and partly according to Burundian values and ideas of respect and hierarchy. People's strategies when electing a leader are socially embedded but unpredictable. This unpredictability is particularly prevalent in situations of rupture like the refugee camp, where old habits and norms are being questioned.

Another criterion for becoming a leader in the camp, it was claimed, was to be able to read and write. It was an advantage to be able to take notes at meetings and to be able to write reports for UNHCR. As one leader put it:

> UNHCR told them that they had to elect someone who will know to make a report, or to represent others. Or when there is a problem, to know to explain the problem fluently.

The kind of knowledge (or 'intelligence' as they would often say in the camp) obtained from formal education is placed in opposition to the knowledge of old men.[12] According to this discourse, old men's knowledge is based on experience, rooted in history, in a knowledge of people's lineages and their past; and it is rooted in locality, a knowledge of the land. An old man in a village knows who has occupied which land for generations and he knows how a certain person treated his first wife thirty years ago, and that so-and-so had a bad childhood. This kind of knowledge was useless in the camp where nobody knew their neighbour, localities were new and the past was irrelevant.

Success in Lukole was about mobility, language skills, education and openness. There was an emphasis on youth and change and the old hierarchies were seen as archaic and useless. However, this process was neither complete nor one-way, as it was not a question of all the old men and all the old traditions being rejected. As we have seen, people were generally ambiguous about change and the status of 'big men'. They also longed for the good old days, they despised the Rwandans for their rude behaviour, they took pride in their distinctly Burundian behaviour as law-abiding citizens, and they believed that women should respect their husbands. In other words, there was a constant struggle between looking forward and looking backward. Public authority could rest on both.

The statistics on refugee leaders do not support such a drastic break as we are made to believe from the interviews with the young leaders, and when I asked ordinary people in Lukole what were the most important features of a good leader, the answers most certainly were more complex. As James said, it depends on your personality. A good leader is humble and kind and knows how to give advice. According to James, it only took a few days to get to know someone's personality in the camp because people lived so close to one another. Being able to mediate in conflicts, being able to find 'the truth' and being kind were abilities that were mentioned again and again in Lukole. To have these qualities, one obviously did not need a higher education; nor did one need to know a lot of languages. In fact, education, language skills and not being shy may play against you – although this was never explicitly mentioned – since shyness, honesty and naivety were good old Hutu virtues. Although the refugees operated with ethnic stereotypes, the character traits of the different ethnic groups were not believed to be completely innate and unchangeable. Hence, the Rwandan Hutu were acting like Tutsi due to Rwanda's postcolonial history, and the Burundian refugees were beginning to act like Rwandans due to contact in the camps. There are a number of other examples of the idea that Hutu would begin to behave like Tutsi if they were in Tutsi positions or the environment was in other ways conducive to it. In other words, there was a risk that these well-educated, young parvenus might forget their background – their humble Hutuness – and become 'too proud'.

So while educated young leaders had the advantage of being able to express themselves to camp authorities and make sure that the refugees were not tricked too much by corrupt Tanzanian staff, an older, more 'humble', man of the people was more respected when it came to solving problems between neighbours.[13]

The *bashingantahe*[14] lead a shadowy existence in Lukole, and they were not part of the official organisational set-up in the camp. It took some time before I learned about their existence at all, and even then it was rather unclear how formalised the institution was and what role they actually played. One street leader explained to me that there was not a fixed group of elders in his street. When a small problem occurred between neighbours, for instance, they would take the problem to the block leader (who was elected and part of the official, UNHCR-instigated leadership) who would then gather five or six elders to help find a solution to the concrete problem. It was rather an ad hoc advisory council, appointed on a case by case basis by the block leader. The *bashingantahe* did not seem to be involved in the power struggles between various factions in the camp – as opposed to the NGO elite and the street leaders who were deeply involved in political rivalry.

To sum up, the refugees were struggling between different concepts of being a 'big man' and different perceptions of how to deal with rupture. Should they opt for the 'liminal expert', the trickster, as the best option for achieving results in the new setting of the camp, or should they opt for the old man who symbolised some sort of continuity and surety? In practice a leader was often a compromise between the two, like James who was young and mobile but was not well educated and not part of the NGO in-crowd. He tried to live up to ideals of being a kind and humble leader, but he also knew the 'mechanisms of the camp', as they say, better than most others in his particular village, due to being an experienced refugee.

Furthermore, the street leader was not the only 'big man' around. People would go to their neighbours, to the block leader, the security guards or a group of elders, depending on the nature of the problem and the kind of personal relations involved. In later chapters, we will see how 'big men' competed to gain the respect of the refugees, and how this was deeply entrenched in violence and politics.

Patrick: Minding His Own Business

I first met Patrick in one of the forty medium-range bars in Lukole A, where you got to sit inside a building made of mud bricks and UNHCR plastic sheeting, sometimes cut in decorative strips. There were homemade tables and benches, and often a radio playing Congolese pop music or Bob Marley. Here they mainly sold *guagua*, banana wine that was more expensive than, and which people preferred to, *mugorigori*, the maize beer that tastes and looks like fermented porridge. Guagua was served in glasses rather than in communal plastic containers. The Tanzanians freighted it from Karagwe by the truckload and sold it at the junction outside the camp to the bar owners in Lukole.

Patrick was hanging out with some friends. They were the ones whom I referred to as 'young traders' in the previous chapter. One of them was unemployed and explained that he almost finished secondary school in Burundi and wanted to continue at the post-primary school in Lukole, although he could not afford the fees. He occasionally came to the market to look for casual jobs, loading pickups with maize that Burundian middlemen sold to Tanzanians or offloading bananas from Tanzanian trucks. His brother bought cooking oil from refugees and sold it to Tanzanians. The TRCS always opened the oilcans before distributing them in order to make bartering more difficult, and this young man explained that they occasionally got caught by the TRCS and had the oil confiscated. For the same reason, they did not trade in the market but down the other end of 10th Street. The last of Patrick's friends had a little shop in the market. He had almost finished secondary school and used to work for AEF.

Patrick was quite an established entrepreneur.[15] In spite of being only twenty-two-years old, he had run his own bicycle-taxi business for three years, transporting goods to and from the junction about two kilometres outside the camp for 200 shillings. He earned enough money to buy the bicycle, working for an NGO as a watchman when he first arrived in the camp.

Patrick's parents were farmers and after finishing primary school he got a job cleaning and cooking for a European priest in Burundi. He liked his job there, although he had dreamed of becoming a soldier. His parents had fled Burundi in 1972 and he was born in Rwanda where the family stayed until

1982. He told me openly about being like a Rwandan, and agreed that the Rwandans were better entrepreneurs than Burundians.

> The reason is because Rwandese have been in government, have been in power. And they had a chance not to be afraid of anyone. But these ones of Burundi have been ruled by Tutsi for many years. That's why they are always afraid of some people ... But this happened before. Because now Burundese are influenced by Rwandese. Nowadays they are equal. They act at the same level. Nowadays, Burundese became more businessmen, like the Rwandese.

Contact with Rwandans had changed the mentality of the Burundians – but only for the better in his opinion. There is an interesting twist to Patrick's account of this well-known theme. In his account, it was not the Rwandan Hutu who had been Tutsified by political power and the Burundians who were the true and pure Hutu; rather, the Burundian Hutu mentality was not natural but the product of many years of oppression. In other words, shyness is a product of historical circumstances and not a natural Hutu character. Only in the camp could they stop being so afraid all the time and become who they really were.

Patrick felt that he had an advantage over other Burundians because he grew up in Rwanda and therefore had the latter's mentality. In fact he claimed to have had the best of both worlds when the Rwandans were still in the neighbouring camps. He used to transport people and goods on the back of his bicycle from Lukole to Benaco, Musuhura and Lumasi.[16] When in Benaco or one of the other Rwandan camps, he would speak Kinyarwanda to attract customers, and when in Lukole he would speak Kirundi. For Patrick, mixing and hybridity was clearly a resource. When asked whether he would have an advantage over those who remained in Burundi if he went back there, Patrick replied, 'Of course we will be more intelligent than those who stayed in Burundi'.

In terms of recapturing Lukole, entrepreneurs were the ones who most visibly marked the ways in which the bureaucratic space of aid agencies was inhabited by people and transformed into lived space. These strategies ranged from the poor refugees who chopped extra firewood and sold it to the more wealthy refugees, to the big entrepreneurs who owned hammer mills, traded maize and ran restaurants. In terms of income, their earnings ranged from 200 to 20,000 shillings a day, although most were reluctant to inform me about this. The big entrepreneurs in the camp earned far more than any of the NGO employees, and some even owned scooters and cars.

In the market in Lukole A alone, there were 48 restaurants, 32 bars, 95 shops (selling shoes, clothes, batteries, salt, rice, and so on), 94 *mugorigori* (maize beer) outlets, and 116 market stalls selling fresh fruit, vegetables and maize. Apart from this, there were hammer mills, hairdressers, radio repairers and a row of other small businesses. The market in Lukole B never really competed with the market in Lukole A in size or variety. These markets not only catered for the refugees but also attracted Tanzanians from the whole district.

The entrepreneurs were not part of the educated elite. Their level of education was not much different to that of the population in general and they seemed to speak less French and English.[17] Nor did they seem to speak much more Swahili than average, which is surprising as it was in relation to business that they were in contact with local Tanzanians. However, the local language, Kihangaza, is so similar to Kirundi that they understand each other, rendering Swahili superfluous for interaction with Tanzanians from neighbouring villages. It was only when communicating with NGO staff, police officers, government staff and Tanzanians from other parts of the country that Swahili became necessary.

In spite of not belonging to the educated elite, many of the entrepreneurs had significantly higher incomes than the NGO employees, and the wealthier among them would often be referred to as 'big men' and respected for their success. Even the poor entrepreneurs represented another way of coping with Lukole and of trying to recapture the camp. The entrepreneurs showed that they were not dependent on UNHCR rations, and that they did not just sit around the *blindé*, waiting to be fed; instead, they took responsibility for their own lives and made a living of their own. What is more, they took responsibility for their families.[18]

The owner of a patisserie explained that he could now afford to buy some decent food for his wife to prepare for the whole family. This relates to the perception of 'UNHCR being a better husband' and hence of a fundamental fear of having one's male identity taken by the white man. The best cure against this emasculation was to prove that one could afford to feed and clothe one's own women. Being able to feed one's wife and children was about rehabilitating the masculinity that the UNHCR allegedly stole and about defying UNHCR laws and the decay of Burundian social customs. It was about taking things into one's own hands and re-establishing some sense of order. A young radio-repairer linked business directly to access to women:

RADIO-REPAIRER: If you give money to your wife, you are considered a husband. So this one who is rich can go with the wife.
S.T.: The wife of other men?
RADIO-REPAIRER: Yes, the wife of other men.
S.T.: So can you take the wives of many other men?
RADIO-REPAIRER: That is easy, if they know that you are rich, they come.

There was a sense among the entrepreneurs, especially the young ones, that they had taken the opportunity to start a business that they would never had dreamed of in Burundi. No longer constrained by the expectations of older generations, they were no longer compelled to become farmers like their fathers and grandfathers before them. They were free to try their fortune as entrepreneurs. In the marketplace the playing field was levelled, as all were equal when they arrive in the camp. As Patrick stated above, he had become much more intelligent than those who stayed in Burundi. This 'intelligence', he claimed, came from contact with Rwandans, while others claimed that it was the product of the hard life in the camp. In the words of a young bar owner:

And when I go back to Burundi, I think that I will be more powerful than these ones who stayed in Burundi. Because here I have to use knowledge. All knowledge I have got – to have something to eat. But in Burundi they are just joking, because they get food from the fields. Here I have to use my head to get something.

He believed that the hardship of camp life hardened and developed you. This was certainly the ideological construction around being a entrepreneur. My survey shows that a great number of the entrepreneurs had had small informal businesses in Burundi as well, selling bananas at the market, repairing radios at the roadside, or running a small bar. However, more than 40 per cent of the entrepreneurs were farmers in Burundi and hence actually had 'made it' in the camp.

Patrick and his friends assured me that they were not interested in 'politics'. Because they worked so hard, they did not have time to listen to the radio and involve themselves in such matters. The radio-repairer echoed their attitude:

RADIO-REPAIRER: Myself, I don't know how that problem happened in Burundi. I don't know because in morning I wake up, I go to work, and evening I came back – and just it was time for eating. So I didn't have time to go and discuss with others about Burundi problems.
S.T.: So businessmen stay away from politics? Who are the ones who are involved in discussing these things?
RADIO-REPAIRER: These people who know more about Burundi, they are these people who are not dealing with business. These villagers who are always staying with Tutsi. These people who are always staying in *blindés*, houses ... farmers and others who do not do business or go to work. They are always in villages with Tutsi and Hutu.
S.T.: So they start discussing these things?
RADIO-REPAIRER: Yeah.

S.T.: Even if they are uneducated?
RADIO-REPAIRER: Yeah.

In other words, there is a self-image of a hardworking man who earns his honest living and can take care of himself and his family. But he also minds his own business and is not interested in getting involved in politics, which is both a waste of time and potentially dangerous. This is in stark contrast to the educated elite, who worked for NGOs and who constantly felt that they had to measure their personal strategies in relation to the 'common cause' of the Burundian people.

To sum up, entrepreneurs were an important component in recapturing Lukole and the more successful among them had most certainly become 'big men'. However, it appears that they represented a strategy that differed from both the NGO employees and the street leaders. Respect was won neither through formal education and language skills nor through age, experience and knowledge of Burundian customs. Their knowledge was a third type that was very much bound-up with the camp context and neither learned in school nor on the Burundian hills. Hence their strategy was very concrete and based in the present context of the camp rather than in a nostalgic past or a utopian future.

Steven, James and Patrick – three ways of recapturing Lukole

In Lukole the fact that an older order seemed to have disappeared gave room for new orders to form. It was these new orders that young men like Steven, James and Patrick attempted to exploit. In the destructured space of the camp, they were able to exploit the liberating potential of liminality and become 'liminal experts'. They managed to carve out a space for themselves in the camp and had, to varying degrees and along different paths, managed to outmanoeuvre the old patriarchy and become the new 'big men' in the camp. No longer inhibited by Tutsi peers taking the best positions, young semi-educated men (and some women) were given important positions with relief agencies in the camp. No longer inhibited by norms and social expectations, young entrepreneurial men started up businesses of all sorts on the basis that they had nothing to lose – and some succeeded and became 'big men' in the camp. And finally with knowledge of locality and history being more-or-less irrelevant in the camp, old men appeared to be losing their grip on leadership while a number of young men were taking up the challenge of being street and village leaders.

However, this shift was not a complete break with the old order of things. The emerging young elite was not uncontested, and neither was the ideology of rejecting shyness and politeness and asserting oneself more powerfully vis-à-vis the international organisations. In Lukole there were ambiguous feelings towards good old Hutu virtues on the one hand and the brave new NGO world of the young educated elite on the other. These competing ideologies were not to be found in their pure, opposing forms, supported exclusively by one or another specific group in the camp. Rather, almost everyone in Lukole had doubts and everyone hesitated. So, when choosing a street leader, people hesitated between, on the one hand, the old man with no education but good negotiating skills and a high degree of respect due to his age and his 'good behaviour' – offering a guarantee of some kind of stabilising force against the social and moral decay of the camp – and, on the other hand, the young man who appeared to understand these foreign languages and strange new laws and institutions. He may not be perceived as capable of guaranteeing the status quo or functioning as a bulwark against the forces of change, but he may be seen as the best bet to promote one's interests with the UNHCR.

In spite of breaking with the ideals of hierarchy and respect to get where they were, these young men continued to draw on an ideology of inequality. A leader continued to be perceived as a patron. A 'big man' – whether due to his wealth or education, respectively important for big traders and NGO employees – was to be respected by the common people in the camp. So by breaking the norms and ideals of Burundian customs, the new liminal experts were not doing away with structures of inequality. Rather, they were building new ones through their strategies of coping with the 'flattening' homogenisation of society in the camp. These strategies for becoming 'big men' challenged the UNHCR's principles of equality and of aiding the weakest.

These strategies can also be seen as attempts to reclaim the masculinity that they perceived the UNHCR to have taken from them. In order to avoid being reduced to cuckolds, these young men fought back and tried to recapture their masculinity by feeding their own wives. An obvious example is the entrepreneur who earned extra money to be able to give some clothes and food to his wife and thus be able to fulfil his role as the superior 'giver of gifts'.[19] Once he had fulfilled his obligations as a superior, he expected his wife to fulfill hers by showing respect and obeying her husband. While creating a new space for themselves in an attempt at recapturing Lukole, these young men broke with old ideologies and old hierarchies in terms of age and class. However, as they were fighting for their masculinity, gender ideals were reinforced rather than transformed, as women were still meant to be the obedient and shy inferiors. By proving themselves as real men, these men also reproduced the ideal of real women.

NGO employees and street leaders were reclaiming their masculinity at another level. As we saw in the case of Steven, NGO employees were usually deeply involved in informal and clandestine political networks in the camp.

These networks were about showing strength and determination, and the young men involved were taking their future into their own hands and acting accordingly, rather than passively waiting in the camp to see what the future might bring. Whereas the entrepreneurs took care of themselves and their close family in the present, the political elite was thinking of the future and of their country. In the camp, politicians were respected – even feared – because they had the courage to defy UNHCR laws and play by their own rules. In this way, they had managed to reclaim their position as men – as those who set the agenda and must be obeyed. Ironically, they used their employment with the UNHCR and other agencies to achieve their goals. In this manner, they managed to fight what they saw as the destructive forces of UNHCR policies in a nonconfrontational manner. Recapturing is not necessarily a heroic struggle against the powerful but rather a question of strategies, and for these young men it was strategic to be employed by an NGO.

In short, this chapter has argued that a group of young men attempted to recapture Lukole by making the most of their position as young and mobile, and by adapting to the new setting, the new rules and new masters. They attempted to avoid being reduced to pure victims – 'bare life' without agency, history or political subjectivity – but they also attempted in various ways to avoid being labelled as 'troublemakers'. Entrepreneurs did so by avoiding politics which they perceived to be dangerous and contaminating. NGO employees and leaders were more ambivalent in this case, on the one hand taking on the role as troublemakers when they defied camp regulations and vowed to fight for their country, while on the other hand playing along with the agenda of humanitarian agencies, learning the development-speak of community participation, and in this sense distancing themselves from 'trouble'. As we shall see in following chapters, the two dominant parties in the camp – CNDD and Palipehutu – took slightly different approaches to the issue of positioning oneself as the victim or the troublemaker.

Finally, there were a number of young men who did not become 'big men' and who applied other strategies to cope with the camp. The majority of young men sat around the *blindés* all day, playing cards or *urubugu*,[20] while others devoted themselves to the Church. But it was the 'big men' who set the agenda in the camp, and it was to a large degree their conflicts that defined the ideological fault lines and the spatial differentiation of the camp.

Notes

1. See Laclau and Zac (1994) for a discussion of the concept of a gap from four
    different angles and of how it produces space for politics and agency (of a sort).
2. This account is based on a taped interview (June 1997), a taped life-story
    interview (24 February 1998), interviews (August 1997, March 1998 and April
    1998), letters (January 1999 and March 2001), and e-mails (September 2005
    and April 2006).
3. The UNHCR regulated the maximum wages that NGOs were allowed to pay
    Tanzanian and Burundian staff.
4. I carried out a survey of 123 NGO employees from Lukole A and B, which can
    be compared with my baseline survey of the adult population in the camp.
5. That this may not be exactly true will be explored in later chapters where we
    see how slander and defamation is used against the elite by discontented
    refugees.
6. All the refugees were counted to verify whether the present feeding figure was
    correct.
7. For the verification, each person dipped their fingers into ink that was
    impossible to remove to avoid 'recycling'.
8. Burundi was subject to an embargo by neighbouring countries after Buyoya's
    coup d'état in July 1996.
9. In November 1991 an abortive Hutu uprising (during which scores of civilian
    Tutsi were killed) resulted in thousands of Hutu being arrested and killed by the
    army (Lemarchand 1996a: 152–59).
10. Based on a survey of sixty-two street and village leaders that I carried out in
    early 1998.
11. According to my survey the leaders' knowledge of Swahili was not significantly
    higher than the average male population (55 per cent versus 43 per cent).
    Seeing as virtually all leaders were male, I am comparing only with the male
    population.
12. Although the leaders were not as well educated as the NGO workers, they
    differed sharply from the average population in this regard: virtually all (98 per
    cent) had some kind of formal education while almost a third (29 per cent) of
    all men in Lukole had no formal education.
13. Often the older leaders in the camp had held similar positions in Burundi, as
    chef du zone or similar, both before and after the democratic reforms in 1993.
14. A council of elders, a traditional Burundian institution that has been revised
    several times by various regimes since independence. See Laely (1992).
15. I use the term entrepreneur. In the camp the refugees would use the term
    business in English (*affaires* in French) for any kind of income generating
    activity that is not wage labour. In Swahili, the term *za shughuli*, which literally
    means 'of the things', nicely covers this informal wheeling and dealing.
16. These were enormous camps within a radius of about 8 km. In late 1996, more
    than 500,000 Rwandans lived in these camps.
17. Based on a survey that I did of 79 entrepreneurs in Lukole A and B (47 and 32
    respectively).

18. Most of the entrepreneurs that I interviewed were men (64 out of 79), and with a few marked exceptions, the female respondents either had small businesses selling vegetables and/or worked with their husbands.
19. Giving gifts has always been central to patron–client relations in Burundi. 'To ask for a gift, say the Rundi, is to honour; to give is to like. It is the superior who gives, the inferior who asks. In order to receive it is necessary to obey, but everything depends on the will and the affection of the superior' (Albert 1963: 273). See also (Lemarchand 1996a: 11–12).
20. A board game. In Lukole it is played with stones in small hollows made in the ground.

6
Rumour and Politics

Refugee agencies may have been trying to void the camp of politics and create bare life, helping and empowering the camp's population, but Lukole remained saturated with politics. In this chapter we explore the local dynamics of establishing public authority and creating political subjectivities through complex interactions of political rivalry, violence and rumours. In this process, political competition not only divided the camp between Palipehutu and CNDD, it also delineated an emerging political field, in part defined by political imaginations from Burundi and in part by local power struggles, converting local power struggles into national political issues and vice versa.

Furthermore, this political rivalry was linked with processes of creating meaningful space in the camp. In this way, the camp was differentiated and ordered into hot spots and cool places, into spaces of action and mobility and spaces of waiting and docility – just as people in Lukole were ordered into us and them, the educated and the peasants, the moderates and the extremists, the hardworking and the lazy parasites, the criminals and the law abiding, the modern and the retrograde. Of course these dichotomies themselves were contested, so the struggle was not merely to dominate the field but equally to define it. This in turn helped to combat the sense of being homogenised by the governing techniques of the UNHCR and of being reduced to bare life.

Joseph's Story

Joseph wanted to talk to me, so we met at the usual bar. I guessed that he wanted something from me in terms of access to funds. I had met him once before, when he had told me about an organisation that he had created in the camp with the ambitious aim of promoting peace and reconciliation in the Great Lakes region.

This time, however, he was not intent on talking about his organisation. Instead he complained about CNDD hijacking the NGOs. He complained that virtually all NGO staff were members of CNDD and that they made sure that nobody else got a job. They told lies to the Tanzanian staff about Palipehutu, so the Tanzanians believed that Palipehutu members were extremists and the ones causing the security problems in the camp. Because of this, Tanzanian staff were very reluctant to employ anyone who was not a CNDD sympathiser, he explained, and it was very difficult to be apolitical when the NGOs were so biased and politicised. Joseph claimed to be apolitical and only interested in the welfare of refugees, although it became apparent during our discussions that he expressed Palipehutu views and sympathies.

He complained that the medical assistants at the clinic openly were wearing Ndadaye badges. Though strictly speaking not connected to a political party and hence difficult for the authorities to clamp down on, these badges, with a picture of the assassinated president on them, were political statements that signified CNDD support. Caps in CNDD colours – white, red and green[1] – also expressed political loyalties in the camp. Joseph complained that if the Burundian hospital staff recognised a patient as CNDD, they would give them good treatment; but if they thought that you were Palipehutu, they would just tell you to leave. 'Go and get treatment from Kabura',[2] they would say.[3]

Whereas Palipehutu received press releases from the internet, downloaded in Nairobi and sent to the camp by refugees, CNDD members would fabricate them on AEF typewriters in Lukole – because so many of them work for AEF – and claim that they were sent from headquarters in Brussels, Joseph claimed. Furthermore, CNDD members working as pharmacists stole drugs from the hospital and sent them to their soldiers in Burundi or, even worse, sold them at the market in Lukole. Joseph asked me if I had seen these medicines for sale, and I must confess that I had, although I had also heard other rumours as to how they got there.

When asked about the security guards, he said that they had become more balanced politically since the reshuffle in 1997, although this did not mean that they were apolitical. He knew exactly which party the security guards in charge of various zones belonged to. The chiefs of Zone A and B in Lukole A were CNDD, he explained, matter of factly, while Zone C and the whole of Lukole B were Palipehutu. Steven, the chief security guard for Lukole A, was a well-known CNDD soldier, according Joseph, while the rank and file guards were mixed.

Joseph was very upset with the refugees employed by AEF in 'community service'. They were all political leaders and thieves, he said. At the moment, CNDD members were busy forging certificates that claimed that the holder used to work for NPA in Kitali, and selling them for 5,000 shillings each. At the time of this conversation, community service and a number of other functions (health and education) were in the process of going from one NGO (AEF) to another (NPA). Therefore, there was a lot of manoeuvring going on in order to secure a new job with the new NGO; hence, the alleged production of forged employment certificates. This was probably also the reason why Joseph approached me at this point in time. Now was his chance to get a foot inside.

It was not the refugee staff alone that was corrupt, he claimed. The Tanzanian youth coordinator, a central figure in community services, was running his own show in the camp, selling blankets, jobs and so on in cooperation with the CNDD leadership.[4]

Joseph's account gives the impression that there existed an elite, working for the NGOs, and that it was this elite – and not the official street and village leaders – that was running the camp. In his view they were not only working for NGOs, and therefore receiving a salary; they were also misusing their position for political and criminal purposes. Furthermore, they managed to keep political rivals at bay by indoctrinating the Tanzanian staff. Meanwhile, Joseph managed to reject the idea that the politics of this elite might be truly political or idealistic, by claiming that they were actually using the political party as a cover for self-enrichment. That is why they forged the press releases, to make it look as if CNDD was active. He later explained that they would dress up in full combat gear and take pictures of themselves in the neighbouring bush, claiming that these were pictures of CNDD on the way to attack Bujumbura airport. It was, of course, Palipehutu that attacked the airport on New Year's Day in 1998, according to Joseph.[5]

Joseph's story can be read in several ways. First, it shows how the camp was structured by political rivalry and how CNDD had managed to forge a powerful network of young men like Steven who exploited their positions as brokers to gain more power. My immediate reaction to his story was also to be quite alarmed by the almost claustrophobic picture that he painted. I knew already that most of the powerful positions in the camp were linked to political parties but the extent to which this was so came as a surprise to me, and I actually contacted a staff member from NPA to tell her what I had heard and enquire whether she was aware what was going on. She did admit that they had probably been misled by CNDD staff during the violent conflict in Kitali camp in December 1996 and had blamed Palipehutu.

However, Joseph's story can also be read as a partial contribution in the struggle to define and hegemonise the political field of the camp. He was obviously embroiled in this power struggle and had a quite specific reason for involving me, the outsider. Through rumour and conspiracy theories he was trying to make sense of the camp. But these conspiracy theories were not free of power relations, and they had the aim of damaging his political opponents through slander and defamation of character.

Joseph's story is a prime example of the kind of rumour-mongering and defamation of character of political rivals that was so common in Lukole. He later went on to explain that CNDD was actually an invention and an instrument of President Buyoya. Buyoya sent CNDD accomplices into the camp to create trouble in order, firstly, to weaken Palipehutu and split the Hutu opposition and, secondly, to have the refugees sent back by the Tanzanian authorities for making trouble.[6]

The fact that his story was based on rumours does not make it less valuable, as rumours about political opponents were important structuring principles in political rivalry in the camp. Therefore, we can use his story – and other stories like it – in two ways: to explore the political rivalry that seemed to penetrate the camp, and to explore the means by which Joseph – and others – sought to delegitimate political opponents. In the end, they both merge to shape the political field. In other words, these rumours help us understand the nature of the political field and the role of political entrepreneurs in creating that field.

The following analysis is inspired by Bourdieu's analysis of political representation (see Bourdieu and Thompson 1991). Bourdieu argues that the political field is like a game where politicians gain a 'practical sense' of the game and learn how to comply with the unwritten rules of the political field. By becoming competent players of the game, they also reproduce it. The positions that political representatives take are less determined by the interests that they claim to be promoting and more by the structure of the field, where they must position themselves vis-à-vis other players in a field that is constructed around polarities (ibid.: 185). A good politician knows how to master the practical skill of positioning themselves in this field, and it is this positioning that we must explore when trying to understand the dynamics of politics in Lukole.

For the political field to function, Bourdieu contends, the representatives must conceal the above-mentioned fact that they are playing this game of taking positions, and instead express devotion to the masses. Bourdieu reformulates Weber's distinction between those who live 'for' politics and those who live 'off' politics to state that 'one can live "off" politics only by living "for" politics' (ibid.: 183). In other words, it is important to show one's devotion to the cause and to the group that one is supposedly representing. And, as we shall see in the case of the camp, it becomes equally important to dismiss an opponent as a mere speculative manipulator who only lives off politics and not for it. Bourdieu argues that it is essential that a representative appears credible in order that a group should invest their belief in them and confer upon them the power to represent the group. In this precarious situation the politician is vulnerable to rumour-mongering and defamation of character by opponents in the political field who are trying to undermine their credibility and hence their right to represent the group (ibid.: 192–93). What they are competing for is basically the right to represent 'the people'. Stories like Joseph's are central to this process.

Networking and Brokering: Political Entrepreneurs in Lukole

It was generally held by refugees in the camp that CNDD was the most influential party in Lukole and had by far the biggest backing among the refugees. It was obviously impossible for me to evaluate these statements at first, as no refugees would openly confide in me about the political situation in the camp. When at last some of them did, they would usually exaggerate the importance of their own party while belittling the opponent, as we saw with Joseph's account. After a while, however, a picture began to take shape where it became apparent that Palipehutu was active in Lukole B and CNDD in Lukole A, and that CNDD was the dominant force in the camp.

As was mentioned in Chapter 5, there appeared to be a group of young, semi-educated men that occupied a central position in the camp. They were centred around the marketplace, NGOs and UNHCR, and had privileged access to and control over flows of resources and information in and out of the camp. However, they were not bound together by their positions as NGO employees or as street leaders or businessmen. Networks of individuals appeared to transcend these categories and make up large networks of 'big men'.

Mousa was an example of one of these influential young men. He had worked for an NGO as a coordinator for community mobilisers, then he went into business for a while, until finally taking up another job with an NGO. Meanwhile, he had a plot of land that he employed another refugee to till for him. He was thirty-years old and married, with two small children, and his wife worked as a schoolteacher. He had finished secondary school and used to work as an accountant in Burundi. He was a member of Frodebu in Burundi and was even mayor (*bourgmestre*) for a short while, after the previous Frodebu mayor fled the country, between 1993 and when he was compelled to flee himself in 1994. In spite of having no official position in the camp – neither street nor block leader, security guard nor social worker – it was to Moussa that neighbours went if they had problems with a ration card. He would go with them to the UNHCR office and explain their problem (in English, French or Swahili) and make sure things were sorted out. He was also awakened at 3 A.M. to help sort out a robbery in his street, negotiating with the security guards and the Tanzanian police. He knew the right people in the right places and could get special treatment at the hospital. With the right handshakes and smiles, he could wander into any NGO office and borrow a typewriter or just have a chat. What tied Mousa and the other influential men he knew together was their involvement in politics.

There is no doubt that these political entrepreneurs were 'in it for the money'. The windfalls of being part of the 'in-crowd' were, as Joseph argues, not negligible. In this way, claiming allegiance to a party was about establishing alliances, finding protection and establishing patron–client relations. In this sense, it appears at first sight that the ideological positions of the parties played only a minor role. However, being active in politics was about more than material gains.

Political entrepreneurs attempted to combat the depoliticised space that the humanitarian regime imposed on them and to regain their political subjectivity. They claimed that they were fighting for the future of the nation and for the common future of the Hutu people rather than just sitting around doing nothing or merely thinking of themselves, as businessmen were alleged to do. In this manner, they achieved a sense of purpose and direction in what was seen as a crumbling social and moral space. Although they defied the rules of the UNHCR and MHA by organising clandestinely, they obeyed far more powerful laws: the rightful struggle of the Hutu people. In a sense, these political entrepreneurs were living out their assigned position as troublemakers, epitomising the stereotypes ascribed to them by the relief agencies. This gave them the respect that they feared losing in the liminal space of the camp. Ironically, however, they also used the humanitarian agencies as an avenue for achieving their position of respect in the camp, many of them being NGO employees, security guards or street leaders. National and international relief staff appeared to have ambiguous relations with these people. While in principle being against politics as such, the only refugees that Tanzanian and international staff had daily contact with were these young men.[7]

It would be beside the point to attempt to estimate to what degree these political networks were about personal gains or about 'true political ideologies' since the two are inseparable, as Bourdieu argues. Politics is a mixture of both, with the political field in any given situation defining the positions that the parties may occupy. The refugees operated with a normative distinction between sordid politics that was based on selfishness and greed, and sublime politics that was linked to unselfish sacrifice for a larger common cause. The objective of most struggle was therefore to show that one's opponents were involved in the wrong kind of politics. In the pragmatics of political struggle in Lukole, anything would go, while in the normative sphere politics was about keeping the moral high ground.

In Lukole, political rivalry – leading to people being killed or forced back to Burundi – frustrated relief agencies, Tanzanian authorities and refugees alike. The latter in particular would have preferred a unified front against the common enemy rather than internal strife among Hutu, and numerous rumours circulated about the Burundi government deliberately splitting the refugees. However, this political rivalry or competition was an important element of defining the political field and hence of defining the political parties. Through this competition and mutual positioning one group managed to present itself as the true political idealists and representatives of people's interests, as opposed to their opponents who were mere selfish troublemakers – not dissimilar to the troublemakers in the UNHCR's perceptions. Rumours about rivals were about finding a position in the political field and about defining the field itself – defining the limits between 'good' and 'bad' politics – in the fragmented reality of the camp.

Producing Political Space

Lukole A was established in January 1994 in response to the first wave of refugees that fled after the assassination of President Ndadaye in October 1993. It was told in the camp that this first wave came from all parts of the country and consisted of people who had reason to fear persecution due to their positions in society and in political life. This, they said, is why CNDD was strong in Lukole A. A strong kernel of active Frodebu members managed to more or less monopolise the camp, and when a more radical faction of Frodebu exiles, led by Leonard Nyangoma, broke away and created CNDD, they followed suit.

A second wave of refugees arrived following the genocide in Rwanda in 1994, and were settled in the newly established Lukole II. It is difficult to establish any reliable socio-economic profile of the various parts of the camp due to these movements. However, in people's minds, Lukole II was perceived to be wealthy, with a large number of businessmen living there. My impression of the place confirmed this picture. It was quite densely populated with a large proportion of the houses being constructed in mud brick rather than shelters of grass and plastic sheeting.

Lukole A had also expanded in terms of the length of its streets. These new areas – far from the main road, the NGO offices, the police post and the market, and close to the swamp – were generally perceived to be marginal. Malaria was said to be rife due to the swamp and bandits were believed to be hiding in the bush close by. Moreover, Streets 50 to 70 were established later than the rest of Lukole A, and housed a number of Rwandans masquerading as Burundians and Burundians who had lived in Rwanda since 1972. This area appeared to be poor and was rather 'rough'.

Finally, there was Lukole B. My first impression of Lukole B was rural tranquillity and peace. Perhaps this was due to the layout of the camp, which had villages instead of streets and an abundance of trees providing shade and camouflaging the *blindés*, markedly different Lukole A's endless rows of blue and white plastic sheeting. However, I was very quickly told that this peace and tranquillity was only a surface phenomenon, an optical illusion; under the surface Lukole B was far more violent than Lukole A.

Most of the refugees in Lukole B had come from Kitali Hills camp in January 1997, and a great number had lived in Keza camp prior to that.

These refugees had typically fled Burundi later than those in Lukole A, fleeing when civil war broke out in their commune, Giteranyi, close to the Tanzanian border.[8]

As opposed to the first influx of refugees, these had not been politically active; neither had they held any prominent positions in the administration. They were mostly peasants who had fled en masse from a general state of violence and insecurity. There were a number of theories in the camp as to why these people should be especially prone to support Palipehutu, among them being that they were less educated. My survey data support the theory that education was higher in Lukole A than in Lukole B.

It seems quite plausible that the Frodebu leadership in Lukole A was quick to establish something like a hegemonic position in the camp, with its interpretation of events becoming the only official one. In Keza and Kitali the organised Frodebu elite was less conspicuous, leaving the field more open for alternative interpretations and discourses. Furthermore, Palipehutu had been operating in Giteranyi commune – some say because it was close to the border with Tanzania, from where Palipehutu originated – and might have influenced them prior to flight. Finally, the conflict in Burundi had escalated significantly from 1993 to late 1995, radicalising and polarising politics, thus making the tolerant views of Melchior Ndadaye and Frodebu rather out-dated and Palipehutu's hard-line approach more appealing.

In any case, political infighting between Palipehutu and CNDD broke out in Kitali as both parties attempted to become the leading party in the camp, representing the refugees and defining the 'truth' about the conflict in Burundi. This dispute came to a head in late December 1996 when around ten people were killed[9] and another ten went missing. Almost 400 refugees were detained and 126 were sent back to Burundi by the Tanzanian authorities, where all but two were shot by the Burundian army at the border crossing on 10 January 1997 (Human Rights Watch 1999).

In an internal note for the file, UNHCR quickly identified Palipehutu as 'the violent group' and recommended the arrest of all their 'ring leaders'. It appears that the UNHCR swallowed the CNDD version of the event hook, line and sinker, just as Joseph feared. According to the UNHCR, the reason why the violence erupted at that specific point in time was that the Palipehutu leadership feared losing its grip on the population if they were transferred to Lukole. According to internal notes within the UNHCR at the time, the Palipehutu leadership feared that it would no longer be able to conduct its 'coercive activities' in Lukole and hence was trying to eliminate rivals from CNDD before being moved.

Once moved to Lukole B, the violence continued at a lower level and caused a spatial reconstruction of the camp as individuals moved from one part of the camp to another, thus homogenising the different spaces in terms of political affiliation. Large-scale violence was no longer needed. The aim of violence was never merely to kill certain individuals but to spread terror and expectations of violence. The fear and anticipation of violence, kept alive by rumours about violence, was enough to cause people to act accordingly and move from Lukole B to Lukole A of their own accord.

It was generally held that CNDD supporters were moving from Lukole B to A in order to avoid threats of violence and being compelled to pay contributions to Palipehutu. Although there were a number of divergent interpretations of why some people had moved from Lukole B to Lukole A, it was certainly held by both parties that most of the NGO employees lived in Lukole A.[10]

By June 1997, the security situation had stabilised, with fewer refugees moving from Lukole B to A and fewer repatriating to Burundi. This relative peace lasted until late March 1998, when new violence emerged. In the meantime, a new group of refugees had entered the camp, which had been rounded up by the Tanzanian authorities from September 1997 onwards and were placed in new villages in Lukole B. This group was generally perceived to be apolitical. In fact, some political leaders in the camp expressed satisfaction with the round-up operation because they now had an opportunity to 'make them aware'.

Just as trouble was attributed to Lukole B by CNDD members, people in Lukole B claimed that certain villages in Lukole B were worse than others. In this manner the inhabitants of other parts of Lukole B would claim that F2 and C2 were full of young men who had been 'causing trouble' in Keza and later in Kitali, and had been forced into hiding in the bush after the conflict with CNDD and the subsequent police intervention in December 1996. They had been allowed into the camp again and had settled in F2 and C2. In this way, violence is circumscribed and ascribed to a certain group of young men and pinpointed in two particular villages. I often visited village F2 and got quite friendly with a number of the young men there. Their version of things was, of course, quite different. They saw themselves as the victims of the elite in Lukole A, who took the best jobs and dominated the market – even here in Lukole B – and then blamed the poor and marginalized people in F2 for the security problems. I return to this underdog ideology, which was prominent in Lukole B in general but particularly pronounced in village F2, later in the chapter.

I have here drawn a rather bleak picture of the way the camp was split into two politically separate spaces, forcing people to move if they did not fit in. Although this was the general picture, it was more a means by which the refugees made sense of the political field and the social space of the camp; a kind of road map with which individuals could manoeuvre. In this way Albert, a young, educated man working for 'community services', managed to stay in Lukole B for a long time in spite of being politically out of sync with his neighbours. He was quite aware about this fact and was very open about his survival strategies when I enquired about them. Not only did he not support Palipehutu as opposed to most people in Lukole B, his father had also supported the ruling Uprona party in Burundi. While Uprona was generally considered 'Tutsi', it was not uncommon for Hutu to be members of Uprona when it had been the only party if they expected any upward social mobility in the state sector. Why he was still a member in 1993, Albert never told me. In any case, an angry Hutu mob from the same village chased Albert's family from their house shortly after Ndadaye's assassination, whereupon they looted the property and killed seven members of Albert's family. Albert explained to me that he knew the perpetrators, and that they were now his neighbours in the camp, some of them even working as security guards: 'And they know that I know. So they are afraid that I will revenge them'. In other words, he was afraid that they would attempt to get rid of him as a witness. His strategy was to remember to socialise with his neighbours in Lukole B. He would buy them beer every now and then and sit and drink and talk with them. 'When they have drunk enough, they usually tell me the truth', he laughed. In this way he kept an ear to the ground in case trouble was on its way, and he also maintained good relations with his neighbours, proving that he was not an arrogant NGO employee who thought he was too good to mix with the peasants. Unfortunately, Albert was forced to move to Lukole A shortly after I interviewed him. When the security guards arrested his sister who was visiting him from Burundi and his younger brother who was staying with him in the camp, he complained to the Tanzanian police who had them released, and then moved with his family to Lukole A the same night.

Political Rivalry: Conspiracy Theories and Slander

While mythico-histories – in the sense of coherent narratives with an explicit moral content – were surprisingly lacking, Lukole was rife with rumours and conspiracy theories which were characterised by being unfixed and short lived, as opposed to myths and legends. Rumours are without specific authors, always fluctuating and adjusting details of context around a kernel of truth.[11] Rumours provide an overwhelming source of knowledge about the ways in which people react to dramatic change and how they attempt to interpret the global through the local and vice versa.[12]

Taking my cues from Allen Feldman's illuminating reflections on violence and rumour (Feldman 1995, 2000), I propose that we should perceive violence and similar crises as destabilising the 'natural order of things', and rumours as ways in which the people subjected to these shocks, try to cover up the cracks in the symbolic order. Violence, flight and exile had jolted the taken-for-granted life-world of these people, and rumours flourished in this as-yet-unstable environment as fantasies that tried to re-establish the taken-for-granted order of things as they once were. In the camp anything could happen, and people were ready to believe anything. The rumours themselves may have been about banal everyday events but often they related to larger issues, expressing the narrators' desires and anxieties.

Rumour is a kind of 'wide-awake dreaming' that intermingles fact and fiction and not only tries to make sense of the past but also tries to be prognostic about possible outcomes in the future. Rumours do not necessarily attack what was once taken for granted. Rather, by its nature of 'wide-awake dreaming', rumour tries to prop up the social-symbolic order while simultaneously revealing the constructedness of this order. In other words, rumours are openly constructed as opposed to other narratives that try to conceal their own constructedness (Feldman 1995: 231).

In rumour-mongering, meaning is given to an event that perhaps never had a meaning. The rumours try to uncover patterns of violence, even if these patterns may not exist. In this way, violence which by nature is transgressive and arbitrary, is made sense of, harnessed and made manageable. So rumours respond on the one hand to disorder and disintegration but produce, on the other hand, an order that is 'over-structured'. Thus, I found that there was a tendency to want to find causal links and ulterior motives in every event in the camp.[13] While conspiracy theories may not alleviate the suffering of the victims, they at least give them some certainty in their misery by pinpointing a cause and an authorial position. As Patricia Turner points out, the vague feeling of 'loosing out' (in her case the diffuse sense among African-Americans of being underprivileged due to race) is replaced by a concrete fear of a certain definable and omnipotent 'other' (Turner 1993). The imaginary capacities of rumours as 'wide-awake dreaming', the fact that they have not yet been reined in by official discourse (as this is no longer hegemonic in the camp), lets them 'run wild'. They managed to express the anxieties, hopes and ideological fantasies of the people in Lukole in ways that other discourse could not.

One of the most common ways to delegitimise a political opponent in the camp was through spreading rumours about the rival party. These accusations and rumours went both ways with both political parties claiming that the other party had lied to the Tanzanian authorities, UNHCR or NGOs about their opponent. In 1997, when there was trouble between the chief security guard (a Palipehutu supporter) and the camp chairman (who was also the chairman in Lukole A and known to support CNDD), the UNHCR received a petition submitted by refugee leaders, proposing the removal of the chief security guard for alleged misuse of authority. According to CNDD supporters, the chief security guard had told the authorities that the chairman was politically active, resulting in the chairman being sent to prison for ten days. In other words, the chief security guard and chairman were accusing each other of being politically biased and misusing their positions of authority to further their own political interests. In this case politics is perceived along the same lines as in humanitarian discourse; namely as selfish power mongering. Simultaneously, they were both accusing the other party of telling tales to the camp authorities in order to delegitimise their opponent and further own interests. These rumours revealed an attempt to prove that the opponent was using dirty tricks to gain power and position in the camp.

Often CNDD supporters would explain that Palipehutu did not actually exist at all anymore and was certainly not fighting inside Burundi. As proof for this statement CNDD supporters claimed that CNDD leaders from Burundi had secretly visited Lukole and had confirmed that Palipehutu was not actively involved in fighting on the ground. Those who claimed to be Palipehutu politicians in the camp – especially in Lukole B – were actually just criminals, according to this account, and the taxes that they collected from the refugees, supposedly for the rebels, were actually just for their own greedy consumption. The most common accusation against Palipehutu was that they were merely criminals, collecting taxes from poor refugees for their own consumption rather than the struggle, or that they were simply robbing people. A more nuanced version of this rumour claimed that Palipehutu used to be better when Rémy Gahutu, founding father of the party, was alive. He also allowed Tutsi membership, and the party enjoyed considerable support in the camps in Tanzania. Several reasons were given as to why the party lost its popularity. Some claimed that the Hutu began supporting Frodebu and later CNDD. Others said it was because Palipehutu became increasingly 'extremist'[14]. Another rumour had it that the refugees began to realise that the party leadership was misappropriating funds for themselves, and that the 'taxes' were not going to the cause but into the pockets of the leadership in the camp.

Many of these attitudes towards political opponents came to me in the shape of rumours about specific events or persons rather than full-blown theories or explanations. For instance, Jean-Claude would ask rhetorically how 'certain Palipehutu leaders' could afford a car, several wives and cattle when they had no job and no shop. Obviously, he was referring to the camp chairman in Lukole B, a known Palipehutu supporter, although he had the prudence not to mention names. Rumours are ambiguous, they adapt to the situation and live off hints and insinuations rather than clear-cut narratives. Jean-Claude went on to explain that Palipehutu had found it increasingly difficult to levy taxes and had therefore gone into theft and robbery. In this way it was clear that Palipehutu politicians, in his opinion, were construed as not living *for* politics but merely living *off* politics. They cynically misused the uneducated refugees' naivety to promote their own self-interest. Evidently, Jean-Claude was an important figure in CNDD.

The issue of Palipehutu members supposedly being uneducated was common knowledge in Lukole. Implied in this claim was the assumption that educated refugees would not let themselves be deceived into supporting the party. When asked, however, if only the elite supported CNDD, the CNDD leadership would be eager to explain that CNDD also enjoyed strong support among the non-educated. If not, its popular backing would, indeed, be meagre in a camp where only a fraction of the population had attended secondary school. But whereas it was implied by CNND supporters that the uneducated masses were harassed into joining Palipehutu, they followed CNDD because of its ideology and its commitment to 'the cause'. In this manner, CNDD managed to explain why so many refugees still supported Palipehutu and how Palipehutu dominated a part of the camp in spite of CNDD's political superiority. Palipehutu was dismissed as an unworthy political rival – as it consisted of a bunch of criminals – and the 'small people' who supported them were exonerated of any guilt or blame as they had merely been lured and coerced into supporting the wrong party. By claiming that things were different during the reign of Gahutu, CNDD supporters also managed to create a split in Palipehutu and explain why it was once so evidently popular. In this context, true politics is perceived in the positive sense of self-sacrifice for the larger cause.

Counter-rumours about CNDD were of a slightly different character, presumably due to the fact that CNDD was actually dominant in Lukole. They went more along the lines of CNDD being elitist without any connection to the masses. As we saw in Joseph's account, CNDD members were seen to promote their own interests through deceiving the outside world. This underdog ideology of Palipehutu tried to explain away the success of CNDD through a number of conspiracy theories. When Palipehutu members experienced the fact that CNDD was everywhere and expanding its power – as Joseph had – conspiracy theories emerged to give an explanation. One persistent conspiracy theory held that CNDD was actually the brainchild of Buyoya, and was created in order to split the Hutu. The Denmark-based leader of a Palipehutu faction, Etienne Karatase explained to me that Buyoya gave Nyangoma (leader of CNDD at the time) weapons and money so that Nyangoma could buy good officers from Palipehutu – effectively splitting Palipehutu between Karatasi and Kabura, who had been bought by Nyangoma. So although Nyangoma may have had a lot of firepower and soldiers, he had been corrupted by Tutsi money and had sold his soul to the Tutsi, according to this rumour. Palipehutu, on the other hand, had fewer weapons and fewer soldiers but the soldiers that were left had resisted the temptations of money and had managed to remain morally 'clean'. 'Nyangoma has no ideology', according to Karatasi. Ironically, it was rumoured in the camp that Karatasi had sided with Nyangoma. First, some CNDD supporters used this rumour as 'evidence' that Palipehutu no longer existed. A few months later, a Palipehutu supporter used it to prove that Kabura was the true leader who knew the harsh realities on the ground and who had managed to remain 'clean' while Karatasi had been bought by CNDD.

This theme of CNDD being morally corrupted by Tutsi power existed in other rumours as well. While CNDD supporters would pride themselves on their party having Tutsi members (usually Ganwa, who were believed to represent the noble Tutsi as opposed to the Hima parvenus), Palipehutu supporters saw this as a big mistake, as these Tutsi infiltrated the party and sabotaged it from within. The same went for the Hutu in the CNDD leadership who married Tutsi women. I heard several rumours from people in the camp that specific 'big men' in the camp and in the CNDD national leadership had married Tutsi women, playing on the stereotype of beautiful Tutsi women who use their beauty to seduce Hutu into bondage.[15] By remaining ethnically pure, Palipehutu may not have had so much power at the moment but what they had was genuine. Palipehutu was conceived as the honest, salt-of-the-earth, people's party – the true Hutu. They may have been losing out because of their honesty and simple manners, but they retained their Hutu values and remained true to their Hutu identity – rendering them pure. CNDD members on the other hand were cunning and speculative – apart from being educated and wealthy; traits that were commonly associated with the Tutsi.

There is a sense in these rumours that CNDD was using its domination to inflate its own importance further. Thus, a rumour told to me by a Palipehutu supporter had it that CNDD had bribed the Tanzanian police to put a woman in prison. Apparently, she had come from Burundi to tell the refugees about Palipehutu's attack on the airport in Bujumbura. However, the CNDD leadership in the camp did not want the truth about the attack to circulate because they had made the refugees believe that CNDD had attacked the airport.[16] When their attempts to bribe her to keep quiet failed, they convinced the police to jail her. Interestingly, this kind of rumour was similar to those about the Tutsi lying to the outside world, thus causing the 'big nations' to support the Tutsi regime, and played on the idea of Hutu being the object of a larger conspiracy where powerful others create a web of lies, a web so tightly woven that it is difficult to penetrate with the truth. It also put CNDD leaders on a par with the malign Tutsi and contributed to a generalized myth of a global conspiracy against the Hutu.[17]

Common to rumours about both parties was the idea that someone was pulling strings and making Hutu refugees fight among themselves instead of uniting against the common enemy. In other words, there was a sense of a master plan, a conspiracy against the Hutu in general and the refugees in particular. This perception of an authorial position was a means of making sense of a senseless situation (Feldman 2000). After all, being the pawns in a grand master plan was better than merely being left to oblivion in the Tanzanian bush.[18] At a more concrete level, rumours about opponents were means of delegitimising the other and of manoeuvring in the political field, as both parties claimed to represent the refugees. The effect of this manoeuvring was twofold: firstly it produced a political field, and secondly it helped to differentiate political space in the camp. This political space was closely interwoven with struggles about access to power and resources in the camp.

Rumours of Violence and Violent Rumours

On 26 March 1998 I attended a meeting with street leaders, NGOs and the UNHCR in Lukole A, in which the issue of security was being taken up by UNHCR's protection officer. He was telling them that important people – leaders, 'some of you sitting here' – were hosting Burundians from Kigoma and from Burundi who were not officially registered in the camp. 'Please tell these people to go to Mbuba[19] to be scanned and registered. Some of these people that you are hosting have been caught for making an illegal training facility, abduction and torture'. He was clearly hinting at political activities in the camp and at the rumour that camps in Tanzania were being used as bases for the rebels in Burundi. But he also linked it to a general deterioration of security in the camp. Crime levels during the past three weeks had been as high as they had in April the previous year.

On the night of 24 March a man was shot dead in his *blindé* and robbed of 375,000 shillings. That same night another shooting had taken place a few hours earlier in the same area of the camp. Burundians from the camp must have been involved, the protection officer said. They knew that this man had money.

The murder happened close to where my assistant lived, and he had been up half the night trying to help. We discussed what it was all about. The facts were that he was shot dead at 2 o'clock in the morning of 25 March. He was a farmer, not a businessman, and was known to be very wealthy. He left two widows. Apart from these basic facts, things got very blurred and it became very difficult to understand why he was actually killed. The event was frightening for neighbours and others in the camp, and they asked themselves what it meant, whether it could happen to them next and how to avoid it. In order to find some kind of certainty, in order to determine the risk of being the next target and apply strategies to reduce it, people in the camp tried to fill in the gaps wherever the facts stopped short of providing answers. This was done through rumours.

The UNHCR protection officer made the first connection – hence laying the ground for local theories and rumours – by mentioning another shooting earlier the same night. Secondly, by mentioning political activity, he opened up the possibility that it might be a politically motivated murder. This was further accentuated by mentioning the crime levels of April 1997, when violence was largely believed to have been politically motivated.

Rumours began to circulate that it was a politically motivated murder that had been disguised to look like simple robbery. The UNHCR's security officer claimed at an interagency meeting that the recent violence was due to Palipehutu killing and robbing CNDD members, and this conviction was shared by many CNDD sympathisers in the camp. Others claimed that it was Rwandans hiding in the bush that were stealing and robbing. A third theory related to me, held that the farmer was the victim of a jealous husband:

His second wife is Rwandan and had been married to a Rwandan soldier. When the Rwandan refugees were told to leave Tanzania, the soldiers hid in the bush. They did not want to return to Rwanda. So this rich Burundian 'married' the soldier's wife. Now the soldier has been sending messages that he wants his wife back. Perhaps it was him that killed the rich Burundian farmer.

The rumours about the murder in Street 9 were attempts to explain what had happened but they were also prognostic, which Feldman claims is a characteristic of rumour. They tried to predict whether it could happen again and to whom it could happen. The rumour was that Streets 1 to 9 were insecure, so people living there took their precautions and did night watches. Rumour also had it that the man had been murdered by thieves, so the wealthy refugees left the area or moved their valuables. Yet other rumours held that he was shot for political reasons by Palipehutu, so CNDD sympathisers would take extra care. Finally, a rumour circulated claiming that he was shot by a jealous husband and that the killer was a Rwandan hiding in the bush. This rumour relegated the event to the realm of the personal, the unique and the exceptional. In this way, it was of little concern for other refugees and was unlikely to happen again. In each of these cases, the rumours were prognostic and prescribed certain kinds of preventative action. The rumours influenced practice and had a tendency to become self-fulfilling prophecies.

Discussing the security situation almost two months later with two CNDD supporters who lived in the same area as the killing, I realised the complexity of the issue.

Someone has been robbed in Street 7. They heard gunshots. Fifteen goats were stolen off an old man. They agree that Streets 1–9 in Lukole A are the worst hit by the recent violence. People in the area have decided to do *urundo* (night watches). Mousa has moved his massive ghetto blaster to another part of the camp. Other wealthy refugees have chosen to leave the area, and stay with friends elsewhere, they say.

I ask whether it is somehow linked to politics. Oh yes, they say. It is only CNDD members that are targeted. These Palipehutu members are never robbed, not even the rich ones, they have not left the area and they do not take part in *urundo*. They just stay in bed at night. Have you noticed, they ask rhetorically, how certain Palipehutu leaders in Lukole B are very wealthy, in spite of not having a shop or a job (referring to the chairman, as we already saw in the last section). Recently, a bar owner in Lukole B was robbed. He was also CNDD, they say.

As with the earlier murder of the wealthy farmer, these events triggered intense speculation and rumours. They were linked to the first murder and interpreted in terms of space, politics and crime.

Often the three dimensions – politics, crime and space – would coalesce in people's understandings of the event. For instance the CNDD sympathiser who saw it as Palipehutu's deed also disclaimed Palipehutu as a political party and called them a bunch of gangsters. So, although CNDD members were allegedly targeted, the motive of the killers was more about personal enrichment than political disagreement, according to this CNDD rumour. Similarly, they reflected on the spatial distribution of violence and safety in the camp, claiming some areas to be safer than others and linking this to the area's exposure to Palipehutu elements. Thus the political, social and spatial structures of the camp were actually reified through these rumours about a specific event. However, the event also caused them to readjust the symbolic order, the taken-for-granted structures in society, where Lukole A used to be considered safe, while violence was associated with Lukole B. However, the robberies and murders in Streets 1 to 9 in March and April 1998 disturbed this pattern and made it necessary to come up with new explanations of violence.

The rumours that emerged in relation to the event of the wealthy farmer's murder attempted to stabilise the world for the refugees, and to cover the gap that the murder had created. But they were not just 'wide-awake dreaming'. The phantasmic attempts to cover the traumatic event were mediated by the structuring principles of the symbolic order; in other words, the rumours fitted into larger interpretative schemes concerning the role of politics, the position of Rwandans and ideas of safe spaces in the camp. In short, the murder of a wealthy refugee temporarily destabilised the taken-for-granted order of things – which was precarious in the first place due to the nature of the camp – and the subsequent rumours, which were attempts to stabilise it again, drew on a number of already known understandings of society. But they did so in new and unexpected ways.

Space, Politics, Violence and Rumour

As the rumours around the event of the wealthy farmer's death illustrate, the event was interpreted according to certain spatial hierarchies. Very soon the whole security issue became a question of where it was safe to be and where the troublemakers came from. Being linked to Palipehutu, violence was also linked to Lukole B, as this was widely perceived to be Palipehutu territory. Consequently, there were numerous accounts of witnesses claiming to have seen or heard the bandits going in the direction of Lukole B.

However, theft and robbery also occurred in Lukole B at the time, when, for instance, someone attempted to rob the owner of my favourite bar. He managed to escape, but the owner of the bar next door was robbed in his *blindé* the same night. They took all his money and a crate of beer, which they drank as they got away.[20] Allegedly, the same gang went to Lukole A and robbed some *blindés* near the swamp that divides the two parts of the camp. This opened the way for alternative interpretations of the spatial hierarchy of security in Lukole.

The chairman in Lukole B articulated such a dissident understanding of space and violence, and claimed that the robbers and thieves came from Lukole A at night. He claimed to cooperate with the Tanzanian authorities, the security guards, the street leaders and the night guards in fighting crime and lamented that the chairman in Lukole A was not keen on catching criminals or on cooperating with Lukole B. He claimed to have banned all political activity in Lukole B, and that Palipehutu and CNDD helped each other in combating crime instead of quarrelling. In other words, it was the others – those from Lukole A – who wanted to divide the people by introducing politics. He just wanted the refugees to be safe, to cooperate and to combat troublemakers, echoing UNHCR perceptions of politics obstructing the creation of 'the community'.

He explained the reason why the thieves were in Lukole A as follows: When Lukole B was settled in early 1997, all the thieves came here from Kitali camp, from the bush and from Lukole A. However, the police intervened and many thieves fled. People with weapons went to Lukole A but kept their ration cards for Lukole B. 'Perhaps these people were causing the trouble' he suggested.

Shortly before I interviewed him, he had found a letter on a tree with a death threat. Apparently the letter read:

> Do not remove before the camp chairman has read this message. We have come from Kitali but you [camp chairman] are bad. Even if many people support you, we will kill [the word 'kill' written in blood] you – even if we will pay with our lives. We will kill you if you continue to be involved in something in Lukole A. If it were not for you, we could have recovered

our things. When you came to Lukole B, it was when there were firearms. You have stopped us from stealing, so now we want to stop you.

The letter was signed with a picture of a gun and bullets, the chairman said, though I myself never saw the letter, which may never have existed. However, it was used by him to express to me his perceptions of a conspiracy against him and to explain why such a conspiracy should occur. He suggested that this was either from robbers or from those who went to Lukole A. He could forbid those who live in Lukole A from collecting their rations in Lukole B but then he would simply be accused of being political, he claims.

Politics was seen at one level to be the source of evil, since it caused so much trouble, preventing ordinary people from getting on with life. At another level, it was the politics of the opponent that was seen to be the problem, paradoxically because it was not political enough. The politics of one's own party was about unselfish loyalty to 'the cause' and to the people. Thus politics was split between the sordid politics of the opponent and the benign politics of one's own party.

Along similar lines, the camp chairman of Lukole B claimed that he had banned all political activity in Lukole B, expressing a desire to 'get on with things' without all this partisan bickering. A CNDD supporter commented that it was true that the chairman had stopped political rivalry, but only by banning CNDD activity. NGO employees living in Lukole A and working in Lukole B would take off their Ndadaye badges and their red, white and green caps when they crossed the river that divides the two camps. Palipehutu supporters, however, would freely wear *kofias* in Lukole B, they said.[21] So while rhetorically dismissing politics as divisive, the chairman in fact privileged Palipehutu members, perceiving only CNDD supporters as the divisive element of politics. Similar constructions of politics existed in Lukole A where CNDD dominated. Here, the term 'extremist' was used about opponents. There was a sense that the politics of CNDD was more moderate, reasonable and more in line with international conventions. Thus it was perceived to be more justified and less problematic than the violent, extremist and marginalised politics of Palipehutu. Often, CNDD members would boast that there was a quiet agreement with the camp commandant who let them carry out their activities.

Although both parties shared a perception of the other party as the troublemaker, they did so in slightly different ways, where ideas of modernity and tradition, urbanity and rurality, isolation and global cosmopolitanism played roles in positioning the other. Here the image of the international community also played a role. Generally speaking, people in Lukole A perceived the refugees from Lukole B with a certain amount of disdain, as uneducated peasants supporting what at best could be termed an extremist and racist party, run by a handful of criminals with guns. In spite of its violent reputation, Lukole B was perceived to be rather rural and stagnant, in part because its inhabitants had previously lived in Kitali camp which was 'in the bush' and in part because the majority came from Giteranyi, a poor, underdeveloped commune on the frontier.

Along with this understanding, the refugees in Lukole A saw themselves as more in touch with modern life. Because Lukole A was closer to the road and Tanzanian villages, it had become the main centre for trade; also, most of the offices of international agencies were there. CNDD made use of this privileged access to the international agencies and its proximity to 'the action'. In terms of ideological self-perceptions, CNDD saw itself as being more in line with the international community and was very preoccupied with gaining recognition from 'the big nations'. It was eager to distance itself from Hutu chauvinism and the *génocidaires* from Rwanda by emphasising democracy and reconciliation in official discourse.

This spatial hierarchy was not unambiguous, however, and would leave room for contentious readings of space. In Lukole B the stereotypical portrait of Lukole A and B was not directly dismissed but rather turned upside down. The refugees in Lukole A were seen to be wealthy – 'they live like *wazungu*' – and arrogant – 'how do they know our problems when they only speak English and French?' The sweet and easy life in Lukole A, having access to jobs and business, had spoiled people there and made them oblivious to the suffering of the masses, it was said in Lukole B. They were forgetting their Hutu-ness and their political commitment due to their search for wealth. This underdog mentality of Palipehutu was also its claim to popular support in Lukole B. It appealed to a certain sense of disgruntlement in a population that felt it was losing out in relation to the more established Lukole A population. In Lukole B people often complained that they were very poor and attributed this to the number of times they had been forced to move. Many had been in Keza, then Kitali and now Lukole B. Their plastic sheeting was worn out, they had never had time to establish a business, start farming or find jobs with Tanzanian farmers or international agencies. Palipehutu clearly played on this sense of being underprivileged. If they did manage to get good jobs with NGOs in Lukole, they mostly moved to Lukole A due to the prevalence of this underdog ideology. In this way, the ideology became a self-fulfilling prophecy, reflected in space.

In the perception of Lukole A as arrogant and wealthy lies also an idea that refugees in Lukole A had lost their true Hutu identity (the theme of purity was a leitmotif in much of Palipehutu's political ideology), while – being rural and backward – people in Lukole B had maintained a sense of community. The camp chairman in Lukole B described how everyone here cooperated against crime, implying that the elite in Lukole A was too busy accumulating wealth and power and ingratiating itself with the international

NGOs to bother with ordinary people. 'They' – the elite in Lukole A - clearly lacked a sense of community because of a successful modernist and individualist orientation to life. Here, the dichotomies from the tales of decay are again at play in a highly ambiguous manner. On the one hand, the market and NGO offices were spaces of action, mobility and change, challenging the stigmatising and immobilising space of the camp. On the other hand, these spaces represented danger, a threat towards tradition, Burundian customs and the natural order of things. It is in line with this latter understanding that Palipehutu ideology positioned itself and Lukole B as protectors of Hutu-ness.[22]

The UNHCR, NGOs and Tanzanian authorities apparently also used these spatial stereotypes of the camp. In a meeting called by the camp commandant for influential refugees from Lukole A, the UNHCR, MHA and police in August 1997, the head of police reprimanded them for continuing to fight with Lukole B. He told them that they should abandon their differences with Lukole B. 'You think you are in the town while Lukole B is in the bush', he said. 'But in Lukole B they know how to cooperate and help with catching thieves. You could learn from them'. By using Lukole B as a threat, he was trying to get the refugee leadership to forget their selfishness and individualism and sacrifice some of their pride for 'the community'. Lukole B was conceived as being less urban and civilised while having what they lacked in Lukole A; namely, a sense of 'community'.

Concluding Remarks

In the fragmented, liminal space of Lukole, all refugees were assumed to be equal, constituting a homogeneous mass of hapless victims. However, historical circumstances around their time of flight, the itinerary of their time as refugees, their social background, and subsequent political developments shaped these people very differently. This was reflected in the various spaces of the camp where levels of wealth, health, education and safety varied dramatically from place to place. Other mechanisms of differentiation were, however, also at play. In the political field, two parties claimed to represent the true interests of the refugees, using rumours and defamation of character to delegitimise the opponent's claims. In practice, political networks coalesced with, and were indistinguishable from, other personal networks that gave access to power and resources. This does not imply, however, that politics in the camp was exclusively about access to resources, as political ideologies also proposed themselves as the answer to people's troubles and tribulations, offering meaning in a meaningless world. Although not all refugees in Lukole were involved in party politics, this chapter has shown that political rivalry dominated and structured the camp to a degree that everyone had to relate to it in one way or another.

In Lukole, the struggle between CNDD, which had been in Lukole A since the beginning, and Palipehutu, whose presence was introduced mainly by refugees from Kitali, took the shape of a mixture of violent political struggles, criminal networks and personal feuds. Violence, which has a tendency to shatter social meaning, was interpreted through some rumours as being political, thus reinserting it in the established order of things while simultaneously delegitimising the opponent. Other rumours tried to make sense of the violence and to contain it by linking it to space, while still others referred to it as simple banditry. Often all three levels were linked in the rumours, so that violence was claimed to be caused by desperate criminals calling themselves Palipehutu supporters and living in Lukole B, or by thieves hiding in Lukole A under the protection of CNDD. In this way, expectations of violence, as created by rumours, structured the camp into more or less safe zones. Rumours also structured the camp into zones of wealth and poverty, selfishness and community spirit, urbanity and rurality. Such rumours and the expectations of violence that they created were prognostic, causing people to act accordingly, avoiding certain areas of the camp, for instance. In this way, rumours of violence influenced action and hence shaped the reality that they claimed to be about, and indeed became self-fulfilling prophecies. As long as people in Lukole acted 'as if' violence had a certain pattern, 'as if' the rumours were true, then rumours became true.[23]

Rumours, politics, violence and space interfaced to create a differentiated and hierarchical order in the camp, thus enabling its inhabitants to start making sense of it. However, it was a precarious order that existed in Lukole. The initial shock of war and flight dislocated the taken-for-granted order of things and revealed its constructedness and inherent contradictions, as we saw in earlier chapters. The fact that even banal everyday events in the camp gave rise to the most fantastic rumours and conspiracy theories, testifies to the fact that this initial shock still rendered Lukole a fragile place that constantly needed reordering, restabilising and reimagining. The formally depoliticised space of the camp – as imagined by the humanitarian agencies – was intensively politicised and reclaimed through a proliferation of rumours. These rumours were short-lived and always in flux, as opposed to the standardized mythico-histories that Malkki (1995a) found in the camps a decade earlier, testifying to the fact that the space of Lukole was still exceptional and liminal and ultimately under the control of the UNHCR, preventing the emergence of any hegemonic 'truth'. Due to the constant pressure to create refugees as pure victims and keep the camp exceptional, preventing the establishment of new hegemonies, the camp paradoxically became a space which was at once depoliticised and hyper-politicised.

Notes

1. Allegedly, the 'politicians' would wear white at the front, while 'soldiers' would wear red at the front, symbolising blood.
2. Cossan Kabura was the military leader of Palipehutu's armed wing, the FNL. In the camp he was perceived to be the de facto leader of Palipehutu since he broke with Etienne Karatase, who is based in Denmark. The movement has split several times since then.
3. UNHCR staff told me that Palipehutu supporters were boycotting the schools and clinics because they believed them to be CNDD strongholds.
4. Although I treat this as a rumour and a conspiracy theory, I am not dismissing the fact that it might be true. Two Tanzanian AEF staff had been sacked a few months earlier for selling blankets that were meant for distribution to the elderly.
5. This attack was one of the strongly contested events around which much rumour-mongering occurred. The secrecy of the Burundi government no doubt helped foment these rumours.
6. These rumours use certain events as 'evidence'. Tanzania had forced the Rwandan refugees home in late 1996. This caused constant uncertainty and fear – and a lot of rumours – that it could happen to the Burundians as well.
7. Joseph claimed that the CNDD elite managed to convince the NGOs of their political position due to their near-monopoly of jobs within these organisations. To some degree, Joseph is right when he claims that they were pro-CNDD, for while they dismissed both parties they usually claimed that Palipehutu was the most extremist and started the problems.
8. Based on my survey of 464 refugees and on a UNHCR census (see UNHCR 1997).
9. There is some confusion about the number of dead bodies found in pit latrines and elsewhere. In various Notes for the File, UNHCR field officers change their figures.
10. My survey data do not unequivocally support this statement. However, there was a tendency for some refugees to live in Lukole A and work in Lukole B, while the opposite did not occur. Furthermore, many refugees living in Lukole A had kept their ration cards in Lukole B. We must also keep in mind that, although there was a tendency for NGO staff to sympathise with CNDD, there were still some who sympathised with Palipehutu while others managed to manoeuvre in Lukole B through a number of personal relations, in spite of political disagreement.
11. This phenomenon is what Gary Fine (1992) terms the 'ecotypification' of rumour
12. For anthropological approaches to rumour, see Feldman (1995), Simons (1995), Scheper-Hughes (1996) and White (1997, 2000).
13. There are certain similarities here with witchcraft stories that also have the tendency to accredit too much malign human agency concerning an event that most probably is due to chance and circumstance. As in conspiracy theories, there are in witchcraft narratives notions of a plan, a person, an ulterior motive

and hidden powers. See Geschiere (1997). For discussions of the concept of hidden realities in Africa, see Todd and Sanders (2003) and Mbembé (2001).

14. In Lukole 'extremist' vaguely implied that a person was excessive in their use of violence and was not willing to compromise. However, it also had a number of other negative connotations and became an empty signifier that was used to delegitimise political opponents.

15. For narratives about the dangers of marrying Tutsi women, see Turner (2009). Images of Tutsi women seducing Belgian peace keepers appeared in Rwandan media propaganda leading up to the genocide in 1994 (see Chrétien et al. 1995: 366). This is also in line with a rumour in Lukole that Tutsi sent beautiful women to seduce President Clinton in the White House.

16. For a discussion of the power of concealing and revealing secrets in Burundi, see Turner (2005b).

17. See also Turner (2002, 2004).

18. Gary Fine (1986) and Patricia Turner (1993) show how rumours and urban legend flourish about big corporations masterminding secret plans against ordinary people. Although this does not remove oppression, it removes the vague feeling of being underprivileged by putting a name on the oppressor. I elaborate these thoughts more in Turner (2002, 2004, 2005b).

19. Mbuba was the registration site for new arrivals.

20. Unfortunately, they did not find any culprits at the end of the trail of empty bottles.

21. Although commonly worn by Muslims in East Africa without any political significance, these hats allegedly signified Palipehutu allegiance in the camp.

22. However, it should not be assumed that CNDD/Lukole A interpreted the dichotomies in one way and Palipehutu/Lukole B in another. Both had ambiguous relations to these classifications.

23. For a discussion of the role of ideology, working 'as if' it were true, see Zizek (1994).

7

Innocence Lost

In spite of refugees in Lukole trying to inhabit the space that they had been allocated and turn Lukole into a lived place, they never completely embraced the camp. It always remained an in-between experience, a 'non-place' (Augé 1995) between an idyllic past and a glorious future. This past and future took place somewhere else than here, namely in Burundi. Lukole was neither completely the bureaucratic dream of the UNHCR nor totally recaptured by the refugees. Neither did it ever quite make sense to either part: it evaded total symbolisation and remained precariously balanced in between. When dealing with their present predicament in the camp, young men had to also cope with their past in Burundi, as there appeared to be a dialectic to-and-fro movement between their memories and their present strategies of managing their lives.

The past was used actively to make sense of the present situation, particularly in ideological battles with other actors in the political field in the camp. By resorting to the past, they could claim to know the 'truth' behind the present conflict and therefore also solutions to it. Individuals made sense of their own incoherent life stories by inserting themselves into broader narratives, related to the repertoire of possible ways of imagining Burundi, as political developments in Burundi and the Great Lakes region set the agenda for what to remember and what to forget. In other words, the production of history in Lukole depended on power struggles in the camp as well as in the region.

Central to their narratives was an idea of loss: not only the loss of peace and harmony, but also the loss of Hutu innocence because, as opposed to those who fled the massacres in 1972, the Hutu could no longer claim to be pure victims. Due to memories of 1972 and a growing awareness of their oppression, the Hutu participated in large-scale violence in 1993, and this loss of the victim position had consequences for which narratives could emerge in the camp, especially with regard to the theme of Hutu becoming more aware and open.

The Narrative Form

Between February and May 1998 I conducted fifteen life-story interviews with young men from different parts of the camp and with different backgrounds in terms of education, occupation, province of origin and time of flight. I knew most of them beforehand through earlier interviews and conversations, enabling me to select a broad spectrum of 'types'. What struck me about these interviews was the way in which concrete, personal accounts tended to slide into generalised, impersonal narratives. Although I controlled the interview relatively tightly and kept returning to concrete questions about personal experiences of conflict and flight, answers remained at an aggregate and impersonal level. Often my respondents would just say 'there was killing' or 'then there was war and we fled'. Øivind Fuglerud observes the same tendency among Tamils in Norway: 'When asked about their background, Tamil refugees tend to slip from the story of their own lives into the field of collective history. The individual and the collective fuse into one standardised discourse explaining 'why I am here now' (Fuglerud 1999: 180). Similarly, Veena Das shows how militant Sikhs in the Punjab tend to refer to violence in the impersonal, passive tense – 'there were some killings' – leaving out agency (Das 1995: 130–34). She deals specifically with violence perpetrated by the narrators, and asks how the Sikh community can erase the memories of Sikh participation in riots, abduction and rape, and relates this 'to the issue of how individual biography becomes social text' (ibid.: 131). In order to understand this we must re-examine the relationship between the self and society.

Citing Heidegger and Ricoeur, Fuglerud claims that we must see the self as self-representation rather than as an autonomous being in itself. This self is 'a result of a semiotic process organising experiential fragments into illusory wholes. In this perspective the person is one of the "things" about which we speak rather than itself a speaking subject' (Fuglerud 1999: 175). The self is not a pre-existing entity; rather, it is something that one tries to make into such an entity through the biographic narrative. Individuals' narratives seek to create wholeness and purpose from a fragmented, contingent life path by inferring meaning and causality.

When I interviewed a young man in Lukole about his life, he attempted to make sense of it. The thought that his life was a more or less contingent string of events without any cause and effect and no underlying driving force, and that there was no clear reason why he should end up in a refugee camp, was quite unbearable to him. So he would look for causality, for a direction and a connection between past and present. This process rests upon 'the reading of the end into the beginning, the recapitulation of initial conditions of action in its projected final consequences.' (ibid.: 175).

This was not an individual process however; the patterns that he sought and around which he constructed his biography were socially constructed. He was attempting to insert his narrative into a larger authorised narrative, a master narrative or what Das calls a 'social text' that could lend authority and meaning to his own muddled, doubtful experiences. As Das comments, individuals who have experienced violence – either as perpetrators or victims – attempt to make cultural sense of horrifying events, in this way relieving the individual of responsibility and suffering (Das 1990: 361). refugees in Lukole were perpetrators and victims of violence, if not in person then by proxy since it is relevant to explore how their narratives relate to this violence.

Because violence is often arbitrary and diffuse, and the individual's experience may be solely a vague feeling of insecurity and fear, collective memories of past events are evoked and parallels drawn in order that individuals can navigate the war zone. Furthermore, violence has a tendency to overflow symbolisation, or at least violence is perceived as outside the social, thus distinguishing it from other forms of discursive practice (see Balibar 1998). That is to say that violent events, like those that occurred in Burundi in October 1993, tend to create a sense of social meltdown, dismantling the known symbolic order of things, and it is this vague sense of the suspension of normality that the narratives attempt to overcome. As both Feldman (1991, 1995, 2000) and Das (1990, 1995) point out, violence is reinserted into some meaningful order through narratives. What is interesting to explore here is how this is done, how violence and conflict are narrated.

Shadrack

Shadrack was a soft-spoken young man with mild eyes who did his best to get his English right, quite a contrast to his heavily built body that had earned him a reputation as a good football player. At the time of the interview, he was twenty-seven-years old and unmarried; working for Oxfam and had lived in Lukole A since early 1994. He was in his final year of secondary school when he was forced to flee Burundi. If he had had the opportunity, he would have liked to become a doctor or a soldier. His father died around the time he was born and his mother brought up her three children and cultivated the land on her own.

I tried in the life-story interviews to pinpoint his and others' own experiences of ethnicity. So instead of asking generally about the differences between Hutu and Tutsi, I asked about the relations that Shadrack had had with Tutsi children when he was a child:

> SHADRACK: At that time … Hutu children were not well taught. That's why Hutu have had no problem. But if I try to analyse it now, I see that at that time we had a problem even [if] it was not easy to see … Now I can see we

had a problem because ... for example, it was not easy to share, for example, the same glass with a Tutsi if you are a Hutu child. That's why if I try to analyse nowadays I can see that at that time it was a problem.

S.T.: Do you think that the Tutsi children themselves were aware? Did their parents tell them: "This one is a Hutu. Don't share!"

SHADRACK: While Hutu were – what can I say – like blind at that time, the Tutsi themselves were well taught about the system, about the Tutsi, and not to cooperate ... to cooperate but to have a certain – what can I call it – not to approach them.

When he was a child, Shadrack had no problems with Tutsi children and could hardly tell the difference between Hutu and Tutsi while the Tutsi children allegedly knew about ethnic identities all along. This is what he referred to by saying 'if I analyse it now': with hindsight he could see many problems between Hutu and Tutsi that he did not see then because he was 'like blind at the time'. Before, when the Hutu could not yet see, there was a semblance of harmony but the Tutsi had other plans all along. This made the crime of the Tutsi all the worse. Not only did they want to discriminate and exterminate the Hutu, but they also hid their true intentions and pretended to be friendly with the Hutu who blindly believed them. When he started secondary school, things got worse:

Yeah in the secondary school the problem was very difficult ... The Tutsi were aware of the problem. But the Hutu – because of that event of '72 – they are afraid of doing anything... The Tutsi were trying to do something for their Tutsi friends. But the Hutu was afraid to do something for his Hutu friends.

The antagonism between Hutu and Tutsi that had been hitherto concealed from the naive Hutu was now becoming visible. The Hutu children – concurrently with their improved education – began to 'see'. They could see what was really going on as the real nature of the Tutsi began to reveal itself, but the Hutu dared not yet act upon their newly acquired knowledge. Tutsi could help Tutsi, according to Shadrack, but Hutu could not show ethnic solidarity. This was due to their memories of 1972 and fears that similar events would occur again if a Hutu student openly expressed Hutu solidarity. Without me asking, he wove big events like the massacres in 1972 into his personal narrative of relations between students at school. He interpreted changes in student behaviour in relation to national politics.

His memories of 1972 were obviously not first-hand, personal memories, as he had only just been born at the time. The teachers did not teach them about the events in 1972, he explains. They learned about them through their parents. The killings in 1972 also affected his village:

SHADRACK: What happened, at that time it was in the coffee season. And at every coffee season, all the businessmen go to the *centre de commerce* to have a meeting about how the coffee is being sold and so on. So they called those businessmen just as usual like there is a meeting. My father didn't go to that meeting. He didn't because he was sick. So my father was not there and the others went, supposing that they were going to a meeting. So all of them, no one returned.

S.T.: Many people were killed.

SHADRACK: Yes! There were a lot of people because they were about forty houses, and each house has a man.

As opposed to other accounts of 1972, 1988, 1991 and 1993, Shadrack's account was very concrete about what happened in his particular village and how his own father fortuitously avoided being killed. However, his account remained very factual without any gore and blood or lengthy depictions of Tutsi atrocities.

Shadrack attended a secondary school run by the Church. When Ndadaye was killed in October 1993, teaching was suspended in all secondary schools. But as opposed to other schools, there was no aggression between Hutu and Tutsi students. 'We were obliged to cooperate. That doesn't mean that a Tutsi was a friend of a Hutu but we were obliged to be friends'. In spite of this, he and some other students decided to flee:

> When we stayed in the compound, even if there wasn't anyone to harm another, we were afraid of the situation. Some of us were trying to persuade one another to leave or to stay. But for us, we left the school at the right time. This is what happened. One Tutsi from the school tried to leave the school. All the Tutsi left the school. And at that morning when they decided, we saw that it was dangerous for us. So we decided to leave the school. The rector tried to calm us but it was in vain. It was on 9 November 1993.

Shadrack's account refers to a diffuse sense of fear – 'we were afraid of the situation'. He never saw any killing or else he was reluctant to tell me about it. When teaching was suspended after the assassination of Ndadaye, they just remained at the school and played football and basketball. What triggered him and his fellow students to leave the school were rumours about violence and the anticipation of violence. At the other schools there were 'too many killings', he says. Similarly, the Tutsi students chose to leave the school and seek refuge at town centres because they were anticipating violence from the Hutu.[1] The exodus of Tutsi from the school was read as a bad omen.

SHADRACK: At the time, if you were in the school you were told that if you leave you will not be allowed to return in the school. So that some of us were afraid in order not to leave the school. But also at that time, there were some soldiers who were guarding us. At that time also, to leave the school was also something like a trick. It was dangerous. We were obliged to pass somewhere in order not to be seen by the soldiers.

S.T.: You were afraid the army might come?

SHADRACK: Yeah. If it was not for the army, then there were no problems. For example in the commune all the Hutu would stay in their homes. But they thought that soldiers would come and kill them in their … that's why many Hutu were obliged to leave their houses and sleep in the bush.

Flight was not just a question of escaping violence. There were certain 'staying put' factors (Van Hear 1998: 20) that made Shadrack and his fellow Hutu students hesitate, such as the risk of being expelled from school, if they left. Although the soldiers did nothing to threaten them, they were perceived as a threat due to memories of 1972 and 1988. Shadrack was convinced that the soldiers had secret plans, and substantiates his argument with reference to what they were allegedly doing in the villages, something that he did not experience first hand either.

SHADRACK: When I left the school I came directly to Tanzania, and it was at that date of 9th, and I arrived at Nyarumana; I stayed there for one night, and then at 11th I arrived at Rulenge, Tanzania.

S.T.: Did you leave alone?

SHADRACK: I was with other students. We were more than fifty people. We went together … At that time in that region there was a kind of peace. So that's why we had that chance to cross the border without trouble.

Shadrack was keen to relate dates, routes and places while leaving out personal emotions and detailed narratives of violence, suffering and atrocities. Neither did he mention the fact that many Hutu were involved in the killings of 1993. This was not mentioned for obvious reasons, as he was making the Tutsi soldiers the villains and the Hutu the victims. This means that he had to remain at an aggregate level in his narrative, otherwise he might have to tell about Hutu looting and burning Tutsi homes. His narrative is the victim narrative. In order to make sense of why he was in a refugee camp it was important that he was the victim of brutal violence.

He explained that there was no 'special problem' in his village – and added with a sarcastic smile that it was not a special problem because it was normal for there to be problems. However, his village appeared to have been relatively peaceful throughout the period and his mother still lived there. He could not return though, he explained, because he was a young man. People there assumed that he was dead, and he would like it to remain that way, as it saved him a lot of trouble.

Pierre

Twenty-four-year old Pierre was unmarried and lived with friends. He had no education, no employment and no business activities, and he lived in the dreaded area of Village F2, Lukole B. I had met him a few times when I had held group interviews in F2, where he had been keen to discuss the political situation in Burundi with me, particularly the split in the Palipehutu leadership between Karatasi and Kabura, despite insisting that he knew nothing about politics. The fact that I had personally talked to Karatase appeared to impress him. This time, however, he had agreed to talk about his own life. To bolster his confidence he had brought his brother-in-law along with him to the bar where the interview took place.

Pierre's parents fled Burundi in 1972 and, like many young refugees in Lukole, he was born and brought up in Rwanda.[2] His experience of Hutu–Tutsi relations was therefore quite different from Shadrack's. However, Pierre's narrative was cast along much the same storyline, as he also talked of a past where Hutu and Tutsi lived together in peace and harmony. This harmony was broken when the Rwandan Patriotic Front (RPF) *inkontanyi* ('tough fighters') started their offensive in 1990.[3]

> Before, when I was in Rwanda, when I was very little, there was no problem between Hutu and Tutsi ... The problem started – became open – when there were fights between the army, the Rwandan army, and the *inkontanyi*, the RPF. Because everyone was taught about Hutu and Tutsi ... Even in Hutu group there were some teachers who were teaching Hutu. And also Tutsi, there were also teachers who were teaching Tutsi ... The *inkontanyi* – the RPF – were hidden in villages by Tutsi who were already there.

Not only did the invasion by the RPF in the north of the country change ethnic relationships; it exposed the 'true' nature of the Tutsi, according to Pierre's narrative. Their Tutsi neighbours, with whom they had so far had cordial and unproblematic relations, were potentially hiding *inkontanyi* in their houses. As Chrétien et al. (1995) show, propaganda in the Rwandan media conjured up this image, of all Tutsi potentially hiding or otherwise supporting the RPF, and encouraged all good Hutu to take necessary steps to prevent the Tutsi from supporting the rebels.

Like Shadrack, Pierre believed the harmony of the past to have been only surface deep. Under the surface the Tutsi had other plans, and it was only at a certain point in history that this 'became open' and the Tutsi showed their true colours. The fact that Pierre's parents had fled Burundi due to ethnic conflict in 1972 and Shadrack's father had almost been killed in 1972 did not alter this narrative of a childhood of ethnic harmony and blindness. The issue of a before and an after often turned up in other discussions with Pierre. When discussing marriage – he was not yet married for fear of being repatriated – we touched on the issue of inter-ethnic marriage. Like everyone else in the camp, he claimed that it was only the Hutu who marry Tutsi women. But this had changed, he claimed; after the assassination of Ndadaye, Hutu no longer married Tutsi. In other words, the Hutu were becoming like the Tutsi due to a specific event that opened their eyes and put an end to their trust.

Pierre's family decided to repatriate to Burundi in 1993 when Ndadaye was elected. In spite of not living in camps in Rwanda and having what he called a good relation with Rwandans, they repatriated to Burundi because, he explained, 'When you are abroad, you don't have all your rights'. They wanted to go back and build their nation as they thought all killings had stopped with the election of a new president. Like other repatriates, they were given a small plot of land. However, when Ndadaye was killed, his family was not slow to decide to leave again. They heard the news that Ndadaye had been caught by Tutsi officers at 10 o'clock, and by 5 o'clock the same day they had left for Rwanda again.

> S.T.: So what happened after Ndadaye was killed in your village?
> PIERRE: When Ndadaye was killed, everybody was threatened. And also I was afraid. We didn't have time to stay and look at what was happening in Kirundo Province or Busoni commune. Because we were used to living abroad, we didn't wait. We just went to look for refuge in Rwanda …
> Because we thought that maybe it may happen what happened in '72.

Pierre did not actually see any violence. He heard the news on the radio, and with the memories from 1972 he fled. Lemarchand argues that the memories of ethnocide in 1972 were strong dynamics in later events in Burundi. Thus a small provocation in Ntega and Marangara in 1988 promptly triggered massive ethnic violence. Likewise it was within hours of Ndadaye's abduction that Hutu put up roadblocks and started killing Tutsi (Lemarchand 1996b). Pierre gave the reason for fleeing so promptly himself: 'We were used to living abroad'. In a number of essays written for me by secondary school students on their experiences of flight, they often gave detailed accounts of their hesitations about going abroad.[4] They had heard rumours that you could not get any food or water in Tanzania and that the camps were full of wild animals. Furthermore, they were insecure about the route and often had to hire a guide to help them cross the border. In other words, choosing whether to stay or go was not solely determined by the insecurity that they sensed in Burundi, but also by their uncertainty about their destination. In contrast, Pierre and his family knew exactly what to expect in exile and had no reservations about leaving.

In May 1994, Pierre and his family left Rwanda and went to Burundi. He gave no details on the circumstances surrounding their choice to leave Rwanda, though 'the war' in Rwanda was implied. While his family remained in Burundi, he decided to continue on to Tanzania. Why did he leave when his family could remain?

> The Burundi government, when they saw someone from foreign country, they pretend that one is a killer. And when he is a young boy or an educated one, or a rich one he is caught … And myself, I was among these people, and I was afraid, and I decided to flee the country.

I would often hear these explanations in the camp. The army was targeting young men because they were potential rebels. The educated and wealthy were allegedly targeted because they were suspected of planning what the Tutsi call the genocide against Tutsi after Ndadaye's killing. And anyone who had been a refugee was suspected of being a *génocidaire*, especially if they had been in Rwanda during the 1994 genocide, as Pierre had. It is certainly quite plausible that the government army targeted these groups in its increasingly desperate counter-insurgency operations.[5] However, for Pierre, these categories and general theories about who was targeted when and where were a means to make sense of a diffuse sense of insecurity. Anxiety about violence was interpreted and ordered through the perception that young men were being targeted. In his case, it meant leaving Burundi while his family remained.

Although the reason given by Pierre for his decision to leave Burundi while the family remained was the war, there may, however, have been a number of other factors influencing his decision, tied up with various livelihood strategies. Likewise, in 1993/4 many refugees chose to return to their farms at harvest time. I interviewed refugees who had lived in Tanzanian villages just across the border and had crossed the border daily to tend their fields in Burundi. However, with Pierre's narrative being a flight narrative, it must invoke the imagery of specifically targeted violence, in other words with a perpetrator, a purpose and a victim. By inserting himself into a master narrative in the victim role, he lent authority to his own – rather contingent – life story.

For Pierre the camp did not just mean loss. He emphasised that he had met many new friends, both while fleeing and in the camp. They were not family or old neighbours but you get to know each other well in the camp, he explained, and the hardship teaches you to cooperate. He reckoned that he was twice as intelligent as those who remained in Burundi. So his narrative of being the victim wass also a narrative of increased freedom and influence.

Jean

We met Jean, the leader of Village B3, in Chapter 5 where he explained about being a good leader in the camp. He was thirty-years old and had been married since 1991, and he had three children. He was originally from Gitaramuka commune in Karuzi province but had lived in Gitega and Bujumbura as well. In 1988 he was in the seventh year in secondary school when some things were stolen from the school. Three Tutsi and some Hutu – himself amongst them – were accused of theft and expelled from the school. However, the Tutsi students were readmitted shortly after. Had he been able to continue his studies, he would have liked to be a medical assistant. Instead, he tried his fortune working for various construction companies in Bujumbura. After some years, he quit his job and trained to get a driving licence. It is like a diploma, he explained, enabling him to seek employment as a driver. Unfortunately, Ndadaye was killed just when he had passed his test and was about to collect the documents. Everything was chaos and all the relevant offices were closed.

> When Ndadaye was killed, in Bujumbura everything has stopped. Such as some activities. And these people who were going to work in different areas, they didn't go. There were many soldiers and many policemen around Bujumbura, and in villages like in Gitega or Muyinga, or somewhere else, there were killings. And because of these killings, Bujumbura didn't get food from these areas, and we had a real hunger in Bujumbura. And when we saw that, we decided to leave the city.

This is the most concrete passage in his account of the situation. Most of his answers to questions about his flight were more general and vague.

> S.T.: When did you flee the country?
> JEAN: I fled in 1993 when Ndadaye was killed. Because I was in Bujumbura, there were troubles, we directly fled.
> S.T.: What happened in Bujumbura?
> JEAN: OK. In Bujumbura, when Ndadaye was killed, everything was worse. Because these putschists said that we don't want to see two staying together. More than two people, we catch them.

It does not appear from his narrative that he had been personally threatened. Neither did he give long and detailed accounts of Tutsi atrocities against Hutu, and certainly Hutu violence against Tutsi was not mentioned. The closest he got was that there were 'some killings' in the provinces around Bujumbura. These killings had no subject and no object and were referred to in the passive tense as if they had a life of their own. We do not know whether it was Hutu killing Tutsi or the army killing Hutu. All we know is that the effect was that there were food shortages in Bujumbura.

His personal experiences of the conflict were that he was not able to collect his driver's licence and a hike in food prices due to shortage. He also saw more police in the streets. This was woven into a large narrative on national insecurity and a city under siege due to fighting in the provinces. As opposed to the first two life stories, Jean did not openly claim that it was the Tutsi who carried out killings. He did, however, mention the 'putschists' banning public gatherings, making them partially responsible for the situation.

What is remarkable about his narrative and a number of other life stories I collected, is the fact that the killing of close relatives was not strongly emphasised. He mentioned that his brother died, in passing while discussing another issue, and I had to inquire directly about the details before he told me that the brother was a teacher and was killed in 1995. He thought it was the army in cooperation with the Tutsi who killed him, 'pretending he was a rebel'. That was all Jean had to say about it. Again, one is surprised by the lack of gory details about the evil acts of the Tutsi.

His narrative depicts quite precisely the sense of disruption, insecurity and invisible violence that resulted from the killing of the president and the failed coup attempt. After two months in this tense situation, he fled with a friend to Tanzania. They passed close by his home village and sent messages about their whereabouts. He was among the first to settle in Lukole camp.

His wife only came to the camp in August 1997 when she heard where her husband was and how to get across the border. Although he was already settled in Lukole A, they went to the registration site, Mbuba, and registered as new arrivals and were settled in one of the new villages in Lukole B. By the grin on Jean's and my interpreter's faces, I guessed that this was a way to get extra rations, so I avoided probing further into it.

When asked about relations with Tutsi students when he was a child, he answered:

> Before the killing of Ndadaye, there was no problem. There was somehow problem but it was not open. It was not clear. It was for those who were clever, who were dealing with the Tutsi and these problems. But we couldn't notice that. We were children. But after Ndadaye the problem was open … When I was at primary school I didn't recognise if it's a Hutu or a Tutsi. I couldn't. But when I went in seventh form, I could.

As in the other narratives, we see 'the problem' lying latently under the surface. The problem only became 'open' in 1993 but it had been visible to the 'clever' Hutu before then. The more naive the Hutu – the less education they had – the more blind they were to the problem. How was it, then, that they became aware of the ethnic groups?

JEAN: We noticed because [at the boarding school] the Tutsi didn't want to share food with the Hutu. They didn't want to share the same plate in the school … When they are sharing a bottle of beer, Tutsi didn't want to share with a Hutu.
S.T.: But the Hutu don't mind sharing beer with a Tutsi
JEAN: No. There is no problem for a Hutu to share with a Tutsi.

The last comment is quite remarkable and quite characteristic of the way people in Lukole perceived the relationship between Hutu and Tutsi. 'We love them, but they kill us', people would say. This perception was also evident in their attitude towards mixed marriages where apparently, it is common for a Hutu man to marry a Tutsi woman while the opposite is virtually impossible.[6] In other words, the Hutu were not interested in 'othering' or excluding at all, they had it imposed on them by the Tutsi who were 'extremists' and racists. The effect of this position was, paradoxically, that the 'other' became far more demonised and the process of 'othering' far more effective by putting the blame for ethnic antagonisms onto the 'other' and taking the victimised position as tolerant and non-exclusive.

In the life stories, the ethnic problem became 'open' either in relation to a specific date or in relation to the Hutu's increased awareness, and could either be an individual process, like entering secondary school or reading books about 1972, or it could be related to collective awareness. Jean claimed that the problems started with the introduction of democracy.

Before Ndadaye government, Ndadaye propaganda, everything was all right. Hutu couldn't recognise that Tutsi were dealing with bad things. And they shared everything.

There is an ambivalent relation to awareness in this quote. On the one hand 'everything was alright' and 'they shared everything', when they were not yet aware; it was the fact that Ndadaye told them about their oppression that made everything worse. On the other hand, Jean explained that the Tutsi were also bad before, only secretly.

But myself, I was in school when Hutu began to be aware of Burundi conflict. And when we went to secondary school, the head teacher was a Tutsi one. And when they want to give mattresses they took the good ones and gave to Tutsi. But secretly. And bad ones they gave to the Hutu. Before Ndadaye propaganda, before Ndadaye government, Tutsi were bad, but they had to do that secretly. Now it is open.

This quote shows how Jean interpreted local events, like the distribution of soft and hard mattresses, in relation to broader narratives about the Tutsi acting secretly and the democratic reforms opening the eyes of the Hutu. In some aspects, it was almost preferable when the Tutsi were openly bad rather than operating secretly. In that way, the Hutu could discover who they really were and wake up from their naive trust in the Tutsi.

> Hutu started to be aware when there were massacres in Ntega and Marangara [in 1988] because Tutsi showed that badness to the Hutu. And every Hutu who was around, was aware of that problem. And those Hutu tried to tell other Hutu who were in other provinces what Tutsi are doing to them. And Hutu began to be aware.

Ntega and Marangara in 1988, the massacres in 1972, the killings in 1991 and Ndadaye's abduction and murder in 1993 were all seen as watershed events that helped open the Hutu's eyes. However painful it had been, it was also perceived as a necessary process to reveal the Tutsi's secret plans, open the Hutu's eyes and hopefully the eyes of the international community too.[7] It was a step in the process of Hutu emancipation. Although the educated were the first to be killed by the army, Jean wanted his children to have an education because only the educated could help solve Burundi's problems. It is, in other words, necessary for the Hutu to become ever more aware.

Steven

Steven's narrative is interesting because it is probably the most analytical and reflective. He had an ability not only to reproduce master narratives, but to skilfully relate his own personal life path to broader national politics. We met Steven, chief security guard in Lukole A, in Chapter 5. He was born in Tanzania and went to stay in Burundi as a child. He was in his final year at secondary school when Ndadaye was killed.

> S.T.: And when Ndadaye was killed, what happened at your school then? You were staying at the school at this time?
> STEVEN: No, we fled. We fled immediately when he was killed. Because when he was killed, the population reacted, and how? The population reacted by killing the Tutsi. They said 'Our president is killed by you. So that is why we will make a revenge on you'. So they started to kill the Tutsi in the different regions. To prevent them[selves] from being killed as it happened in 1972.

Steven was one of the very few people I met in Lukole to mention Hutu killing Tutsi. He explained that it was due to fear that 1972 might be repeated. He was keen to emphasise that it was the uneducated and illiterate people who did this killing and that their reaction was spontaneous.

S.T.: And were they organised in any way?

STEVEN: No, it was a spontaneous reaction. Spontaneous. Because they experienced what happened in the past for Burundi. They have seen by their own eyes. They have witnessed what happened in Burundi. So it was a spontaneous reaction. Even the government is saying that they are being mobilised by Hutu intelligentsia. But it is not true. The reaction has been spontaneous.

By the number of times the word 'spontaneous' is mentioned, it becomes apparent how important it was for Steven to emphasise this fact. He was well aware that the government had another reading of the event, namely that it was a genocide that was planned and orchestrated by the Frodebu elite, and he was anxious to dismiss these accusations. Steven expressed the educated CNDD elite's version of the events. His narrative was thus neither built merely on his own impressions and personal experiences of the conflict, nor on fragmented master narratives based on rumours and native theories as the other life stories above to a large degree were, but in direct dialogue with, and in opposition to, other political discourses.

As opposed to most refugees in Lukole, Steven's narrative did not deny or ignore the fact that Hutu also killed Tutsi. Rather, it took issue with the nature of the killings. A central issue in the political field in Burundi has been to define whether the Hutu committed genocide in the days that followed 21 October 1993 or whether they reacted spontaneously and in anticipation of 1972 repeating itself. If it were genocide, then the army was in its full right to clamp down strongly on all Frodebu leaders, such as governors and mayors. Furthermore, the Hutu opposition could be dismissed as *génocidaires* and denied any right to participate in the political field. If, on the other hand, it was a spontaneous reaction by an uneducated and intimidated population, the Hutu leadership was exempted from responsibility and it was the Tutsi army that carried the responsibility for reacting too harshly and for making the Hutu population fearful in the first place (through the 1972 massacres).

In this way, Steven reproduced the victim narrative. In the mythico-histories that Malkki (1995a) encountered in Mishamo there was blood and gory details about the killings, but that was because the Hutu had not been involved. In this way the narratives strengthened the picture of the Hutu as innocent victims of the violence of the cruel Tutsi. However, with the violence in 1993 (and 1988), the Hutu lost their innocence. It was not an issue whether Shadrack, Pierre, Jean or Steven took part in the violence or not. What was at issue was the collective Hutu narrative. This narrative was imposed on them from outside and made tangible by my presence in the camp and my questions about the past. The violence in 1993, and in particular the genocide in Rwanda in 1994, had made all Hutu potential *génocidaires* in the eyes of the international community. It was this image that the refugees had to fight, and this was done either, as Steven did, by emphasising the difference between Rwanda and Burundi and by emphasising the spontaneous character of Hutu violence in Burundi, or, as the other interviewees did, by downplaying Hutu violence and avoiding details.

At Steven's school the army came to protect them but some of the students drew parallels to 1972 and decided to leave: 'They said they came to protect us, but we thought they would kill us. Even in 1972 they said they came to protect the schools. But it was to kill Hutu'. In their memory, 1972 loomed large, and present events were interpreted according to this pattern. The fact that educated Hutu, including secondary school students, were said to be the main target in 1972, further emphasised their fears at the secondary school. Steven fled to Rwanda with roughly eighty fellow students. Others remained at the school and it later turned out that they were not persecuted and merely continued their studies.

After four weeks in Rwanda, Steven went to Tanzania and stayed with his mother who lives near the border with Burundi. However, his father sent a younger brother to fetch him back to Burundi. The brother told him that it was peaceful, some Tutsi were displaced and the schools were guarded by soldiers. When Steven returned to Burundi, he dared not return to school and instead stayed with his father. When the presidents of Rwanda and Burundi were shot down in a plane over Kigali on 6 April 1994, triggering the genocide in Rwanda, he was still in his village.

> I was in my village. And I fled once again when the Tutsi militia came and burned the trading centre in which I was. They came and burned. They burned many of the kiosks, and they looted many goods from Hutu. And then they killed some of the people who were living there.

This account was common in the narratives that I heard in Lukole. I heard many times how Tutsi would come with machetes and petroleum, usually escorted by the army, and burn, kill and loot trading centres. This was when Steven decided to flee again. He left on his own and his father followed a few weeks later, while his father's wife remained in Burundi.

I asked Steven why some people decided to leave the country while others stayed put. I expressed surprise that anyone should wish to stay in a place like that. He explained that it had to do with education because only the educated could see that the Hutu were being persecuted. As with the other narratives, Steven operated with an idea of the problem being hidden versus open. He claimed that there was inequality in precolonial times but it was worsened by the Belgians who said that Hutu were not as intelligent as Tutsi. Also education during the colonial period made the Hutu gradually aware.

Little by little they gained some conscience and they became aware of that discrimination which has been taking place for a long time … when they became aware of the oppression, they tried to fight.

It was with education that they became aware of their oppression, and that was when the problems began. They were taught at school that there were no differences between Hutu and Tutsi. However, 'in 1988, with the massacres of Ntega and Marangara … they were compelled to talk about Tutsi and Hutu'. Here we see how swiftly Steven was able to link his school experience to political events at the national level. Similarly, when talking about his grandfather's cattle, he switched into a general description of *ubugabire* in Burundi. And when discussing why he attended a seminary school, he explained that the government had downscaled secondary schooling in regions that were predominantly Hutu, like Muyinga where he lived. Therefore, the Church had tried to compensate by running more schools in these areas. He then went on to say that he believed that that was the main reason behind the former president, Bagaza's, hostility towards the church. Bagaza was infuriated to see that Hutu were still attending university, in spite of there being no secondary schools in the Hutu-dominated regions. This is to say that when I inquired about his own life and schooling experience, he managed to relate it to broader issues.

Steven was very politically active at school and had been receiving clandestine propaganda material from Palipehutu from as far back as 1988, but with the legalisation of Frodebu, 'which is recognised even by the international community', all the moderate Palipehutu members shifted. Only the radicals remained in Palipehutu, he explained.

Politics was for him connected with awareness and education. It was almost a duty for an educated person to involve themselves in politics and take responsibility for the future of their nation. These were the ideas he brought with him to the camp: it was his duty – and everyone else's – to try to study as much as possible, and for those who have studied to help develop the country in the future. If he so wished, he could easily stay in Tanzania due to his mother being Tanzanian and his language skills in English and Swahili, but he preferred to remain a real refugee in the camp, not putting down roots in Tanzanian soil.

Master Narratives and Political Ideologies

In order to fully grasp the production of narratives in life stories in Lukole, we must explore how they were linked to available political ideologies that provided interpretive frameworks and linked to the political field in Burundi. For the refugees in Mishamo who fled the massacres in 1972, the master narratives at hand did not only bring ontological security to the refugees whose symbolic order had broken down, they were also attempts at fundamentally subverting the official government discourse on ethnicity and history in Burundi. By recasting the Hamitic thesis in new terms, Palipehutu was able to claim that the Hutu had privileged rights to Burundian soil due to autochthony. In other words, their position in the political field in Burundi in the 1970s and 1980s was reflected in the way that refugees talked about the conflict.

In Mishamo, Malkki found detailed narratives on Tutsi atrocities, spelling out in great detail how pregnant women were disembowelled and forced to eat part of the foetus, how penises and breasts were cut off the victims and bamboo sticks were inserted into the vagina or anus to the brain (Malkki 1995a: 87–95). These macabre narratives were not the result of individual refugees relating their own traumatic experiences, but standardised narratives, told in the impersonal tense at any given opportunity.

The detailed, gory narratives of violence in Mishamo confirm a belief in Tutsi evil, and indicate Palipehutu's hegemonic position in sanctioning and providing truths in that camp. I did not come across mythico-histories to the degree that Malkki did, and the standardised narratives that I did encounter differed in a number of ways from the ones that she encountered in Mishamo. One explanation could be that Palipehutu did not hold such a position in Lukole, and neither was CNDD hegemonic, though it was more powerful than Palipehutu. This means that there were not the same ready-made answers for the refugees when searching for explanations as to what went wrong. Steven's explanation of Hutu spontaneously killing Tutsi is the closest we get to official CNDD discourse concerning the events in late 1993. And although Shadrack and Pierre tended to blame the Tutsi more than Jean and Steven did, it is still far from the mythico-histories that Malkki found in Mishamo.

As I showed in Chapter 2, the political field in Burundi changed dramatically in the early 1990s. While the political taboo on ethnicity was removed, Hutu opposition had to reorient its oppositional discourse, rendering Palipehutu's ethnicist ideology anachronistic. It was no longer enough to claim that Hutu and Tutsi were indeed different races, and the conflict age-old which meant that ethnicity lost a lot of its power as an explanatory factor of the conflict in Burundi. This shift in the political field in Burundi and in the political discourse of the Hutu opposition in the 1990s had consequences for the narratives in Lukole. While ideology had to relate to the problems of the refugees and to their memories, it was primarily shaped in relation to other ideologies. Thus, although Pierre's experience of war and his Tutsi neighbours may have been similar to his father's experience twenty-one years earlier in 1972, there were very different interpretative schemes available related to the prevalent political ideologies through which they could make sense of these events.

While the mythico-histories of the 1972 refugees positioned the Tutsi as 'radical other', the life stories from Lukole expressed an ambivalent relation to the Tutsi. Probably, the concept of 'us' liking the Tutsi but them not liking us, illustrates best the perception in the camp. Here, the self was presented as essentially multiethnic and tolerant while was is the 'other' who tried to undermine ethnic cohabitation and harmony.[8]

As we saw in the previous chapter, Frodebu/CNDD was keen to present itself as modern, rational, educated and moderate in opposition to Palipehutu, which played the authentic, populist note. Apart from being a local struggle in the camp, this related to larger political issues and also influenced narratives on ethnicity and conflict.

It was imperative for CNDD members in the camp to achieve recognition from the international community and they were well aware that the international community had put the searchlight on Hutu *génocidaires* – for instance, in the shape of the international tribunal in Arusha. Therefore, it was important for any Hutu who wanted to be taken seriously, to distance themselves from all kinds of Hutu 'extremism' that might link them with the *génocidaires* of Rwanda. This was complicated by the fact that many Hutu did take part in the killing of tens of thousands of Tutsi civilians in the days after President Ndadaye's assassination, something that many Tutsi were quick to use as a reason for excluding Hutu from power. Any essentialistic categorisation of Tutsi in public discourse or reference to a Hutu nation would imply associations with Hutu power in Rwanda in the early 1990s, thereby jeopardising any attempt to be taken seriously by the international community. Therefore, we find this vague definition of ethnicity in the life stories – on the one hand rejecting it while on the other clearly blaming the Tutsi for ethnic conflict. Hutu involvement in killings in 1993 also lead to a general avoidance in the narratives of too many explicit details about violence, which was merely referred to as 'the war' or 'the problems'.

Palipehutu and the refugees in Mishamo envisaged a Hutu nation as the solution to all their suffering. In their view Burundi was truly a Hutu nation that had been conquered by Tutsi, thus disturbing the authentic relation between people and national territory. This 'blood and soil' ideology was not so obvious in Lukole. Here, the solution that most refugees would mention was democracy. If only Burundi could return to the democracy that it experienced so briefly in 1993 then peace and harmony would reign. In this ideological construction the 'true Burundi nation' is the democratic nation where one ethnic group does not get to oppress the other because the people's voice is heard. This true character of the Burundi nation had been blocked by the Tutsi elite which had hijacked the state and prevented it from taking its place among the democratic, civilised nations, according to CNDD discourse. The refugees would emphasise the political rather than ethnic nature of the conflict, thereby projecting ethnicist manipulation onto a cynical Tutsi political elite.

The fact that political ideologies influence narratives of the past does not imply that all members of Palipehutu in Lukole told detailed narratives of violence and atrocities while all CNDD supporters avoided it. Rather, the general shift in the political field had made it less relevant to relate narratives of Tutsi atrocities. Thus even Palipehutu supporters such as Shadrack and Pierre avoided talking about violence. Conversely, CNDD supporters in Lukole would have an ambivalent relation to these narratives, at times falling into narratives about the evil doings of the Tutsi.

To sum up, life stories in Lukole were rather vague on the nature of the conflict, avoiding the bloody details, and they showed no obsession with ancient history. This may in part be due to the fact that political ideologies were not yet as strongly sedimented in the camp as they were in Mishamo in the mid 1980s, as the two main political parties continued to contest each other's credibility; in other words there was not one, politically sanctioned, truth that the refugees were fed with. Furthermore, the ideology of the dominant party in the camp – CNDD – was itself fragmented and contradictory when it came to explaining ethnicity and the historical causes of the conflict due to the changes in the political field in the early 1990s. Finally, the memories of Hutu being involved in the killings in 1993 and an awareness that international opinion was sceptical towards the Hutu after the genocide in Rwanda, divested them of a pure victim position and forced them to avoid anything that slightly resembled Hutu nationalism.

From Hidden to Open

In the political field in Burundi it is imperative for all factions to define when the conflict began. This is what Lemarchand terms the metaconflict (Lemarchand 1996a), giving history an important role. Dating back to the Hamitic thesis and the academic and political contestations over the true nature of the conflict, it is vital for all parties to the conflict to assert whether Hutu and Tutsi are ethnic categories and the Tutsi have always oppressed the Hutu on the one hand, or whether they are merely a figment of the German and Belgian colonial imaginations which split an essentially homogeneous and united people on the other.

In the camp, I saw similar disputes as to when the conflict started in Burundi. Apparently it was an indicator of political orientation, with CNDD pinpointing the start in the 1960s and Palipehutu in the precolonial period. I therefore chose to ask respondents in my survey when they believed that the problems between Hutu and Tutsi started.[9] I hoped in this way to be able to establish the most commonly held understandings of the past in the camp. A majority of the refugees in Lukole believed the problem to be recent. My survey revealed 268 respondents believed that it occurred after independence, while 19 claimed that it started during the colonial period. This indicates that a Palipehutu version of history was not dominant in Lukole, although the number of respondents who believed the conflict to be age-old was not negligible either (119 claimed that it had started before colonial times). However, the problem with a question like this – especially in a questionnaire where it is not possible for the respondent to elaborate – is that people did not have a fixed idea of when the problem started. The question therefore made no sense to them.

This came out in the life-story interviews where it was less a question of when the problems started and more a question of the problems becoming 'open'. Here, we see, firstly, that the problem was there all the time but became open at a certain point in time. Thus the respondents may at times believe to be answering 'how long has the problem existed' and at times be answering 'when did the problem become open'. Secondly, the same individual could give several dates and criteria for when the problem became open. The same person may at times refer to the concrete event that triggered their flight – Ndadaye's assassination – and later talk about becoming 'aware' at secondary school, or that the problem became open in 1972. So, rather than asking refugees when the problems started, it would make more sense to ask when the problems became open – and even then, each respondent would have multiple answers. This illustrates how most flight narratives depict the conflict as latent, under a harmonious surface, only breaking out at certain points in time.

It is apparent from the life story interviews that the perception of things becoming open was pervasive and that this was linked to certain dates and events, either at national level or in the individual's life path. Usually, they would say that they had no problems with the Tutsi when they were children – they did not even know how to tell a Tutsi from a Hutu. This changed either when the Hutu became more aware, due to school education or due to democratic reforms and 'Ndadaye's propaganda', or when the Tutsi went too far and showed their 'true colours' by openly killing Hutu.

There are two aspects to this that will be dealt with here. One concerns the need to explain how Tutsi individuals with whom one had previously had no problems could become part of an ethnic 'other', and how ethnic harmony could be replaced by hatred and violence. The other aspect concerns the idea that awareness was painful but necessary.

The Tutsi's secret identity

When asked to explain why they fled – or even when asked to describe their lives – the young men I interviewed tried to reconcile their experienced memories of the Tutsi with grand narratives of conflict and flight. How did they reconcile the fact that most Tutsi behaved and looked like Hutu with the fact that they had ended up in a refugee camp due to large-scale ethnic conflict? With the construction of a before and an after, they were able to reconcile the two facts. Before, the Tutsi were like the Tutsi of our memories. After, they were what political ideology tells us – the ethnic 'other'.

In a study of Bosnian Muslim refugees in Denmark, Anders Stefansson (1997) observes a similar construction of the past. The Muslim Bosnians alluded to a harmonious, rich life in Yugoslavia and emphasised their friendly relations with Serbs and Croats. However, there was an ambivalent relation to this idealised past. For while, on the one hand, ethnic harmony was emphasised, on the other, 'the past was meticulously investigated for "traces" which seemed to lead to the outbreak of violence' (ibid.: 5). Every little sign that could reveal that the Serbs had behaved as if they had secret plans, was scrutinised and analysed retrospectively to prove that their friendship was only superficial – a disguise that the naive Muslims at the time believed was true friendship.

The similarities with Lukole are striking. But while Stefansson concludes that the Bosnian refugees were gradually building an essentialist ethnic identity, claiming ancient ethnic roots, the interesting point for me – in both the narratives of Bosnians in Denmark and the Burundians in Lukole – is the insistence not on age-old antagonisms, but on ethnic harmony in the past. In part, as mentioned earlier, this has to do with the fact that they had experiential memories – that is, their individual memories from their life path – of relatively peaceful relations with neighbours of the other ethnic groups. However, young men born in Burundi the 1960s and 1970s would emphasise this harmony among ethnic groups during their childhood, in spite of the large-scale massacres of Hutu that took place in 1972. This indicates that the picture of ethnic harmony was perhaps not merely a historical fact, born from concrete memories but rather a discursive construct. It certainly appears to be something that was emphasised rather than pushed aside in their narratives. Refugees from Mishamo, on the other hand, who had not experienced wide scale ethnic violence prior to 1972, were keen to emphasise the deep roots of the conflict rather than ethnic harmony (see Malkki 1995a).

One might propose that this discourse of a harmonious past was connected to a self-perception as tolerant, multicultural and non-essentialist, while the Tutsi disliked the Hutu and started all the problems. In this way, the Tutsi were to blame for the horrific events of 1993, while the Hutu were merely the victims of this process. The Tutsi had secret plans all along, and their friendship was phoney. Tutsi children were taught about the differences, while the Hutu children remained naively blind to the truth.

While we may see ethnicity as a construct – as is now common practice in academia – the Hutu refugees, on the other hand, saw non-ethnic national unity as a construct that was hiding a deeper 'reality', the reality of ethnicity.[10] When they became aware of the 'reality', there was a strong sense of having been deceived and betrayed by the Tutsi who 'knew' about this all these years while pretending to be people's friends. In this manner, the real Tutsi was the stereotypical 'other', while the false one was the one pretending to be your friendly neighbour.

The concept of deception is central in a forceful article by Appadurai on the brutality of ethnic violence in the era of globalisation (Appadurai 1999). Appadurai argues that the body of the ethnic 'other' can be deceptive. Thus Tutsi do not always have long noses and Hutu do not always have thick shins: 'In a word, real bodies in history betray the cosmologies that they are meant to encode. So the ethnic body, both of the victim and the killer, is itself potentially deceptive' (ibid.: 311). In other words, the Tutsi schoolmate who appeared to be just another little boy from the village (perhaps even with a flat nose) was deceiving you by hiding his true identity. It is the sense of betrayal and uncertainty about the other that pushes people to commit horrific acts of what Appadurai terms 'vivisectionist violence' against neighbours and old friends. One tries to stabilise the body of the ethnic 'other' through these macabre acts of unmasking the specific body in order to find the true ethnic body of the generic 'other'. Appadurai is, in other words, arguing how individuals come to terms with the incongruence between individual experiences of the specific members of the 'other' ethnic group and larger ideological constructs about the true nature of the 'other' – hence his remarks elsewhere about the 'ethnic implosion' (Appadurai 1996). Ethnic conflict does not come from within or below, but from above. And when it is linked to and played out at the local level, ethnic violence gets cruel.

Whereas Appadurai's point is to show how ethnic violence between neighbours occurs, this chapter has explored how refugees who had experienced such ethnic violence gave narrative form to it. It is obvious from the life stories that the issues of betrayal and uncertainty about the ethnic 'other' were strong elements in these narratives. This uncertainty only left them – according to the narratives – when the Tutsi showed their true intentions by killing tens of thousands of Hutu and their beloved President Ndadaye.

The painful process of revealing secrets

The other issue that comes forth in these narratives of 'before and after' concerns the way openness was seen on the one hand to be painful, while on the other hand being a necessary step on the Hutu's road to emancipation and self-realisation.

The narratives give the impression that things were agreeable before the problems became open, when there was peace, and they got along with their Tutsi neighbours. There were, however, ambivalent feelings about this time 'before' because the Hutu were also 'blind' then, and harmony was just an illusion. If the Hutu had remained blind, the Tutsi would have been able to continue with their secret plans. Therefore, becoming aware may have made things worse but it was also necessary in order to reveal the Tutsi for what they were.

These narratives relate to ethnic stereotypes, where the Hutu are portrayed as naive and honest and the Tutsi as cunning and secretive. However, the stereotypes are not fixed, as it is possible for a Hutu to become less shy and less naive through education or acculturation, while it is also possible to reveal Tutsi secrets. These secrets are empty – they conceal the fact that Tutsi are not inherently more intelligent than Hutu. As long as the Tutsi keep their secrets and conceal this fact, they can maintain the illusion that they have privileged access to the secrets of power.[11]

Becoming aware through education or through political awakening changes the Hutu by giving them knowledge and enhancing their ability to reveal Tutsi secrets. Gérard realised that the Tutsi had a secret plan when he was at school and he discovered the system of marking Hutu exam papers with a 'U' and Tutsi's with an 'I', making sure that the Tutsi got the best marks.

> You see, to succeed in national examination it was difficult when you were a Hutu. Because there was a sort of selection, when they were giving marks of that examination … They have a system to use a U and I. When you were at primary school, your teacher was a Tutsi, and he has a system to mark I and U in front of your names. And when they were collecting, they were giving marks to the examinations, they have to check if you are I or if you are U. And the I one, even if he had failed, he had chance to have marks.

This theme of using I and U on examinations was repeated countless times in the camp. It epitomised the idea that the Tutsi officially did not discriminate, while unofficially they had an intricate system to keep Hutu out of higher education – something that in itself would reveal their secrets. By using the I/U system, the Tutsi could make the Hutu believe that the Tutsi children were inherently better at school (provided, of course, that the Hutu did not discover the I/U system). Thus they were concealing the fact that the Tutsi were not more intelligent. However, the actual act of hiding – the whole set-up of the I/U system – was an instance of Tutsi intelligence. A real Hutu would never think up such a plan. It is as if there were two kinds of intelligence that the refugees operated with: true intelligence like mathematics, biology and so on, and the false intelligence of scheming and deception. Interestingly, these were bound up with Hutu and Tutsi subjects at university. The Hutu were traditionally allowed to study natural sciences while political science, law and economics were allegedly reserved for Tutsi. Malkki observed a similar distinction between benign and malign knowledge, among refugees in Mishamo who believed that the mission schools had brought benign knowledge to the Hutu. This knowledge was perceived as an avenue for Hutu equality and strongly contrasted to the malign, secret knowledge of the Tutsi that was used to keep the Hutu away from power (Malkki 1995a). Paradoxically, it was this – impure – knowledge that the Hutu strived for, since it was only through studying law and political science that they could wrench power from the Tutsi and reveal their secrets. In the process, the Hutu had to become more Tutsified in order to gain power.[12]

Whenever things become open – when the Tutsi secrets are threatened – the Tutsi become desperate and start killing Hutu indiscriminately. That is why some Hutu decided to take their children out of school and why quite a few people – especially among the less educated – would blame democracy for their misfortune. They were attempting to avoid Hutu awareness and trying to keep things 'closed' in order to prevent Tutsi wrath. The general feeling in the life stories, however, was that the wheels could not be turned back. Now that they had opened their eyes and seen Tutsi oppression, it was no good returning to the days when the Hutu lived at peace with the Tutsi, naively accepting their lot in society. Most people in Lukole wanted democracy back and most wanted themselves or their children to have an education. So, although they nostalgically longed for the harmony of the good old days, they were also aware that return was not possible once you had knowledge and once the Tutsi had (at least in part) revealed their true nature. Furthermore, the harmony was an illusion in the first place. The only thing the Hutu could do was continue what they started on continuing to gain more knowledge and more awareness and in order to reveal the Tutsi's secrets. Only then would a new kind of harmony reign.

Loss of innocence

Most refugees simply avoided going into too much detail about violence. We saw how this was connected to politics in the camp. However, their superficial narratives of violence also related to the fact that they were told to me – the outsider. And whereas the outsider in the 1980s, like Malkki, was presented with standard narratives on the cruelty of the Tutsi and the innocence of the Hutu, this narrative was difficult to maintain in 1997/8 because the refugees in Lukole knew very well that I was familiar with the genocide in Rwanda.

Therefore, just as their narrative was about becoming aware and opening their eyes, it was also about losing their innocence, as only the naive victim is innocent. As the Hutu liberated themselves of their naivety, they no longer let themselves be killed without resistance as they did in 1972. Many refugees emphasised this point directly, or they hinted that it had happened in 1988, 1991 and 1993 when the Hutu knew what to expect and therefore fought back. Hence, the Hutu had matured but they had also lost their innocence and their victim position. When they narrated their story to me, certain things were left untold, as the Hutu now had something to hide as well.

In other words, the life stories avoided gory details for several reasons. One was because the political situation in Burundi had changed in the 1990s, leaving the mythico-histories of Palipehutu obsolete and anachronistic, so that new master narratives avoided direct mention of the ethnic 'other'. But the vagueness of the life stories was also and more importantly due to a perceived loss of Hutu innocence. This loss was linked to a growing Hutu 'awareness' – either individually or collectively. And it was linked to the fact that Hutu had taken part in large scale violence – most notably in Rwanda but also significantly in Burundi since 1993. Ironically, the loss of innocence lead to a less essentialist and explicitly anti-Tutsi ideology. Being cast as the pure, innocent victims, gives the right to accuse the alleged perpetrator. Everyone agrees that the victim is right and the perpetrator is in the wrong and any action against the perpetrator is therefore justified. If, on the other hand, the victim position is not so obvious, one has to justify one's actions and prove one's innocence. This is the transformation that the Hutu had been through.

One way to reclaim the victim position in the camp was to present oneself as tolerant, multiethnic and democratic. In this manner, one could elegantly construct the Tutsi as the 'other' while claiming that 'they' were doing the othering, not 'we'. 'We love the Tutsi' people would say in the camp. The irony is that they constructed an 'other' by claiming that the Tutsi were the ones that were 'othering', while the Hutu were the innocent victims, the objects rather than the subjects. The 'other' in this case was not just the Tutsi 'who don't like the Hutu'. It was also the other Hutu, who were 'extremists': the Rwandan Hutu who organised the genocide and Palipehutu members in the camp. While this was the position of CNDD supporters, Palipehutu claimed the right to the victim position in slightly different ways. In part they were the victims of CNDD conspiracies and in part they had managed to defend Hutu purity, as opposed to the Tutsified CNDD. Ethnic purity was linked to the purity of the victim. Furthermore, Hutu-ness guaranteed a measure of innocence, as Hutus stereotypically are naive, honest and hospitable.

The life stories revealed a deep split in relation to loss of innocence, which on the one hand, gave the Hutu the chance to open their eyes, reveal Tutsi secrets and to progress, while on the other hand, this loss of innocence was dangerous. It had caused a lot of pain so far, they claimed, as intelligent Hutu had provoked the wrath of the Tutsi who feared their secrets would be uncovered. Furthermore, by striving for intelligence and power and by losing their innocence, they risked becoming Tutsified in the process.

In line with the discourse of international relief agencies, refugees are supposed to be innocent victims, stripped of political subjectivity. The life stories show, however, that the refugees were strongly imbued with political ideologies and closely tied up with the political field in Burundi. This does not, however, entail that the refugees rejected the concept of innocence or the victim position. On the contrary, the various narratives manoeuvred ambiguously in relation to the victim position – perceiving innocence as both a burden and a resource.

Notes

1. After Ndadaye was killed and the Hutu population started killing Tutsi, most Tutsi sought protection in town centres where they were installed in municipal buildings and protected by the army.
2. Very few refugees in Lukole had made a simple one-way movement from Burundi to the camp. They had moved around the whole region for a mixture of reasons. However, the image of the homeland still remained strong in their flight narrative.
3. The term inkontanyi is used about the Rwandan Patriotic Front.
4. In August 1997 I asked 20 eighth form students from Lukole Post Pimary School to write an essay on one of four subjects related to the camp. Thirteen of the students chose the following subject: 'Describe your personal experience of fleeing from Burundi and of living in a camp. What were your feelings when you were forced to leave? How has your life changed in the camp?'
5. For details on these operations, see Adekanye (1996).
6. In Burundi it is the man who marries while the woman gets married. In Swahili the verbs differ for men and women, one is the active verb 'to marry', the other is the passive 'to be married'. Ethnographies of Burundi confirm this picture: see Trouwborst (1962) and Albert (1963).
7. This was a recurrent theme in the discussions I had with people in Lukole. They could not understand why the international community or the 'big nations' did not intervene when it was so obvious that the Tutsi were oppressing the Hutu. They were not sure whether this was due to Tutsi covering up the truth or whether the big nations knew 'the truth' perfectly well but did not wish to help. See Turner (2004).
8. In a sense, this ideological construction is a mirror image of the government's construction of ethnicity in the 1970s and 1980s. The government insisted on being non-ethnic, and accused Hutu dissidents of inciting ethnic hatred.
9. Question 39 of the survey asked: 'When did the problems between Hutu and Tutsi start?'
10. No doubt the government's doublespeak – banning the use of ethnic labels and promoting 'one people, one nation' while at the same time favouring Tutsi Hima from the south in the administration – strengthened this image.

11. Interestingly, the Hutu were partly aware that the secrets concealed the fact that there were no secrets; the secrets concealed Tutsi impotence (see also Turner 2005b). Along a similar vein, Taussig argues in relation to public secrets that the secret is that there is no secret (Taussig 1999: 7).
12. For an elaboration on the power of concealment, see Turner (2005b).

8
Conclusion

I set out to explore how competing historical narratives and everyday politics combined in people's attempt to (re)create moral order in a world that was circumscribed by bureaucratic governmental action, a world where politics and history were relegated to the margins of society and the inhabitants were meant to act as innocent victims without a past. This world was at once extremely bureaucratic and tightly managed while simultaneously being full of rumours, myths, politics and historicity, as people inhabited the camp through everyday strategies.

If refugees are constructed by the international community as 'bare life' (Agamben 1998) because they are outside 'the national order of things' (Malkki 1995b), what we witnessed in Lukole were attempts by the refugees to recreate political subjectivity by anchoring themselves in history and politics and by creating new hierarchies. This involved a constant negotiation of meaning, power and being – creating competing truths and pockets of sovereignty beyond the sovereign power of the UNHCR.[1] In the exceptional space of the camp nothing was taken for granted and everything was up for negotiation, resulting in an excess of violence and rumours very different to the stabilized, hegemonic mythico-histories that Malkki (1995a) found in Mishamo a decade earlier. The attempts to void the camp of power and politics paradoxically created a space that was hyper-politicised.

Life outside the nation-state was full of uncertainties, giving rise to moral crises, but this amoral space also provided new liberties and opportunities. Central but hitherto overlooked actors in this game were the young men that relief agencies only concerned themselves with when they caused trouble and disturbed the 'community spirit' of the majority of innocent refugees through their political actions and personal assertiveness. These young men were cast by the UNHCR as potentially dangerous and as threatening to the image of refugees as victims. They played an important role in transforming the camp from an alienating space into a lived place that made sense to the refugees, as they seized this same opportunity to rid themselves – and the

Hutu as such – of their position as eternal victims by breaking with the stereotype of Hutu naivety and recapturing, or reinventing, the camp. This was an ambiguous ordeal: On the one hand, they asserted themselves as real men and as producers of their own history; in other words as political subjects. On the other hand, their political past haunted them in the camp; as potential *génocidaires* they would cling to notions of victimhood and innocence. The genocidal violence in Burundi – whether committed by Hutu or Tutsi –entailed a loss of Hutu innocence and blurred the boundaries between victim and perpetrator, between power and resistance, and between inclusion in and exclusion from the political community.

Humanitarian agencies attempt to manage refugees that tend to defy the hegemonic nation-citizen-territory constellation by producing them as apolitical victims that need helping in the name of humanity. Such victims are by definition innocent and without roots or a past. If they have a past it should remain there and not be brought into the present. Through governmental practices of everyday interventions in the physical and mental well-being of the refugees, the UNHCR attempted to create an 'empowered' community out of the refugees. Empowerment in the eyes of humanitarian relief agencies was an apolitical and ahistorical process of forming 'the community' and forcing party politics to the margins of the camp. Political activity was thus perceived by the camp authorities as introducing divisiveness and selfishness into 'the community'. Being political excludes the possibility of being a pure victim, and victims are the only refugees that the UNHCR can cater for. These governmental actions have the effect of gendering the refugees: women embody the helpless refugee victim and the self-sacrificing cornerstone of the community while men embody 'trouble' in the shape of political activity and rule-breaking.

With closer scrutiny we see that the governmental practices of the relief agencies had quite unintended consequences in the camp. Certainly they did not manage to purge the camp of politics or create refugees as pure victims without a past. Rather than becoming self-governing citizens of governmental practices, acting according to the categories that the humanitarian intervention had produced, the refugees interpreted the camp according to a narrative of social and moral decay. The symptoms of this decay were identified by the refugees as a lack of respect for men, the elders and the 'big men' by women, youths and 'small people'. There was an understanding that the camp was 'flattening' and homogenising the population and thereby destroying Burundian customs, which were conceived to be hierarchical but harmonious. The refugees were, in other words, interpreting their experience of flight and exile in line with a narrative of loss, in which the UNHCR's equal treatment of all refugees, the quasi-urban nature of the camp and cultural mixing with Tanzanians and Rwandans were seen to have disturbed Burundian culture.

However, the narrative of loss was ambiguous. On the one hand, the camp was a threat to the self-evident social order. On the other hand, these processes of alienation were perceived as painful but necessary steps in the progress of the Burundian Hutu. This relates to a recurrent theme in the camp: the narrative of the Hutu losing their pure Hutu-ness. As much as they cherished the virtues of the stereotypical Hutu who is honest and hardworking – stereotypes that date back to early colonial categories – some of the Hutu characteristics were also seen as anachronistic, keeping the Hutu in darkness and oppression. For the Hutu to succeed, according to this narrative, they had to become more assertive and less naive, just as the Hutu from Rwanda had. In other words they had to become more Tutsified if they were to manage against the Tutsi – and if they were to manage in the camp. The camp appeared to accelerate this process of becoming more aware. The hardships and challenges of camp life were perceived to strengthen the Hutu and prepare them for the challenges of the future. If they remained aligned with the ideals of yesteryear they would lose out, both in the camp and in Burundi.

Three groups had taken advantage of the possibilities that the camp opened up for them: the street leaders, the NGO employees and the entrepreneurs. In all three groups young men were strikingly present, becoming 'liminal experts' who were able to take advantage of the possibilities that the camp opened up, learning to play by new rules and outmanoeuvring the older generation. These young men had managed to free themselves from customary norms and had been able to shape their own destinies. They tried to rehabilitate the masculinity that they perceived to have lost to the UNHCR; showing strength and determination through taking the camp back from the UNHCR.

Breaking with past norms and conventions – challenging the virtues of Hutu 'shyness', honesty and naivety and becoming more assertive – characterised these young men and expressed a transformation in the camp. Did this then imply a break with the past, an exclusive orientation to the present? Ironically, this was far from the case. The past was evoked and brought into the camp – not as fixed mythico-histories but in a number of ways which reflected the unstable and unqualified character of Lukole. The past emerged in tales of decay about the harmonious past, the good old days. The past emerged in the political rivalry in the camp to define the true nature of the conflict in Burundi. And the past emerged as memories of conflict and violence.

No doubt this past was constructed in the camp as an answer to present preoccupations. But it did not merely 'emerge' out of thin air, and its discursive elements were not produced in isolation in the camp. The narratives that were constructed in the camp drew on a repertoire of images that were related to the political struggle in Burundi to define the 'truth'.

Such images or discourses had a past and were linked to broader political discourses. Thus when a refugee explained that the conflict was age-old and due to Tutsi invaders from the north, they were drawing on a repertoire of images of Burundi dating back to colonial racial theories on the origin of the interlacustrine kingdoms of Central Africa. This repertoire was linked to political projects that were determined to prove that their particular version of Burundi's past was the true one. Such projects involved more than historiographic disputes and were discursively linked to ideas such as socialism, anti-imperialism and democracy.

In Lukole rival political parties offered competing readings of the past and of the nature of the conflict in Burundi. On the one hand, Palipehutu presented the conflict as primordial and the Tutsi and Hutu as racial categories. CNDD, on the other hand, presented a more moderate and contradictory understanding and exhibited less of an obsession with the past. In Lukole, one would rarely be told about the somatic differences between Hutu and Tutsi, and the hope for the future was of a return to the democracy of 1993 rather than the liberation of the Hutu people. This shift in perception was due in part to the change in the political field in Burundi, where it was increasingly difficult to articulate an oppositional Hutu discourse within the terms of race and territory. Along with the shift in government discourse on ethnicity in the early 1990s, the Hutu opposition had to rearticulate its oppositional discourse around issues such as democracy and human rights.

While the political parties offered competing ideological frameworks that could explain to the refugees why they had ended up in the camp, these ideological frameworks were also important as structuring factors in the struggle to define and dominate the camp. Political rivalry was intermeshed with personal networks and patronage systems that secured access to power and resources. These struggles had the effect of turning the homogeneous, alien space of the camp into space that was differentiated, contested and hierarchical, consequently investing the different parts of the camp with meanings that the refugees could decode and relate to, however contested they might have been.

Because political activity was banned by the camp authorities it took on a clandestine and hence criminal nature. The effects were to split the camp into CNDD and Palipehutu territory through violence and rumours of violence. Operating underground, politics was at once dangerous and appealing. It was dangerous because it was illegal and associated with selfish, power-hungry individuals by the relief agencies; it was appealing because it offered an alternative to the bureaucratised space of the relief agencies. Politics transcended the camp: it pointed towards a broader horizon, beyond the food rations and women's committees of the UNHCR. Being involved in political activity offered not only an answer to the question 'Why am I here?' It also offered a solution to the problems of the future. A politician might have been breaking the law of the UNHCR but they were fighting for a much larger and nobler cause. This is the other side of politics. It is the side of politics that the UNHCR could not see and that the refugees only saw at times. From this perspective, politics is far from sordid or selfish. It is about self-sacrifice and finding a purpose in life.

But politics brought the past as well as the future into the camp. Although the young 'liminal experts' appeared to create themselves anew in the camp, rejecting old structures and hierarchies, they still related to the past in various ways. In life-story interviews individuals inserted their personal memories into larger narratives in order to lend them authority as coherent meaningful narratives rather than merely a string of contingent events. But as opposed to the gory, detailed accounts of Tutsi atrocities that were told by the Hutu who fled the 1972 massacres (see Malkki 1995a), these narratives were rather 'sterile', avoiding too many details of either Tutsi or Hutu violence. Certain aspects of the past were avoided and recounted in vague and general terms like 'then there was violence, and we fled our country'.

These perceptions related to the recurring narrative of Hutu loss of innocence. In this narrative there were harmonious relations between Hutu and Tutsi until a certain point in the individual's life path or in the collective past; this was the point when the Hutu became aware of the Tutsi's true nature. This would happen either because the Hutu had become sufficiently 'intelligent' and 'opened their eyes' or because the Tutsi had showed their true colours and started killing Hutu. This killing was in turn seen as a reaction to the newly awakened Hutu exposing Tutsi secrets. As the Hutu became more intelligent, they shed their Hutu naivety and no longer passively accepted their lot in society. This, I have argued, brought further loss of Hutu innocence, as Tutsi intelligence was seen as malign intelligence that corrupts the mind. Very concretely this innocence was lost when the Hutu – remembering how they had been killed without resistance in 1972 – started killing Tutsi in 1988, 1991 and 1993. Their involvement in these killings, together with their awareness of the genocide in Rwanda, meant that the Hutu could no longer claim a role as a pure victim, and therefore they avoided detailed descriptions of violence in their narratives. According to this narrative the Hutu had embarked on a one-way track with no way of turning back. Once the Hutu open their eyes, they cannot just close them and forget what they saw. Likewise the Tutsi cannot undo their deeds once they come out in the open – although they can attempt to hide them by killing all intelligent Hutu.

Palipehutu and CNDD drew on these issues of innocence and victimhood in slightly different ways. CNDD was attempting to downplay ethnicity and appear as democratic and reconciliatory. In this way, they tried to maintain the victim role in relation to violence, in particular when portraying their rivals as 'violent extremists'. Palipehutu on the other hand was more explicitly anti-Tutsi and ethnicist (although this was also modified in official language), while on the other hand it played on the fact that it represented true Hutu values and had therefore not eaten of the apple of wisdom as its rivals had. In this sense, Palipehutu had restrained itself from the temptations of malign Tutsi knowledge and thus remained pure and innocent.

First and foremost the camp was not an island unto itself. Narratives, imaginations and political ideologies flowed in and out of the camp and were closely linked to the political history of the region. With the massive violence that Rwanda, Burundi and Congo (DRC) have experienced over the past fifteen years, issues of innocence and culpability have become central to political discourse as well as to everyday narratives, mythico-histories, rumours and gossip. A constant struggle is taking place to avoid the genocide label and pin it on political adversaries, while the position of the victim can provide moral high ground. In this struggle old ethnic stereotypes re-emerge in new and unexpected ways – often inverting their original meaning. Likewise, old oppositions dissolve and new ones emerge in the fluctuating and unstable political landscape of the Great Lakes. Meanwhile, the 'international community' lurks as a backdrop to the conflicts – the subject of numerous rumours and conspiracy theories but also the ultimate source of recognition and hence of hope.

At the time of writing, Burundi has been through a lengthy, and to a high degree successful, peace process. After a three-year transition period, Pierre Nkurunziza, leader of the last faction of CNDD's rebel groups to give up fighting, was elected president in the first elections since 1993. Ethnicity is now on the table in Burundi, open for negotiation and all sides are expressing their hopes, fears, doubts and demands. Perhaps it is this recognition of the political nature of ethnic conflict – letting the conflict 'become open' to paraphrase the refugees in Lukole – that is the secret behind the apparent success of Burundi's path to peace.

Notes

1. See also Turner (2005a).

Postscript:
What Happened to the Camp?

It is more than a decade since I was in the camp and much has happened in Burundi, and hence in Lukole, since then. The Arusha peace accords that were signed in August 2000 paved the way for peace, democratic reforms and reforms of areas such as the army, the judiciary, and the media. After a transition period, Pierre Nkurunziza, a former rebel leader, was elected president in 2005 and the last international peacekeeping troops left the country according to plan on December 31 2009. Despite devastated infrastructure and economy, a GDP of only 341 dollars per capita - ranking Burundi at number 174 of 182 countries in the human development index, corruption, breaches of human rights, and constant infighting in government, there are grounds for optimism in this small country that has suffered so much over the past decades. There is a well-established and vibrant free press that will not let itself be bullied by state officials, and as opposed to its false twin, Rwanda, people dare speak their minds – openly discussing ethnicity and criticizing those in power. Interestingly, as the taboo on ethnicity has been lifted, the conflicts have shifted from being locked in a Hutu-Tutsi antagonism to a more fragmented political field where intra-ethnic conflicts are at least as common.

This has not, however, been a smooth transition for all. Since I left Lukole, the various Hutu rebel movements have split into factions several times, each faction discrediting their opponent and claiming to represent the whole party. Due to their clandestine and transnational character it was almost impossible to gauge the legitimacy and popular support of these factions. The leader of any rebel group who would sign a peace agreement was given a government position while his soldiers were either integrated into the Burundian army or supported by the internationally sponsored demobilization programme. As a result, leaders were often accused of being opportunists who were merely scrambling to be part of the peace negotiations and get a share in the peace dividend in the power sharing agreements. In other words, rebel leaders were accused of creating new factions simply to reap the benefits of the peace agreements. For instance, while I was doing fieldwork among clandestine Burundian refugees in Nairobi in 2004, I was told that representatives of Nyangoma's faction of CNDD – which by that time was de facto very weak – tried to recruit officers among the young men living in Nairobi, simply in order to bolster his reputation and so that they could be integrated into the government army. One of the young men I interviewed accepted this offer despite no fighting experience and now has the rank of captain in the Burundian army.

Even while I was in Lukole, CNDD split in two, as Jean-Bosco Ndayikengurukiye attempted to oust Leonard Nyangoma as leader – de facto creating two parties. Similarly, Palipehutu split when Cossan Kabura accused Etienne Karatasi of being out of touch with the reality on the ground. Later, both Kabura's Palipehutu-FNL and Ndayikengurukiye's CNDD-FDD split further into factions, due to regional differences and strategies relating to the peace process. While some factions chose to join the peace process, others decided to continue the armed struggle. One of the latter factions was Pierre Nkurunziza's faction of CNDD-FDD which turned out to be the largest rebel group. Nkurunziza signed a peace accord with the transitional government in October 2003, his party won a landslide victory in the municipal elections and the elections for the National Assembly in 2005 and he was consequently appointed president in August 2005.

In the meantime, what happened to the Hutu refugees in Lukole while the country was experiencing this apparent success story of transition to peace and democracy? A common assumption is that they must have returned, once they were convinced that life was safe on the hills where they came from. Predictably, the Tanzanian and the Burundian authorities put pressure on the refugees to repatriate by making life in the camp even tougher, while UNHCR and international NGOs were concerned with the safety of returnees and attempted to assist their repatriation in terms of livelihoods, land rights, etc. In this world of aiding refugees, security is an important issue, not just in terms of secession of hostilities but also in broader terms of human security, and UNHCR was aware of the fact that some regions of the country remained unsafe despite the political progress. When I visited Bujumbura in June–July 2003, peace was volatile, temporary and far from countrywide, which meant that NGOs were negotiating with authorities on both sides of the border to make sure that repatriation was not forced and did not jeopardize the security of the returnees. However, they were struggling with the fact that patterns of return were completely unpredictable, with some refugees refusing to leave the camp, despite the safety in their home region and the assistance that they could receive from UNHCR in terms of transport and material assistance, while other refugees were returning to unsafe regions in large numbers. The latter were termed 'spontaneous repatriations' simply because they were not organized and supported by UNHCR – although there is no reason to believe that their choice to return was less planned than other refugees' choices. The unpredictability of movement in the eyes of the government and the relief agencies – who had done their best to manage and govern the return movement through coercion and assistance respectively – is indicative of the assumptions they had about security and mobility and how little knowledge they had about the political power relations of the camp. Relief agencies operate with measurable levels of security and expect all refugees to act rationally, according to these security levels. If refugees choose to act otherwise, their choices are dismissed as 'spontaneous'.

When I visited Bujumbura again in 2008, I was fortunate to meet some of the people whom I had met in Lukole a decade earlier. They painted a very different picture of what the peace process had looked like from inside the camp. In 2003–4 the split between the different political factions resulted in widespread violence in Lukole. Nkurunziza's faction, which was powerful in the camp, urged the refugees to return to Burundi – not because they found the security levels adequately low but because they needed the refugees to go home and fight. In other words, repatriation was not about individuals taking rational, informed choices in relation to human security and livelihood strategies. Repatriation was part of political strategic reasoning where Nkurunziza needed to mobilise as many men in arms as possible – not in order to win the war but in order to be in the best possible position for winning the peace. The more soldiers he had under his command, the better terms he could negotiate in terms of power sharing and support for demobilization. So whereas UNHCR perceived security as an ontological reality – something out there that could be objectively measured in absolute terms, the reality of Lukole was that security and peace were active ingredients in – often violent – political maneuverings.

After Nkurunziza managed to convince and coerce his supporters to leave the camp and go home to fight, the camp was left in a power vacuum which Palipehutu – always the underdog in camp politics – immediately sought to fill. This move to fill the power vacuum created increased levels of violence, targeting refugees who did not support Palipehutu, and forcing many to return to Burundi despite fears for their safety. One of those to get caught in this situation was my research assistant who continued to support Nyangoma's faction of CNDD, even after the split. In 2004 he and a friend decided to visit Burundi clandestinely in order to check the security situation in the country and see whether it might be safe to return with their families – if not to their home town then to Bujumbura or somewhere else where he was not known. After a successful visit to Bujumbura they passed through their hometown en route to Lukole. Unfortunately, they were recognized and 'arrested' by Nkurunziza's soldiers and taken to the prison, never to be seen again. This was before Nkrunziza came to power. My assistant's sister made enquiries about their whereabouts and started legal proceedings against the person who she assumed had killed them, but she was also shot.

This story tells us how the camp continues to be a volatile place – at once depoliticized and hyper-politicized due to its indeterminate nature. It also underlines one of the main arguments of this book, namely that relief agencies have no chance of grasping the dynamics of the camp, as long as they ignore the political context and continue to perceived refugees as passive victims. As long as the repatriation exercise simply focuses on relative security and perceives the refugees as apolitical, innocent victims, they cannot grasp the complex mechanisms of repatriation, political mobilization and violence in the years after 2002.

References

Adekanye, J.B. 1996. 'Rwanda/Burundi: "Uni-Ethnic" Dominance and the Cycle of Armed Ethnic Formations', *Social Identities* 2(1): 37–72.

Agamben, G. 1998. *Homo Sacer: Sovereign Power and Bare Life.* Stanford, CA: Stanford University Press.

—— 2000. *Means without End: Notes on Politics.* Minnesota: University Of Minnesota Press.

—— 2002. *Remnants of Auschwitz: The Witness and the Archive.* New York: Zone Books.

Albert, E. 1963. 'Women of Burundi: A Study of Social Values', in *Women Of Tropical Africa*, (ed.) D. Paulme. London: Routledge and Kegan Paul.

Anderson, M., A. Howarth and C. Overholt. 1992. *A Framework for People-oriented Planning in Refugee Situations: Taking Account of Women, Men and Children.* Geneva: UNHCR.

Anthony, A.C. 1990. 'Rights and Obligations of Rural Refugees in Tanzania: A Case Study of Mpanda District', *African Review* 17(1/2): 21–39.

Appadurai, A. 1996. *Modernity at Large: Cultural Dimensions of Globalization.* Minneapolis: University Of Minnesota Press.

—— 1999. 'Dead Certainty: Ethnic Violence in the Era of Globalization', in *Globalization and Identity: Dialectics of Flow and Closure*, (eds) B. Meyer and P. Geschiere. Oxford: Blackwell.

Armstrong, A. 1990. 'Evolving Approaches to Planning and Management of Refugee Settlements: The Tanzanian Experience', *Ekistics* 342/343: 195–204.

—— 1991. 'Resource Frontiers and Regional Development: The Role of Refugee Settlement in Tanzania', *Habitat International* 15(1/2): 69–85.

Augé, M. 1995. *Non-Places: Introduction to an Anthropology of Supermodernity.* London: Verso.

Balibar, E. 1998. 'Violence, Ideality and Cruelty', *New Formations* 35: 7–18.

Bauman, Z. 1989. *Modernity and the Holocaust.* Ithaca, NY: Cornell University Press.

Bayart, J.-F., S. Ellis and B. Hibou. 1999. *The Criminalization of the State in Africa.* Oxford: James Currey.

Bourdieu, P. 1977. *Outline Of A Theory Of Practice.* Cambridge: Cambridge University Press.

Bourdieu, P. and J.B. Thompson. 1991. *Language and Symbolic Power.* Cambridge, MA: Harvard University Press.

Chaulia, S.S. 2003. 'The Politics of Refugee Hosting in Tanzania: From Open Door to Unsustainability, Insecurity and Receding Receptivity', *Journal of Refugee Studies* 16(2): 147–66.

Chrétien, J.-P. 1990a. 'Burundi: Social Sciences Facing Ethnic Violence', *Issue* 19(1): 38–41.

——— 1990b. 'L'ethnisme au Burundi: tragédies et propagandes', *Politique Africaine* 39: 182–90.

——— 1996. 'Ethnicity and Politics: The Crisis of Rwanda and Burundi since their Independence', *Guerres Mondiales Et Conflits Contemporains* 181: 111–24.

——— 2003. *The Great Lakes of Africa: Two Thousand Years of History*. New York: Zone Books.

——— 2008. 'The Recurrence of Violence in Burundi: Memories of the "Catastrophe" of 1972' , in *The Recurring Great Lakes Crisis: Identity, Violence and Power*, (eds) J.-P. Chrétien and R. Banégas. London: Hurst.

Chrétien, J.-P., Reporters Sans Frontières and UNESCO. 1995. *Rwanda: les médias du génocide*. Paris: Karthala.

Christensen, H. 1985. *Refugees and Pioneers: History and Field Study of a Burundian Settlement in Tanzania*. Geneva: United Nations Research Institute for Social Development.

Comaroff, J. and J. Comaroff. 2000. 'Millennial Capitalism: First Thoughts On A Second Coming', *Public Culture* 12(2): 291–343.

Connell, R.W. 1995. *Masculinities*. Cambridge: Polity Press.

Cruikshank, B. 1999. *The Will to Empower: Democratic Citizens and Other Subjects*. Ithaca, NY: Cornell University Press.

Daley, P. 1991. 'Gender, Displacement and Social Reproduction: Settling Burundi Refugees in Western Tanzania', *Journal Of Refugee Studies* 4(3): 248–66.

——— 1993. 'From the Kibande to the Kibali: The Incorporation of Refugees and Labour Migrants in Western Tanzania, 1900–87', in *Geography And Refugees: Patterns And Processes Of Change*, (eds) R. Black and V. Robinson. New York: Belhaven Press.

——— 2006. 'Challenges to Peace: Conflict Resolution in the Great Lakes Region of Africa', *Third World Quarterly* 27(2): 303–19.

——— 2007. *Gender and Genocide in Burundi: The Search for Spaces of Peace in the Great Lakes Region*. Bloomington: Indiana University Press.

Das, V. 1990. *Mirrors of Violence: Communities, Riots, and Survivors in South Asia*. Delhi: Oxford University Press.

——— 1995. *Critical Events: An Anthropological Perspective on Contemporary India*. Delhi: Oxford University Press.

Dean, M. 1999. *Governmentality: Power and Rule in Modern Society*. London: Sage.

Douglas, M. 1966. *Purity And Danger: An Analysis of Concepts of Pollution and Taboo*. London: Routledge and Kegan Paul.

Duffield, M. 1996. 'The Symphony of the Damned: Racial Discourse, Complex Political Emergencies and Humanitarian Aid', *Disasters* 20(3): 173–93.

——— 2001. *Global Governance and the New Wars: The Merging of Development and Security*. London: Zed Books.

Feldman, A. 1991. *Formations of Violence: The Narrative of the Body and Political Terror in Northern Ireland*. Chicago: University Of Chicago Press.

——— 1995. 'Ethnographic States of Emergency', in *Fieldwork Under Fire*, (eds) A. Robben and C. Nordstrom. Berkeley: University Of California Press.

——— 2000. 'Violence and Vision: The Prosthetics and Aesthetics of Terror' in *Violence And Subjectivity*, (eds) V. Das, A. Kleinman, M. Ramphele and P. Reynolds. Berkeley: University Of California Press.

Ferguson, J. 1990. *The Anti-Politics Machine : 'Development', Depoliticization, and Bureaucratic Power In Lesotho.* Cambridge: Cambridge University Press.

——— 1999. *Expectations of Modernity: Myths and Meanings of Urban Life on the Zambian Copperbelt.* Berkeley: University Of California Press.

Fine, G. 1986. 'Redemption Rumors: Mercantile Legends and Corporate Beneficence', *Journal of American Folklore* 99: 208–22.

——— 1992. 'Rumours of Apartheid: The Ecotypification of Contemporary Legends in the New South Africa', *Journal of Folklore Research* 29(1): 53–72.

Foucault, M. 1978. *The History Of Sexuality: An Introduction.* New York: Pantheon Books.

Foucault, M., G. Burchill, C. Gordon and P.M. Miller. 1991. *The Foucault Effect: Studies In Governmentality.* London: Harvester Wheatsheaf.

Frazer, E. 1999. *The Problems of Communitarian Politics : Unity and Conflict.* Oxford: Oxford University Press.

Fuglerud, Ø. 1999. *Life on the Outside: The Tamil Diaspora and Long Distance Nationalism.* London: Pluto Press.

Gahutu, R. n.d. *Persecution of the Hutu of Burundi.* Unpublished document. translated from French by Hugh Hazelton and Peter Keating. Design and production: Productions Paperasse.

Gasarasi, C.P. 1984. *The Tripartite Approach to the Resettlement and Integration of Rural Refugees in Tanzania.* Uppsala: Scandinavian Institute Of African Studies.

——— 1990. 'The Mass Naturalization and Further Integration of Rwandese Refugees in Tanzania: Process, Problems and Prospects', *Journal Of Refugee Studies* 3(2): 88–109.

Geschiere, P. 1997. *The Modernity of Witchcraft: Politics and the Occult in Postcolonial Africa.* Charlottesville: University Press Of Virginia.

Giddens, A. 1991. *Modernity and Self-identity : Self and Society in the Late Modern Age.* Cambridge: Polity Press.

Gilmore, D.D. 1990. *Manhood in the Making: Cultural Concepts of Masculinity.* New Haven, CT: Yale University Press.

Guichaoua, A. 1991. 'Les "travaux communitaires" en Afrique Centrale', *Revue Tiers-Monde* 32(127): 551–73.

Hall-Matthews, D. 1996. 'Historical Roots of Famine Relief Paradigms: Ideas on Dependency and Free Trade in India in the 1870s', *Disasters* 20(3): 216–30.

Harrell-Bond, B.E. 1986. *Imposing Aid: Emergency Assistance To Refugees.* Oxford: Oxford University Press.

Harvey, D. 1990. *The Condition Of Postmodernity: An Enquiry Into The Origins Of Cultural Change.* Oxford: Blackwell.

Hatungimana, A. 2008. 'Political Crisis and Social Reconfigurations: The Problem of the "Disaster Victims" In Burundi', in *The Recurring Great Lakes Crisis: Identity, Violence And Memory*, (eds) J.-P. Chrétien and R. Banégas. London: Hurst.

Hindess, B. 2001. 'The Liberal Government of Unfreedom', *Alternatives* 26(2): 95–113.
Human Rights Watch. 1999. 'In the Name of Security. Forced Round-Ups of Refugees In Tanzania'. New York: Human Rights Watch.
——— 2000. 'Seeking Protection: Addressing Sexual and Domestic Violence in Tanzania's Refugee Camps'. New York: Human Rights Watch.
Hyndman, J. 2000. *Managing Displacement: Refugees and the Politics of Humanitarianism.* Minneapolis: University Of Minnesota Press.
Indra, D.M. 1999. *Engendering Forced Migration: Theory And Practice.* New York: Berghahn Books.
Kadende-Kaiser, R.M. 2000. 'Interpreting Language and Cultural Discourse: Internet Communication among Burundians in the Diaspora', *Africa Today* 47(2): 121–48.
Kaiser, T. 2000. 'Promise and Practice: Participatory Evaluation of Humanitarian Assistance', *Forced Migration Review* 8: 8–12.
Kay, R. 1987. *Burundi since the Genocide.* London: Minority Rights Group.
Kibreab, G. 1993. 'The Myth of Dependency among Camp Refugees in Somalia 1979–1989', *Journal Of Refugee Studies* 6(4): 321–49.
Kimmel, M. 1997. *Manhood In America: A Cultural History.* Oxford: Blackwell.
Laclau, E. and L. Zac. 1994. 'Minding the Gap: The Subject of Politics', in *The Making Of Political Identities*, (ed.) E. Laclau. London: Verso.
Laely, T. 1992. 'Le destin du *bushingantahe*: transformations d''une structure locale d'autorité au Burundi', *Genève-Afrique* 30(2): 75–99.
——— 1997. 'Peasants, Local Communities, and Central Power in Burundi', *Journal of Modern African Studies* 35(4): 695–716.
Landau, L. 2001. 'The Humanitarian Hangover: Transnationalization of Governmental Practice in Tanzania's Refugee-Populated Areas', New Issues In Refugee Research, Geneva, UNHCR (Working Paper No. 40).
——— 2003. 'Beyond The Losers: Transforming Governmental Practice in Refugee-affected Tanzania', *Journal Of Refugee Studies* 16(1): 19–43.
——— 2007. The Humanitarian Hangover: Displacement, Aid and Transformation in Western Tanzania. Witwaterstand: Wits University Press.
Lefebvre, H. 1991. *The Production Of Space.* Oxford: Blackwell.
Lemarchand, R. 1970. *Rwanda and Burundi.* London: Pall Mall Press.
——— 1989. 'Burundi: The Killing Fields Revisited', *Issue* 18(1): 22–28.
——— 1990a. 'L'école historique burundo-française: une école pas comme les autres', *Canadian Journal Of African Studies* 24(2): 235–49.
——— 1990b. 'Response to Jean-Pierre Chrétien', *Issue* 19(1): 41.
——— 1996a. *Burundi: Ethnic Conflict and Genocide.* Cambridge: Cambridge University Press.
——— 1996b. 'Burundi: Genocide Forgotten, Invented and Anticipated'. Occasional Paper. Copenhagen: Centre Of African Studies.
Lemarchand, R. and D. Martin. 1974. *Selective Genocide in Burundi.* London: Minority Rights Group.
Lennox-Cook, C. 1996. *Kitali Camp, Ngara, Tanzania: A Year in the Life of a Rwandese and Burundese Refugee Camp.* Unpublished report. Ngara Field Office: GOAL.
Lentz, C. 1998. 'The Chief, the Mine Captain and the Politician: Legitimating Power in Northern Ghana', *Africa* 68(1): 46–65.

Lund, C. (ed) 2007. *Twilight Institutions: Public Authority and Local Politics in Africa*. Oxford: Blackwell.

Macgaffey, J. and R. Bazenguissa-Ganga 2000. *CongoParis: Transnational Traders On The Margins Of The Law*. Oxford: James Currey.

Malkki, L.H. 1995a. *Purity And Exile: Violence, Memory, And National Cosmology Among Hutu Refugees In Tanzania*. Chicago: University Of Chicago Press.

—— 1995b. 'Refugees And Exile – From Refugee Studies To The National Order Of Things,' *Annual Review Of Anthropology* 24: 495–523.

Mamdani, M. 1996. *Citizen And Subject: Contemporary Africa And The Legacy Of Late Colonialism*. Princeton, NJ: Princeton University Press.

—— 2001. *When Victims Become Killers: Colonialism, Nativism, And The Genocide In Rwanda*. Princeton, NJ: Princeton University Press.

Maquet, J. 1961. *The Premise Of Inequality In Ruanda; A Study Of Political Relations In A Central African Kingdom*. London: Published For The International African Institute By The Oxford University Press.

Massey, D. 1992. 'Politics And Time/Space', *New Left Review* (196): 65–84.

Mbembe, A. 2003. 'Necropolitics', *Public Culture* 15(1): 11–40.

—— 2001. *On the Postcolony*. Berkeley CA: University of California Press.

Mendel, T. 1997. 'Refugee Law And Practice In Tanzania', *International Journal Of Refugee Law* 9(1): 35–60.

Millwood, D. 1996. 'Joint Evaluation Of Emergency Assistance To Rwanda'. Copenhagen: Steering Committee Of The Joint Evaluation Of Emergency Assistance To Rwanda, DANIDA.

Mitchell, J.C. 1983. 'Case And Situation Analysis', *The Sociological Reader* 31(2):187–211.

Mworoha, É. Ed. 1987. *Histoire Du Burundi. Des Origines À La Fin Du Xixe Siècle*. Paris: Hatier.

Ndjio, B. 2008. 'Cameroonian Feymen And Nigerian "419" Scammers: Two Examples Of Africa's "Reinvention" Of The Global Capitalism'. Leiden: African Studies Centre Working Paper.

Nyers, P. 1998. 'Refugees, Humanitarian Emergencies, And The Politicization Of Life', *Refuge, Canada's Periodical On Refugees* 17(6):16–22.

Olivier De Sardan, J.P. 1999. 'The Moral Economy Of Corruption In Africa', *Journal Of Modern African Studies* 37(25–52).

Ong, A. 2006. *Neoliberalism As Exception: Mutations In Citizenship And Sovereignty*. Durham and London: Duke University Press.

Pottier, J. 1996. 'Relief And Repatriation: Views By Rwandan Refugees; Lessons For Humanitarian Aid Workers', *African Affairs* (95): 403–429.

Pred, A. 1986. *Place, Practice And Structure: Social and Spatial Transformation in Southern Sweden, 1750–1850*. New Jersey: Barnes and Noble.

Prunier, G. 1995a. 'Burundi: Descent Into Chaos Or A Manageable Crisis?': Writenet. Available at http://www.unhcr.org/refworld/docid/3ae6a6c00.html [accessed 14 October 2009].

Prunier, G. 1995b. *The Rwanda Crisis, 1959–1994: History Of A Genocide*. London: Hurst & Company.

Rajaram, P.K. 2002. 'Humanitarianism And Representations Of The Refugee', *Journal Of Refugee Studies* 15(3):247–64.

Republic of Burundi. 1972. 'The White Paper On The Real Causes And The Consequences Of The Attempted Genocide Against The Tutsi Ethny In Burundi'. Washington D.C.: Embassy Of The Republic Of Burundi.

—— 1989. 'Rapport Final' of the Commision nationale chargée d'étudier la question de l'unité nationale. Unpublished document. Bujumbura, May 1989.

Reynolds, R. and P. Baynard-Smith 1996. 'Community Services And Repatriation', *Refugee Participation Network* (22). Available at www.fmreview.org/HTMLcontent/rpn22.htm. Accessed 13 October 2009.

Reyntjens, F. 1990. 'Du Bon Usage De La Science: "L'école Historique Burundo-Française"', *Politique Africaine* (37): 107–113.

—— 1993. 'The Proof Of The Pudding Is In The Eating – The June 1993 Elections In Burundi', *Journal Of Modern African Studies* 31(4): 563–83.

—— 1995. 'Breaking The Cycle Of Violence'. London: Minority Rights Group.

—— 1996. 'Burundi – Landet Med Kupen Utan Slut'. Uppsala: Nordiska Afrikainstitutet.

Roitman, J. 2004. 'Productivity in the Margins: The Reconstitution of State Power in the Chad Bassin'. In *Anthropology in the Margins of the State*, Eds. Veena Das and Deborah Poole. Santa Fe, New Mexico: School of American Research Press. 191–225.

Rose, N.S. 1996. 'The Death Of The Social? Re-Figuring The Territory Of Government', *Economy And Society* 25(3): 327–57.

—— 1999. *Powers Of Freedom: Reframing Political Thought.* Cambridge, United Kingdom; New York, NY: Cambridge University Press.

Sanders, E.R. 1969. 'The Hamitic Hypothesis; Its Origin And Functions In Time Perspective', *Journal Of African History* 19(4): 521–32.

Scheper-Hughes, N. 1996. 'Theft Of Life: The Globalization Of Organ Stealing Rumours', *Anthropology Today* 12(3): 3–11.

Schmitt, C. 1985. *Political theology: Four Chapters On The Concept Of Sovereignty.* Cambridge, Mass: MIT Press

Simons, A. 1995. 'The Beginning Of The End', in *Fieldwork Under Fire*, (eds.) Carolyn Nordstrom And Antonius Robben. Los Angeles, Berkeley, London: University Of California Press.

Simonsen, K. 1993. *Byteori Og Hverdagspraksis.* Copenhagen: Akademisk Forlag.

Soguk, N. 1999. *States And Strangers: Refugees And Displacements Of Statecraft.* Minneapolis: University Of Minnesota Press.

Sommers, M. 2001. *Fear In Bongoland: Burundi Refugees In Urban Tanzania.* New York: Berghahn Books.

Stefansson, A. 1997. 'Essentialist Representations Of Violent Conflicts: The Case Of Bosnia-Herzegovina'. Unpublished Paper.

Stoler, A.L. 1995. *Race And The Education Of Desire: Foucault's History Of Sexuality And The Colonial Order Of Things.* Durham: Duke University Press.

Taussig, M.T. 1999. *Defacement: Public Secrecy And The Labor Of The Negative.* Stanford, Calif.: Stanford University Press.

Trouwborst, A.A. 1962. 'Le Burundi'. In *Les Anciens Royaumes De La Zone Interlacustre Meridionale*, (ed.) A. Trouwborst M. d'Hertefelt, J. Scherer. London: International African Institute.

Turner, P. 1993. *I Heard It Through The Grapevine: Rumor In African-American Culture.* Berkeley: University Of California Press.

Turner, S. 2002. 'Dans L'œil Du Cyclone. Les Réfugiés, L'aide Et La Communauté Internationale En Tanzanie', *Politique Africaine* (85): 29–45.

—— 2004. 'Under The Gaze Of The "Big Nations": Refugees, Rumours And The International Community In Tanzania', *African Affairs* 103(411): 227–47.

—— 2005a. 'Suspended Spaces – Contesting Sovereignties In A Refugee Camp'. In *Sovereign Bodies: Citizens, Migrants And States In The Postcolonial World*, (eds) Thomas Hansen And Finn Stepputat: Princeton University Press.

—— 2005b. '"The Tutsi Are Afraid We Will Discover Their Secrets" – On Secrecy And Sovereign Power In Burundi', *Social Identities* 11(1): 37–55.

—— 2008. 'Cyberwars Of Words: Expressing The Unspeakable In Burundi's Diaspora', *Journal Of Ethnic And Migration Studies* 34(7): 1161–80.

—— 2009. 'Betraying Trust And The Elusive Nature Of Ethnicity In Burundi'. In *Traitors: Suspicion, Intimacy And The Ethics Of State – Building*, (eds) Tobias Kelly And Sharika Thiranagama. Philadelphia: University of Pennsylvania Press.

Turner, V.W. 1967. *The Forest Of Symbols; Aspects Of Ndembu Ritual.* Ithaca, NY: Cornell University Press.

UNHCR. 1991. 'Guidelines On The Protection Of Refugee Women'. Geneva: Office Of The United Nations High Commissioner For Refugees.

UNHCR Sub-Office Ngara. 1997. 'Preliminary Registration And Demography Report'.

US Committee For Refugees. 2000. 'More Male Refugees Than Previously Thought'. Washington DC: US Committee For Refugees. Refugee Reports 21(2). Available at http://www.refugees.org/world/ articles/males_rr00_2.htm. Accessed 26 September 2003.

Uvin, P. 1998. *Aiding Violence: The Development Entreprise In Rwanda.* West Hartford: Kumarian Press.

Van Hear, N. 1998. *New Diasporas: The Mass Exodus, Dispersal And Regrouping Of Migrant Communities.* Seattle, WA: University Of Washington Press.

Van Hoyweghen, S. 2001. 'Mobility, Territoriality And Sovereignty In Post-Colonial Tanzania', *New Issues In Refugee Research*, Geneva: UNHCR (Working Paper No. 49).

Van Velsen, J. 1967. 'The Extended-Case Method And Situational Analysis'. In *The Craft Of Social Anthropology*, (ed.) A.L. Epstein. London: Tavistock Publications.

Waters, T. 1997. 'Beyond Structural Adjustment: State And Market In A Rural Tanzanian Village', *African Studies Review* 40(2): 59–89.

West, H. and T. Sanders (eds) 2003. *Transparency and Conspiracy: Ethnographies of Suspicion in the New World Order.* Durham, NC: Duke University Press.

Whitaker, B. 1999. 'Changing Opportunities: Refugees And Host Communities In Western Tanzania', *New Issues In Refugee Research*, Geneva: UNHCR (Working Paper No. 11).

—— 2002a. 'Changing Priorities In Refugee Protection: The Rwandan Repatriation From Tanzania', *New Issues In Refugee Research*, Geneva: UNHCR (Working Paper No. 53).

—— 2002b. 'Refugees In Western Tanzania: The Distribution Of Burdens And Benefits Among Local Hosts', *Journal Of Refugee Studies* 15(4): 339–58.

White, L. 1997. 'The Traffic In Heads: Bodies, Borders And The Articulation Of Regional Histories', *Journal Of Southern African Studies* 23(2): 325–38.

White, L. 2000. *Speaking With Vampires: Rumor And History In Colonial Africa.* Berkeley: University Of California Press.

Zizek, S. 1994. 'How Did Marx Invent The Symptom?' in *Mapping Ideology*, (ed.) Slavoj Zizek. London and New York: Verso.

Index

Lightning Source UK Ltd.
Milton Keynes UK
UKOW05f0609081013

218656UK00004B/29/P